The
AESTHETICS
of
ACTION

A Note on Illustrations

Figure 1 appears on page 27, figure 18 on page 144, and figure 19 on page 145. All other figures, the photographs by Michael Katakis, are printed in the photo essay.

The
AESTHETICS
of
ACTION
Continuity and Change in a West African Town

Kris L. Hardin

SMITHSONIAN INSTITUTION PRESS
WASHINGTON AND LONDON

The author has donated royalties and the indexing costs for this book to the Smithsonian Institution's book famine program for Africa

This book was designed by Kathleen M. Sims and edited by Nancy L. Benco

Photographs reproduced in this book are by Michael Katakis

Library of Congress Cataloging-in-Publication Data

Hardin, Kris L.
   The aesthetics of action: continuity and change in a West African town / Kris L. Hardin.
   p.   cm. — (Smithsonian series in ethnographic inquiry)
   Includes bibliographical references.
   ISBN 1-56098-235-7
   1. Kono (African people)—Social life and customs.
   2. Aesthetics, Kono.
   3. Aesthetics, Comparative.
   I. Title.
   II. Series.
   DT516.45.K65H37   1993
   306'.09664—dc20
   92-20747   CIP

For permission to reproduce illustrations appearing in this book, please correspond directly with the author. The Smithsonian Institution Press does not retain reproduction rights for these illustrations or maintain a file of addresses for photo sources

Cover illustration: Kono man on his way home from his farm

For Michael

CONTENTS

PREFACE

This volume has been a long time in coming. I
began my fieldwork in Sierra Leone in the spring of 1982. At that time
I was interested in critiquing the idea that the world of art is somehow
naturally separate from the world of everyday life. That starting point
led me to an exploration of Kono history, aesthetics, politics, creativity,
change, and a realm of other topics. My first field trip lasted until the
spring of 1984. In 1988 I was able to return to Sierra Leone for two more
months of research.

By the time I first arrived in Sierra Leone, I had already decided to
work in the Kono area because I was interested in exploring aesthetics in
a region where people did not seem to have a category of "art" and were
not actively engaged in the production of what might be termed "high
art" in a Euro-American sense, in other words, painting, sculpture, or
performance genres that have marked distinctions between performer/
artist and audience. What the Kono do produce falls more into the Euro-
American category of crafts—weaving (including spinning and indigo
dyeing), some basketry and mat-making, ceramics, and blacksmithing.
The Kono also have a vibrant tradition of dance occasions associated
with such events as initiation into Poro or Sande societies and funerals.
In most dance performances musicians and singers incorporate the audience into the performance rather than perform for a non-participating

audience. I later found out that the Kono have also adopted newer forms of performance that were originally introduced by missionaries but now are the main dance form used at regional and national fairs and competitions. These dance forms place more emphasis on individuals as performers and on the audience as appreciators of, rather than as participants in, the dance.

While I had selected Kono as the site of my research, I had no idea of exactly where I would settle. During several trips through the region, I discussed my project with the elders of a number of chiefdoms and learned where weaving, ceramics, blacksmithing, and other production processes were being carried out. This information was reinforced in conversations with Kono officials from the National Diamond Mining Company, missionaries, and Peace Corps volunteers. Eventually, I settled on Soa Chiefdom, an area where music and dance traditions were still thriving, where weavers, blacksmiths, and potters still practiced their skills, and where most farmers were still engaged in subsistence agriculture. Equally important, Paramount Chief S. E. K. Foyoh III was interested in having the Kono language and customs documented and agreed to allow me to work in the chiefdom.

My research has been funded by numerous institutions and grant-giving agencies. I would like to thank the Fulbright-Hays Doctoral Dissertation Fellowship Program, the African Studies Program of Indiana University, and the Graduate School of Indiana University for supporting my initial field research, and the University Museum, University of Pennsylvania, for funding the research done in 1988.

During my time in Sierra Leone, I accumulated debts that are too numerous to name. The research itself could not have been pursued without the cooperation of the Institute of African Studies at Fourah Bay College and its former director, Dr. C. Magbaily Fyle. During both stays in Sierra Leone, I was the guest of Paramount Chief S. E. K. Foyoh III and the people of Soa Chiefdom in Kainkordu, a town of about 1,200 inhabitants and the site of the chiefdom headquarters. I would like to express my deepest thanks to Paramount Chief Foyoh and his family for their overwhelming hospitality during my stay in Soa and to the residents of Kainkordu who patiently allowed me to share in their lives. I am especially grateful to Aiah Fengai Johnny, colleague and guide, who introduced me to much of what I learned about Kono culture during my initial trip to Sierra Leone. Equally, I am grateful to Fengai's wife, Sia Johnny, who welcomed me into her household, and to Aiah Njemina, his wife Finda, and their children, who taught me much about Kono agriculture and, in doing so, about Kono culture. Agnes (Kumba) Sebba, midwife and friend, also shared much of her time and companionship in ways that are difficult to repay. Aiah David James was also very helpful in numerous ways during my initial days in the field. During my second trip, Sahr Foyoh was invaluable as both translator and guide, and I thank him for his assistance. I would also like to thank Sia Gbenda and her daughter Kumba for their assistance, and David Gbenda for providing lodging during my 1988 stay in Kainkordu.

There are many others who assisted my fieldwork in numerous ways. These include the Honorable A. B. L. Abu, Mr. A. A. Koroma, Fathers Patrick McGeever and John Skinnader, Sister Carol Kleba and the School Sisters of Notre Dame, Peter Anderson, Sally Fowler, and Lori Rubin. I would especially like to thank Dr. Julie Nemer whose hospitality, friendship, and insights into anthropology and Sierra Leone were ever helpful.

The list of people who have somehow assisted in writing this volume is equally long. At various times my writing has been supported by the African Studies Program at Indiana University, the Fellowship Program at the Smithsonian Institution, the School of American Research, and generous leaves from the Anthropology Department and the University Museum at the University of Pennsylvania. My greatest debt is to Ivan Karp. His insights and criticism have been invaluable during the entire course of this project. I would also like to thank Paula Girshick for her careful critiques and timely insights in the preparation of the first draft of this volume. Sandra Barnes, Adrienne Kaeppler, Patrick McNaughton, Simon Ottenberg, and Anya Royce have also made comments on various parts of this volume during its long preparation. I am also grateful to Mary Jo Arnoldi and Rob Leopold for their comments, their constant support, and their friendship over the last ten years. More recently, Yvonne Teh and Amanda King have helped with bibliographic work and other tasks that freed me to write, and I thank them for their generosity and time. Nancy Benco's editorial assistance in preparing this volume has been invaluable. I would also like to thank the anthropology students in the graduate program at the University of Pennsylvania for their comments and insights in numerous discussions of aesthetics, fieldwork, and other topics. As always, however, any mistakes are mine.

My deepest gratitude goes to my parents for their unflagging support over the years and to Michael Katakis who was my companion on the 1988 trip to Sierra Leone. The extraordinary photographs that accompany this volume are his. For his unending questions about Kono life, for his encouragement, and finally for his patience, I will always be grateful.

I

AESTHETICS AND CHANGE

This is a study of aesthetics and changing sociocultural forms among the Kono of Sierra Leone. Essentially I am interested in the ways in which old Kono ways both shape and are shaped by new situations. The Kono of eastern Sierra Leone, like many other groups today, find themselves pulled in at least two directions. On one side is a subsistence economy that emphasizes kinship and the dispersal of goods and services in ways that extend family ties and social obligations. On the other side is a rapidly growing cash economy that favors individuation in ways that reshape ties of kinship because of the potential such ties have for draining resources. As educational opportunities expand and household formations change, conflicts between individual aspirations and socially prescribed ideals of behavior emerge. Social mores and traditions provide both resources for and constraints on action in a world where social forms and everyday practice are continually influencing each other, and individuals find themselves choosing between what are often competing and incompatible goals.

With each decision or choice new paths take shape. Some options open to view, and others become less desirable. The patterns and forms that emerge in the nexus between kin-based and market-based social systems are largely unpredictable as well as uniquely culture specific. In other words, what are sometimes considered hegemonic forces of globally based economic influences are tempered by the ways in which particular cultures appropriate and manipulate new social and economic formations as new forms mesh with and are transformed by already-existing social and cultural forms. The path each society takes, as well as the final outcome, is the result of unique articulations between past orientations and the choices and contingencies that individuals of a given society face on a daily basis.

My approach to this problem is not from an economic viewpoint, which assumes that individuals make rational choices based on what they perceive to be most advantageous for them. Rather, my approach is from the field of aesthetics—how people decide that particular forms (behavioral or objective) are appropriate. This approach entails a consideration of how new patterns of acceptable action emerge; how behavior and its evaluation draw from and transform previously accepted social or objective forms; how such changes are justified; and how, in what can best be considered a series of chain reactions, such new forms and arrangements of structural properties provide an arena for contesting and reshaping norms and traditions. I am certainly not alone in suggesting that traditions and norms are constantly in a state of simultaneous construction and deconstruction (see, for example, Kratz n.d. and Hobsbawm and Ranger 1983). But what I have tried to do in this volume is to present ethnographic descriptions that acknowledge the role played by affect, aesthetics, and values in the construction of new social and cultural forms.

In this book I argue that the decisions made in the course of everyday life utilize social and cultural forms as resources for action. As social and cultural forms are reproduced, they are altered through new insights, substitutions, and other transformations as people respond to the contingencies of everyday life. Because new actions are perceived as anomalous when they are compared to the background of tradition, habit, and norm, such alterations are initially rationalized and explained as deviations from ideals or norms. They are also evaluated. With repeated use or with shifts in power relationships, however, what were once perceived as anomalies or alterations take on the shape of habit or norm, and the background against which subsequent actions are evaluated shifts. What was once habitual becomes problematic, contested, and subject to debate. New habits become the essence with which people conceptualize themselves, their social worlds, and their future actions. My investigation, then, focuses on the interplay between structure and action. It seeks to consider both agency and the processes through which individual actions are melded into the social and cultural forms that structure future action.

Aesthetic evaluation, then, is seen here as one of the mediators between structure and action, a dynamic force in constituting sociocultural formations rather than a mere reflection or aftereffect of such formations. Viewing aesthetic evaluation in this way allows us to consider the role that aesthetic criticism plays in the construction of social and cultural identity, to examine the mechanisms through which aesthetic criticism affects social and cultural processes, and to begin to view the relationship between aesthetic evaluation and change, especially the ways in which new forms may be transformed by old ones (or vice versa). Such a project requires an understanding of how people recognize form as appropriate, extraordinary, or beautiful and the range of forms that have aesthetic impact in a particular society (in other words denying the universalist perspective that pervades so much of the literature on aesthetics). The project I present here also requires an acceptance of evaluation as an act with social and political consequences that can only be understood by examining the mechanisms by which individual aesthetic preferences are translated into norms.

It is probably clear that, when I am talking about aesthetics, I am not necessarily referring to forms that might be called "art" in a Euro-American setting. In addition, given the fact that much of the writing on aesthetics is currently dominated by discussions of art, I feel it would be helpful to preface this volume with an explanation of my use of aesthetics.

The ethnographic material on Kono ideas of preference and value provides an approach to aesthetics that emphasizes linkages between artistic and everyday experiences rather than conceptual separations of the two domains as is typically found in the Euro-American elite art world. Other studies suggest similar linkages for other non-Western societies and for subcultures within Euro-American societies that are peripheral to or separated from elite art worlds. And yet disciplines that study non-Western arts have tended to reproduce the boundaries between art and everyday life in problematic ways. Since at least the mid-sixties, the anthropology of art has been stalled by an inability to define a field of study for itself. It is difficult enough to define art in a Western setting,[1] but attempts to locate and thus define a distinct category of art cross-culturally have certainly failed.

4   Kris L. Hardin

Underlying the debates about art in non-Western and pre-colonial settings is a search for universals and the identification of things or concepts that have validity across cultural boundaries. It is assumed that if
clear commonalities can be identified, the study of art cross-culturally
will proceed, much as the study of religion, politics, or economics has
proceeded over the last decades. As a result, the search for things to study
in the anthropology of the arts has primarily been restricted to our own
categories of the arts—music, dance, sculpture, painting, and, sometimes, textiles, ceramics, and verbal performance.[2] As more research is
completed outside Euro-American elite art worlds, however, it is clear
that the categories we have relied on are, at best, artificial and, at worst,
shield our view from both the intricacies of expressive culture in other
places and insights into the connections between art and everyday life in
our own world.

While many authors have criticized the use of western categories in
the anthropology of art, notably d'Azevedo (1958), Riesman (1975), and
Schneider (1971), the categories still persist implicitly, if not explicitly.
Those who have tried to tackle the problem find themselves caught between two questions that continually stifle effective analysis of the problem. The first is whether or not non-Western sociocultural systems have
"art," if they lack a linguistic category that corresponds somehow to our
own. Answering "yes" to this question implies opting for an etic explanation of human experience because it has been impossible to determine
what art is, if it is something other than music, painting, dance, sculpture, etc. At the same time, most scholars have been unable to answer
"no" because of the political implications of such a stand.

The second stumbling block is whether or not an aesthetic system exists without a category of art. This question is as problematic as the first.
Answering in the affirmative sets one squarely against those who limit
the idea of aesthetics to discussions of art. Those answering "no" are
again perceived to be making negative statements about non-Western societies. Our inability to move beyond this double-bind has crippled research in the anthropology of art, in the anthropology of aesthetics, and
in studies of aesthetic evaluation in general, to the point that the field has
remained at a virtual standstill for twenty years.

To move beyond such dilemmas, we need an expansion of our concepts and a reexamination of the definitions we use and where they come
from. Even a cursory look at the history of the word "aesthetics," for
example, shows that the tendency to consider aesthetics in terms of art

alone is a relatively recent phenomenon. The Greek root of aesthetics, *aisthetikos,* is related not to the perception of art specifically but to sensory perception in general. Until the beginning of the nineteenth century, discussions in aesthetics considered appreciation of natural beauty along with artistic or man-made beauty (Osborne 1972:5). Only in the twentieth century has the field of aesthetics been increasingly limited to evaluating works of art in a strict sense of the word.

The narrow focus on aesthetics in the twentieth century reflects and reproduces particular aspects of our own social world. For example, the increasingly privatized experiences characteristic of late capitalism can be seen in the Euro-American art world in several ways—the increased value given to the individual creation or perception of artistic experience over the last fifty years; an economic system increasingly characterized by a hierarchy of specialists with limited access to knowledge about "high" culture, especially the making and appreciating of art; the increased commodification of expressions that are deemed "artistic"; and an emphasis on goods as things that are accumulated rather than dispersed. What I am suggesting, then, is that our conceptual categories, with their increasing tendency to separate art from everyday spheres and to distinguish between those who know about art from those who do not, help to create a particular cultural configuration and, in doing so, inhibit us from seeing beyond that configuration. Searching for our categories in other societies, the direction many researchers in the anthropology of art have taken, implicitly sets up comparisons and rankings of other societies with our own that are reminiscent of nineteenth-century evolutionist thought. At the same time, such rankings tend to reify our system of categories, our expectations for the "development" of other societies, and, to some extent, their expectations for themselves. This perspective is similar to arguments made by others about how theories of culture or notions of "the other" reflect and reify cultural interests rather than provide a basis from which to explore them (R. Williams 1981; Said 1979; Mason 1990). The narrowing focus of discussions in aesthetics, then, tells us more about the trajectory of our own system of categorization, based on particular historical and socioeconomic formations, than it tells us about the specifics of aesthetic response in another place or time. This is similar to Mudimbe's (1986) criticism of analyses of African art that rely on Western conceptions and models. By following these criticisms to their conclusions, our penchant for searching in other societies for our own arrangement of sociocultural phenomena is not only a dead-end but is also dangerously close to much of what contemporary social theory has seemingly tried to avoid.

The solution to the dilemmas currently posed by the limited questions we ask of art and aesthetics is to revise the problems we define for ourselves. The search for universals—how to define art or aesthetics in ways that are applicable cross-culturally—is outdated. What is needed, instead, is an examination of local or indigenous categories of production or experience and forms of evaluation that does not set a priori boundaries on the kinds of forms that will be examined. By recognizing the possibility of alternative boundaries for research we can shift the focus of questions in aesthetics away from locating Western configurations of meanings and forms in other cultures to identifying and exploring the various kinds of valued experiences actually found in any particular setting.

While there have been attempts to broaden the definitional framework in the study of non-Western aesthetics, most of this work has been viewed as peripheral to the major concerns of the study of anthropology and the arts because of the overwhelming tendency to employ Western concepts and definitions when dealing with questions of aesthetics. In fact, however, the numerous forays into local or indigenous ideas of art, value, or aesthetics form a body of work that has the potential to redirect anthropological research on arts and aesthetics. For example, Alan Merriam (1964) compared six components of what he defined as a "western aesthetic" with features of American Flathead Indian and BaSongye musical traditions.[3] He concluded that some non-Western groups may not have the concept of aesthetic as we know it. He also suggested, however, the possibility of other kinds of aesthetic systems when he wrote (1964:270) that ". . . the western aesthetic is but one manifestation of a broader set of principles . . ." Unfortunately, Merriam failed to describe or elaborate on the nature of this broader set of principles. I suggest that these principles have to do with the capacity, even the necessity, to evaluate, which then has culture-specific manifestations. This means that our focus should not be on particular objects and forms and how they are evaluated but rather on how evaluations take place and how aesthetic systems articulate with behavior, especially motives and ideals, in a particular place. By comparing aesthetic systems from this vantage point, we are in a position to look at aesthetics cross-culturally in ways that tell us something about the human capacity to evaluate, as well as the social, political, and behavioral aspects of particular kinds of aesthetic systems.

In addition to Merriam, numerous other studies have tried to broaden our view of non-Western aesthetics. One fruitful approach has been a focus on patterns and the habitual aspects of production processes,[4] and how these relate to appreciation. Adams' (1973, 1977) analysis of Sumbanese textiles, for example, suggests parallels in the organization of textile designs with the organization of trading, village space, and gift exchange. Adams further suggests that these parallels are the source of specific textile designs and thus can be related to Sumbanese aesthetic preferences.

Lechtman's (1977) work on pre-Columbian casting deals similarly with the repetition of patterns across a variety of cultural domains.[5] Briefly, the casting process involves the emergence of gold from within the mixture of molten elements poured into a mold rather than the addition of a layer of gold plate onto the already-cooled metal. Lechtman shows that this particular choice of techniques was an idiomatic reference to a principle at a higher level of abstraction that was manifested across a range of domains of experience, which include both social and material forms. The higher order principle emphasizes the emergence of desired ends from within forms (either behavioral or material) rather than the addition of significant elements (such as a layer of gold plate), once the construction of an event or the production of an object has begun. Lechtman's conclusion is that patterns in the production of material culture can be shown to draw from the patterns that structure production in a variety of domains, and that these patterns structure action, solutions, and ways of conceptualizing cause-and-effect relationships in general. While Adams and Lechtman show a direct relationship between the organization of "art" and "non-art" domains, they unfortunately also imply that art draws its patterns from other domains rather than actually participates in the construction of the principles or predispositions for action that they discuss.

Similar kinds of parallels have been shown in studies of African aesthetics. Fernandez (1971, 1973, 1976), focusing primarily on form, has explored the principles of opposition, vitality, and asymmetry that crosscut and structure a range of contexts among the Fang of Gabon. Rubin (1975) suggested there is a relationship between the way some African peoples conceptualize such values as social cohesion and cultural continuity and the representation of those values in sculptural forms that emphasize the accumulation of material over time. As long as the logic is maintained the forms are considered appropriate.

Pattern and analogy were also important in Thompson's (1973) early work with Yoruba critics. Thompson suggested that there were complex connections among the concepts of linearity, civilization, and facial scarification in Yoruba sculpture that paralleled ideas about the opening of roads in forest areas and ideas about the meaning of the open human eye. He then connected these analogies to the Yoruba ideal of "allowing the inner quality of [a] substance to shine forth" (1973:19). According to Thompson, aesthetic criticism can be related to emotional ideals and can "reveal the hidden unities which impose meaningful design upon the face of a culture" (1973:19).

When taken as a group, these studies and others suggest that the search for patterns, repetition, and analogies may provide a useful tool for research on aesthetics, one that demonstrates how aesthetic expressions connect with culture or how artistic forms come to have meaning and importance. Much of this research, however, still begins from objects considered to be "art" in a Euro-American sense and from criticism related to these objects. Fernandez, Rubin, and Thompson, for example, all began their work with sculpted forms. Their analyses then shifted to the discovery of like features or related patterns and habits in other cultural domains. An alternative approach, and the one used in this study, however, reverses this orientation by first examining the categories of production or experience in general and then the forms of criticism related to these categories, regardless of whether or not they are considered to be "art" forms.

As will be clear from the Kono data, the Kono use similar kinds of criteria to judge what are to us "art" and "non-art" forms. When the same principles or concepts can be seen to organize production in dance events, agricultural labor, and a range of other domains of experience, the question becomes how to distinguish between the aesthetics of "art" and the aesthetics of action. Where are the boundaries? For the Kono, and probably for many other groups as well, the answer can only be that such a distinction either does not exist or that it is shaped very differently than we might expect it to be. Likewise, I would argue that the kinds of appreciation applied to art and non-art forms do not differ significantly for the Kono. Preference and value, then, are socially constructed phenomena, and there are few qualitative differences between the way they are applied to art and non-art forms as a Westerner would define them.

In addition to relying on Western categories, anthropological studies of arts or aesthetics have been criticized for their emphasis on stasis and homogeneity. We have long assumed that forms of evaluation and culture are integrally related. Today, we know that culture changes and that styles and taste change, and we assume a link exists between the two. Yet that link has not been thoroughly examined. We are also aware that there are different dynamics to change, that not all things or individuals change at the same rate, and that even with change the traditions, styles of behavior, and forms of a place often retain the flavor of what went before. We also know that when new forms are adopted they are in some way domesticated or altered by previous forms. As this happens, the new forms become somewhat unique, or at least distinguishable from the forms originally borrowed. Neither aesthetic anthropology nor the anthropology of art have been able to describe the mechanisms through which such transformations occur.

The lack of attention to change and variation is partially a result of tendencies to see preference not as individual choice but rather as socially dictated adherence to norms or traditions. We have produced a literature in which there are few debates about form and no arguments about whose interpretations are correct. Few writers on aesthetics have considered the role of consensus in evaluation, the mesh between individual evaluations and social or cultural norms, the implications of consensus building for questions of power, or how consensus and choice translate into the choices people make in everyday life. As early as 1958, d'Azevedo (1958) noted the importance of individual experience in aesthetic response, and yet that seemingly productive avenue of investigation remains unexplored. Thompson (1973:22, 27), for example, solves this problem by writing that Yoruba qualitative criteria are consensual but that there are only a few Yoruba individuals with the skills to actually criticize. He implies that differences of opinion among critics can be attributed to differences in talent and familiarity with various art forms. D'Azevedo's (1973b) work on Gola artists probably goes as far as anyone else's toward recognizing heterogeneity by suggesting there are categories of people with particular skills, personality traits, and specialized areas of knowledge. But he, too, provides little of the information on the range of variation or the conflicts in evaluation that occur within or among these categories.

There are probably several reasons why topics that connect aesthetics with change and variation have not been more thoroughly investigated. First, until very recently the arts have been seen only as a reflection or mirror of culture, something that occurs after the fact. Researchers have tended to ask questions about what an object means, symbolizes, or represents, tying the object to what is already known about the culture itself. Until very recently, investigators have not explored how an object and its production participate in the construction of larger cultural meanings. Some would argue that it is impossible to get at the latter without an understanding of the former, but in many cases the reflective aspect served as the final step of inquiry.

Second, the market for "traditional" art objects has made it more difficult to focus on change in studies of aesthetics in non-Western settings. An argument can be made that the point at which social theory in general shifted away from functionalism and other perspectives that implicitly viewed action synchronically and moved towards the analysis of the constituting or constructive aspects of action was precisely the time when commercial markets for the kinds of objects anthropologists were investigating in non-Western settings were expanding. One criterion for value in these expanding marketplaces has been authenticity and tradition. The more traditional or authentic an object appears, the more value it has. I have argued elsewhere (Hardin, Arnoldi, and Geary n.d.) that the history of art historical and material culture studies, especially in Africa, has been so tied to commercial interests that the emphasis on action, change, and variation that currently tends to dominate other areas of anthropological inquiry has yet to be fully explored in studies of non-Western art and aesthetics. As a result, questions of variation and change have tended to be downplayed until very recently.

A third factor in the tendency not to explore questions of change in studies of African art and aesthetics has to do with politics. The general public in the United States became interested in non-Western arts in the mid-sixties, a time of political upheaval. Clearly at that point in American history people had vested interests in exploring the "high" arts of their own cultural heritages, particularly in African-American communities. While the events of the sixties encouraged the study of traditional art, they also mitigated against the analysis of the Western definitions and categories used in much of this arts research. Western standards defined which African objects were included in art collections, such as those in the Metropolitan Museum of Art or the National Museum of African Art, with little regard for the ways in which these objects were defined in the contexts in which they had been produced. Using African objects in this way made important statements about Africa, Africans, and the heritage of African-Americans, but it also tended to reify particular African traditions and forms as "authentic" in ways that reinforced both the markets' emphasis on traditional objects and the scholarly interests in uncovering traditions at the cost of exploring how those traditions have changed over time.

THE THEORETICAL FRAMEWORK

The approach to aesthetics that I present here turns around three concerns: redundancy, agency, and power. It moves the study of aesthetics and value away from a focus on the art/non-art dilemma and applies contemporary social theory to questions of change and variation. It is fueled by several related theoretical approaches. The first is derived from studies that examine the arts as systems of nonverbal communication that embody modes of classifying the natural and social order. The significance of the meanings conveyed by these nonverbal systems is derived from the perception of relationships between the components of form rather than through the form's direct representation of other cultural facts, such as mythology or religion. These nonverbal relational meanings are not restricted to the art sphere but derive their significance from their expression or modification of basic principles that are used to organize all of social life (Fagg 1973; Munn 1973; Simmel 1968). Because they can be shown to operate in a wide variety of contexts, they provide individuals with a framework or the predispositions for action that simultaneously mirror and shape what has been termed the aesthetic dimension of social life (d'Azevedo 1958; Geertz 1976; Karp 1980; Riesman 1975). Thus, material or social form or, more precisely, the production and use of form by human agents can be seen to both embody and be involved in the process of constituting the social wholes within which human action becomes meaningful. In this way one begins to see a larger picture, one that more adequately addresses questions of context, the place of evaluated forms within a cultural whole, and the specific meaning of forms.

The second concept that this analysis draws from is redundancy. While the principles that organize social life and the forms to which they are applied may vary between cultures, the Kono material suggests it is the very adherence to, and successful representation of, principles that elicits positive aesthetic response. The primary mechanism here is redundancy. Bateson (1972a) suggests it is redundancy that makes something remarkable, noticeable, apparent, even meaningful. It is the very repetition of form that leads to appreciation and the sense of fitness or appropriateness associated with aesthetic judgment (Adams 1973, 1977; Baxandall 1972; Fernandez 1971, 1973, 1976; Kaeppler 1978, 1986; Thompson 1973). It is this kind of repetition that produces similarities in different spheres of experience, but similarities that are not causally connected. Thus, agricultural or subsistence patterns in general do not structure action in other spheres; rather, it is the repetition itself and the perceived similarities between different spheres that provide patterns for action and value and the framework that people use to construct, and deconstruct, tradition.

In social science research, an obviously related approach is the notion of "total social phenomena" (Beidelman 1963, 1966, 1986; Durkheim 1915; Evans-Pritchard 1940, 1956, 1960; Hertz 1960; Lienhardt 1961; Mauss 1966). This approach implies that the numerous spheres of social life usually conceived of by the social scientist as discrete are actually structured by a core of principles that provides the framework and idioms for individual action. These, in turn, become resources for the interpretation of experience and the reproduction of that framework over time. The "whole" that this position implies, however, should not be taken as homogenous; instead, it must be considered in terms of the inner conflicts and multiple voices jockeying for power and expression in ways that subtly shape social and cultural forms. Methodologically, the approach I outline here entails the observation of social phenomena as part of an integrated and comprehensible whole "whose parts cannot be adequately comprehended in isolation from each other" (Needham 1963:xxxiv).

A third approach that I draw on in this volume comes from recent work in social theory that addresses the role of human agency and production processes in the construction of social and cultural formations (Bourdieu 1977; Giddens 1976; Jackson and Karp 1990; Karp 1986). Social science has generally defined the patterns or principles that shape social and cultural forms as structure. The perspective taken in this volume draws from Giddens's more flexible notion of structural properties. Essentially, he argues that structural properties are "temporally present only in their instantiation, in the constituting moments of social systems" (Giddens 1979:64). In other words, structural properties emerge at various times and in varying configurations. These organizing principles are never present in identical forms over time but are always in the

process of becoming through human action. In this way "social structures are both constituted *by* human agency, and yet at the same time are
the very *medium* of this constitution" (Giddens 1976:121). To explore
this further, I have focused on the relationships among structural properties, the idioms in which they are manifested, and patterns of action.[6]
As patterns of action are increasingly practiced, they become more idiomatic and apparent in a variety of domains. As such paradigmatic associations are established, they become increasingly important resources
for structuring meaning and perception in ways that allow for the constitution of particular arrangements of structural properties. As a result,
structural properties have the potential to guide (but not determine) action, but simultaneously action has the possibility of affecting the emergence of structural properties.

While this is not central to my argument, it is important to point out
that structural properties are probably meta-cultural principles. What is
culture specific are the idiomatic patterns and associations that manifest
the ever-changing arrangements of structural properties and the shape of
the structural properties guiding action at any particular point in time.
Change in the arrangement of structural properties, then, results from
changes in action and the potential such changes have for reconstructing
or resorting the perception or evaluation of action at the level of idiomatic forms. While redundancy and its appreciation is one of the means
that people use to reproduce particular configurations of structural
properties, reproduction in a world of constant flux necessarily implies
changes in action; thus, reproduction is as inherently problematic as
change itself.

Incorporating practice-oriented theories of scholars such as Anthony
Giddens, Pierre Bourdieu, and others also allows a move away from the
"art as a reflection of culture" model and toward an examination of
what individuals do, the choices they make, and the rationale for their
choices. Looking at individuals in this way reveals the process by which
change occurs over time in at least two ways: when tensions between individual interests and socially held values are resolved and rationalized
in the contingencies of everyday situations, and when individual interpretations of situations change.

Looking at production and aesthetic evaluation in this way reveals
the degrees of slippage and variation that potentially lead to constructing new values and tastes over time. In 1958 d'Azevedo (1958:708)
wrote that aesthetic effect emerges from "the correspondences perceived

between the qualities of an aesthetic object and their affinities in the subjective experience of the individual." In other words, appreciation stems from recognition of formal analogies, the recognition of already-known principles in particular forms.[7] Sieber (1985) captured this emphasis on repetition and recognition when he said in a lecture "I may not know anything about art, but I know what I like"; this should be changed to "I may not know anything about art, but I like what I know." It is what people know, then, from their own subjective experience, shaped as it is by culture, personal experience, interests, and repetition in various guises, that imbues expressive forms with a sense of appropriateness and value. But even here, the ways of knowing, or the mechanisms by which meaning becomes associated with form or action, are related to the perceptions of individuals. How these perceptions are constructed must be understood in order to understand affect.

This approach takes an investigation of aesthetics far beyond the realm of what we, as Westerners, would call "art." In fact, it often makes art an irrelevant point. Instead, it opens the way for examining local categories of experience and production, analogies among these categories, and similarities in the attribution of value across domains of experience. Then the emphasis becomes discovering indigenous systems of value, defining the range of social or material forms to which value is applied, and at the same time understanding how, and perhaps why, value is applied to specific forms at specific times. From such comparisons, the outsider begins to have a picture or map of the principles, predispositions for action, and habits that shape social life as well as appreciation and criticism.

Equally important for the goals of this volume, looking at agency and practice provides a way of examining the constitutive and constructive potential of aesthetic evaluation, and this raises questions of power. If aesthetic perceptions and responses are tempered by the subjective experience of individuals, as d'Azevedo (1958) suggests, then groups of individuals must somehow arrive at an approximation of agreement about how they view the world and actions in it. Such agreements are tempered to some degree by shared histories, but allowing variation and subjective experience into the equation opens the analysis to include the possibility of viewing the interpretations of action and form as indeterminant, negotiated, and constantly in flux. Thus, interpretation can have significant consequences as particular interpretations are given more weight or import than others. Personal reputations play a role here, in the sense that individuals with power tend to be given more weight in group situations. Similarly, if background and personal history color individual interpretations, then those with similar backgrounds and interests will be more likely to arrive at similar interpretations.

Individual interests in particular situations also affect interpretation and evaluation. Thus, reputation, personal history, and interests are all factors that must be dealt with in the building of consensus or the politics of interpretation, but these factors are only made visible through accounts of the lives and actions of individuals.

Giving one set of evaluations precedence over others raises questions about power and the consequences such decisions have for future action and for ideas of morality. What will become clear is that many of the idioms discussed in this volume are moral idioms. How people account for success or failure of action often has to do with judgments about character. The potential for evaluative statements to take on moral significance was first noted by Leach (1954:37) when he wrote that "[e]verywhere there is some intimate relationship between ethics and aesthetics and, since ethical systems vary from one society to another, so aesthetic systems must vary too." When taken in moral terms, aesthetic evaluation is no longer an exercise in "taste." Instead, it takes on the aura of a powerful tool for framing categories of people and action, as well as for generating expectations and the very principles that will frame evaluation in the future. The generative aspect of particular kinds of power has been noted by Foucault (1977). For a more recent exploration of the creative aspects of power, see Arens and Karp (1989).[8]

METHODOLOGY

The approach to aesthetics and change presented in this volume can only be operationalized through the interweaving of many kinds of data—life histories, participant observation, documentation on the production of a wide variety of objects and occasions, and the understanding of the way language is used to appreciate or evaluate objects, occasions, and everyday life. Most of all, however, collecting data for this kind of research implies an attention to values and patterns of action in a way that allows recognition of the qualitative features of everyday life. In most situations the qualitative features of everyday life are best apprehended at an experiential level as insights to be checked verbally, or in other ways, at a later time. In settings or situations where the experiential level cannot be reached, careful attention to language, gesture, innuendo, and other cues must serve to round out what will always remain an incomplete and inadequate picture.

At this writing I have made two research trips to Sierra Leone— March 1982 to April 1984 and June to July 1988. During my initial months in the field, I alternated between participant-observation and informal interviews. Formal interviews were used to clarify questions or ideas that had been raised in more informal settings. Language training was also an invaluable source of information for me as I tried to get at categories of experience and criticism. Eventually, I found myself increasingly aligned with several large extended families. I was able to come and go as any other household member in these families, and this provided me with exposure to the range of activities and emotions that make up the ebb and flow of everyday life. Close ties to these families also allowed me access to family farms where I was able to begin to comprehend some of the complexities of subsistence agriculture.

There were two reasons for using such an open-ended and informal approach to data collection. The first has to do with my preference for working informally and my commitment to the importance of combining verbalized and observational/participatory data that is collected over a long period of time in a variety of contexts. Equally important, I felt that what distinguished my project from other studies of aesthetics was a commitment to examining local categories of experience and finding ways to trace relationships between those categories. This implied not only using methods such as direct questioning but also apprehending and, hopefully, learning how the Kono came to experience and use these categories. As a result, I spent much of my initial two years in the Kono area listening, watching, and participating. Not only was I looking for categories of experience, but I was also searching for the cues that signal categories, appreciation, or displeasure. Some of these cues are verbalized in response to questions, but there are other layers of the repertoire associated with appreciation that can only be apprehended over time through attention to such cues as gesture, the use of space, and other kinds of information.

A major part of my research also relied on efforts to learn various production processes firsthand. This meant spending long days on farms where I learned the stages between clearing a farm and harvesting rice. I also learned how to process harvested rice, how to make palm oil, how to fish, and a variety of other tasks. Emphasizing firsthand knowledge meant accompanying women when they went to collect firewood or to do laundry, helping to take care of children, and learning to cook. I also became an apprentice in order to learn the skills of indigo dying and ceramic production. At the same time, I learned about the responsibilities of a student towards a teacher. To learn to spin I did what any young woman might do—I went to an older woman with kola and other small gifts and asked her to teach me. In these various ways I was able to learn about making or doing certain things, but I was also able to examine how the Kono teach, learn, and judge abilities or skills. In tasks that women do not undertake I made a conscious decision to rely on interviews, observations, and photographs, rather than to learn firsthand.

It is also important to explain that, as a result of my choice of field methods, much of my ethnographic and observational data shares the point of view of my Kono contemporaries. As an unmarried student between 1982 and 1984, I had the most access to young women and men, those who were contemplating marriage, those who had recently married, and those who had small children. From this perspective I was privy to debates about access to land, problems with marriage and household formation, aspirations for the future, and complaints and concerns about the responsibilities of marriage. In my return trip in 1988 I was able to observe how the positions and concerns of my contemporaries had shifted with their changing positions in domestic and lineage groupings. At that time as a professional and a married woman, I had more access to political debates and to the life histories of older women and men. I expect that each return to the Kono area will open a different set of doors as my contemporaries pass through the life cycle. In the chapters that follow I have tried to distinguish and contrast the various voices and perspectives that have been collected up to this time.

As a final note, I should add a word on language. Before beginning fieldwork I studied Bambara, a language related to Mandingo, Kuranko, and, somewhat more distantly, to Kono. Variations of Bambara are spoken in Mali, Guinea, Senegal, and northeastern Sierra Leone. After I arrived in Sierra Leone I spent several weeks in Freetown working intensively on Kono, building on my training in Bambara. Once I arrived in the Kono area I continued studying and attempting to use the language. By the end of the first six months I had no trouble carrying on everyday conversations. If I wanted to talk about more difficult things, however, I would switch the conversation to Krio (an English-based pidgin) or I would use an interpreter who would continue the conversation in Kono and speak to me in either Krio or English. In these cases I could understand much of the Kono spoken but felt less able to frame conversations myself. Krio is fast becoming the lingua franca of Sierra Leone and is relatively easy to learn, particularly the up-country variety that emphasizes less Yoruba than coastal versions. In the rural parts of Kono today Krio is spoken by most adult men, many women, and almost all of the younger generation. Elderly men and especially elderly women, however, often do not speak Krio. A relatively small group made up primarily of teachers and government officials speak English.

STRUCTURE INTO ACTION/ACTION INTO STRUCTURE

After a brief introduction to the regional and national setting of the Kono, this book is divided into two parts. Part I—Structure into Action—considers the ways in which structural properties, in the guise of ideas about tradition and appropriate action, shape Kono history, ideas of personhood, social organization, and techniques of production. The dialectical relationship between structural properties and behavioral idioms is important here. Equally important are the choices that individuals make on a daily basis and the potential such choices have for reshaping both habits of action and, by extension, structural properties. Chapter 3 focuses on the ways that jural norms of the descent system intersect with aspects of the domestic domain in ways that produce identity, affect, and sentiment. I am particularly interested in tracing how actions in a variety of domains interpenetrate to reproduce certain actions over time. One of the points here is that the actions of a single domain are not causal in this process. Rather, it is the coordination of actions across domains that tends to produce or reproduce structure. Chapter 4 considers the ways in which aspects of identity established through attachments to particular places limit claims to identity that might be available through the manipulation of patrilineal or matrifilial affiliations. Embedded within this discussion is a recognition of the constant struggle between two dimensions of personhood—the objectively or culturally defined expectations of others and the subjective interpretations of self that are idiosyncratic to each individual. The limitations on an individual's actions are related to the efforts made by human agents to live up to the values established by tradition (essentially particular con-

figurations of structural properties) to meet the expectations of others
and to be seen as good or moral people while they simultaneously try
to meet personal goals. Some of the limitations discussed come from
the intimate knowledge of genealogical ties that those living in the same
community share and the periodic rituals that continually reattach individuals to particular places. Another kind of limitation stems from
modes of enculturation that foster group identity over individual intention. As individuals strive to live up to the ideals of what it means to be
a good person, they find subjective goals channeled along avenues that
foster group cohesion and ideals. Chief among such modes of constraint are a system of birth-order naming that restricts certain kinds of
knowledge about the individual and concepts of the human body that
work to distinguish between moral (socially sanctioned) and amoral (socially uncontrolled) emotions and actions in physically or somatically
charged ways.

Chapters 5 and 6 focus on the ways in which structural properties
emerge in everyday action. The Kono material suggests that aesthetic
preferences are rooted in habitual patternings or predispositions for action that crosscut domains of life. Specifically, Chapter 5 looks at agriculture, cloth production, and the construction of a successful dance occasion to explore the ways in which particular habits of action emerge.
These analogies are interpreted as idioms that habitually reproduce, although in potentially ever-changing forms, the principles that organize
social life. Positive aesthetic response is produced only when appropriate
idioms are perceived as effective in particular circumstances. The key
here is that the perception of relationships is rooted within individual or
subjective experience. By recognizing the powerful role of individuals in
aesthetic determinations, aesthetic judgments become one of the primary
mechanisms through which structure and action impinge upon each
other, and aesthetic judgments become a primary factor in change.

Chapter 6 also demonstrates the mutually reinforcing relationships
among structural properties, categories of production, and forms of aesthetic criticism. Implicit within this analysis is the idea that only in action, as in the process of categorizing the surrounding world, are structural properties reproduced over time. Given the integral relationship
between structure and action it is not surprising to see that the Kono arrangement of categories of production is somewhat unique. While the
Kono do not have a category of "art" in a Euro-American sense, it is
clear that aesthetic judgments inform production in a variety of domains

and that these judgments are integrally related to the stuff of which social life in general is composed. The ethnographic data also show that aesthetic criticism, whether applied to what we would call "art" or "non-art" domains, crosscuts forms of production in specific and patterned ways and thus can be used as a way of further exploring categories of production and the ways that aesthetic evaluation works to reproduce structural properties.

Part II—Action into Structure—deals with the ways in which actions impinge on structure. Chapter 7 focuses on the relationships among action, knowledge, and power and authority in Kono life, how children learn about these interrelationships, and how Kono adults manage power and authority. Power here refers to the ability to have one's interpretations or evaluations of action count.

The first part of Chapter 8 discusses the importance of variations in the interpretation of action as a result of differences in personal experience or interests. I use interpretation here in the sense of recognition and incorporation, even embodiment, of the habits of action that carry meaning over time and serve as models for action in the future. Aesthetic judgments, then, reflect the mesh of personal differences in the habits of interpretation as well as in the habits of rationalization in vogue at particular points in time. From this vantage point aesthetic judgments can be used to explore the politics of subjective experience. Essentially I am interested in the ways that criticism is manifested in everyday life and the potential of such variations to transform the structural properties outlined in Part I.

The last section of Chapter 8 considers structural transformations and change in more depth. Change is taken as an inherent aspect of the process of production. As individuals make adjustments based both on personal differences and the contingencies of everyday situations, new kinds of associations or configurations of meaning come into use. I focus particularly on how these relationships or resonances provide insights into the ". . . ways that actions in different social fields have consequences for each other" (Karp 1978a:157). As once-accepted forms are contested and re-negotiated, the very shape of structural properties changes, as do ideas about what constitutes appropriate action.

In Chapter 9 I summarize the various points raised in previous chapters and consider the implications of my argument for anthropological research. I also examine other aesthetic systems. I am particularly interested in exploring the relevance of the approach used in my research for elite Euro-American art worlds.

By way of closing this introduction, I would emphasize that the division of this volume into two parts is not meant to suggest that such divisions have any reality in real life. Rather, the division is an heuristic device that merely provides a way of separating like factors away from the chaos of everyday life long enough to explore and analyze them. Neither half of the book can be read alone or without an understanding of the processes discussed in the other half. The analysis of structure or structural properties in the first half can only be fully understood through an understanding of the ways in which action and agency work together to constitute and reconstitute structure over time.

2

THE REGIONAL SETTING

The Kono are a northern Mande-speaking ethnic group living in an area of about 2,178 square miles in the Kono District of the Eastern Province of Sierra Leone. The Mende live to the south and the Kuranko live to the north. The eastern and western boundaries of the Kono area are marked by the Kissy and Temne ethnic groups, respectively, and it is not unusual to find Kono who speak one or all of these languages in addition to Kono, Krio, and English (Fig. 1). I consider the history of relations among these various ethnic groups in Chapter 3. At the time of the 1974 government census there were approximately 13,000 Kono living in the Kono area (Thomas 1983).

The research for this book was conducted in the eastern part of Kono, an area characterized primarily by low-lying hills, savannah, and secondary forests. Boulders, rocky outcrops, and swamps are scattered among the hills and forested areas. During the rainy season (*saama*), which occurs from March to September, the hills are hidden in rain and mist. Most of the rainfall in Kono, which measures between 100 and 120 inches per year, falls in the rainy season. The heavy agricultural labor is undertaken during the rainy season, with farmers relying on the rains to water their various crops. By contrast, the dry season (*tehma*), which runs from October to February, is a time of rest, celebration, and feasting. For much of the dry season the atmosphere is heavy with waves of dust brought by the *harmattan* winds that sweep in from the Sahara. On the occasional clear day in Kono, however, it is possible to see all the way from Guinea in the east to central Sierra Leone in the west from many of the higher hilltops in the area.

Currently, Kono can only be reached by road.[1] Government buses, privately owned trucks, and *poda podas* (Volkswagen buses and other vans altered to take as many passengers as possible) regularly ply the 200 miles between Koidu, the Kono district headquarters and the second largest city in Sierra Leone, and Freetown, the capital of Sierra Leone. From Koidu, unpaved roads spread out to connect various parts of the Kono District. An unpaved road also connects Koidu with Kenema, a major population center in the south of the country. In addition to people, the roads carry trucks loaded with dried fish, imported rice, and imported goods, such as cloth, clothing, tinware, plastics, petrol, kerosene, and building supplies from Freetown to the provinces. On their return trip, the vehicles carry people and commodities, such as palm oil, *gara* (dyed cloth), vegetable goods, and other products from Koidu to supply the markets of Freetown. Imported goods that eventually make their way to rural towns in the Kono area usually come from Freetown by way of Koidu. Some foreign goods, however, are smuggled into the Kono area across the Guinea border, and many of these end up in the markets of Koidu.[2]

KOIDU

Koidu serves as the market and transportation center for the Kono area and as the administrative headquarters for the Kono District. While the economy of eastern Kono depends primarily on agriculture, the economies of Koidu and other westerly Kono areas are based primarily on diamonds, which have been mined in the areas around Koidu, Yengema, and Sefadu since the early 1930s when British surveyors discovered the gem deposits. Since that discovery, the diamond mining concession (National Diamond Mining Corporation) has been owned and operated first by the British, then by several companies that included both British and Sierra Leonean managers, and since 1988 by the Sierra Leonean government, which has been looking for a foreign company to take it over. Several studies have been done on the impact of the mining industry on the Kono area (see, for example, Conteh 1976 and Rosen 1973) and on the history of diamond mining in Sierra Leone (van der Laan 1965).

Koidu has been called the wild west of West Africa because of the glut of workers who have migrated there in search of quick riches. The city's population consists of Kono along with migrants from all over Sierra Leone and neighboring countries. The economy has always been focused on alluvial mining, a labor intensive process in which gravel is dug during the rainy season as new deposits are exposed by each rain. The gravel is then sifted for gems. Some workers remain in the area during the dry season, but many go back to their homes until the next rainy season begins.[3] The composition of the labor population varies with changing government regulations about access to the mining fields. In 1988, for example, after the government had opened up mining to anyone able to lease land, the road into Koidu was lined with squatter camps of migrants hoping to strike it rich. In some cases, the ethnicity of the migrants could be identified by the style of their makeshift mud-walled houses along the road. These houses were occasionally interspersed with cement and zinc-roofed houses, testimony to the fact that a few diggers do, indeed, make big money in the diamond fields.

Most diggers spend their days, and sometimes nights, in the backbreaking work of exposing, sifting, and washing gravel under the watchful eyes of a gang foreman. The lucky ones are paid a few leones for a day's work. The rest work with the hope that they will uncover the next legendary stone. Every season, new stories detail where large stones were exposed and how much the digger was paid for them, fueling the dreams of those not so lucky. Stories of large finds have become part of the folklore of the area, uniting strangers through the aspirations they instill in what is an otherwise disenfranchised population.

The majority of diggers are male, young, and poor. At nightfall in Kono, one can see hundreds of these workers trudging home alongside the main road from Freetown to Koidu. The lucky ones have wives or girlfriends who have prepared dinner for them in the squatter settlements. The rest will have to buy food from women who have migrated to the area to cater to the needs of the largely male population. While this volume does not discuss workers in the western Kono area in any detail, it is important for the reader to have a sense of the options available to eastern Kono men and women. Work in the mining areas is one of these options.

Western Kono shows the scars of the mining industry very clearly. Rumors of a find in a particular area are followed, virtually overnight, by an influx of hundreds of workers with shovels and picks. As a result, vast areas of potential farmland have been denuded to expose the potentially diamond-rich gravel. Areas that were once lush, green forests have been transformed overnight to red clay expanses that are covered with man-sized pot holes and trenches. When the digging season is over, the land is left barren. In an otherwise verdant tropical environment the diamond tailings are the only areas of the region that fail to return to the greenery typical of the tropics in the rainy season. Instead, these areas are caught up in their own cycle, alternating between muddy washes in the rainy season and packed red clay or dust in the dry season. It is impossible to estimate the effort it will take to return this region to agricultural production, but the diamond fever is so high-pitched at the present time that few worry about it. Even essential parts of the infrastructure of the area fall prey to diamond fever. Some of the roads in the area have gone from two lanes to one as diggers pick away on either side. I fully expect that by my next visit several of these roads (some of which are main arteries to and from the eastern agricultural areas) will be gone entirely.

Koidu also has a government hospital, several secondary schools, and the largest market in the district. The main streets of Koidu are lined with pharmacies, banks, mosques, and shops that sell imported goods. The Koidu market extends along one side of the main street. Not far in the other direction is the lorry park where lorries (large flat-bed trucks) and taxis begin their journeys to Freetown and the western region or to the towns and villages of eastern Kono (Fig. 1).

Walking through the streets of Koidu can be sheer bedlam for a foreigner. Rural Kono sense the bedlam as well, but for them it is tinged with excitement, much the same as an American might feel on a visit to New York City or any other large metropolitan center. Koidu has electricity and running water sporadically, and the diversity of goods is overwhelming compared with what is available in most up-country towns and villages. Aside from the businesses, many of which are owned by Lebanese traders[4], Koidu's streets are lined with hundreds of small-scale, independent merchants—groups of women roaming the sidewalks selling cucumbers, roast corn, or whatever is in season, goats being led to market, stalls of Mandingo merchants with blankets or leather work from Mali, young Fullah men hawking eggs (fresh or boiled), and Muslim men in flowing robes selling medicines and cures for every illness. Everywhere there are men, women, and children selling bread, watches, cassette tapes, soap, and imported pharmaceuticals. Five times a day the three main mosques of the city use their taped and amplified prayer calls

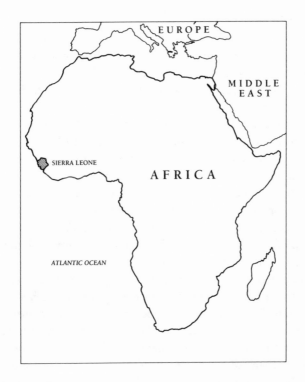

Fig. 1 Map of Africa and detailed map of Sierra Leone.

to compete for supporters. There are also beggars—the blind, crippled, and otherwise unfortunate. Many are Muslim and are only too eager to help those more fortunate than themselves dispose of their alms and win a place in heaven.

City services in Koidu have declined radically over the last decade. In 1982, when I arrived in Koidu, running water and electricity were taken for granted. By 1984, they were available only sporadically. By 1988, they were virtually nonexistent, except to those with their own generators. Petrol, the life blood of any transportation center, also has a history of being unpredictable, and even a rumor of an impending shortage is enough to generate day-long lines at petrol stations.

Sharp decreases in the availability of city services and imported goods over the last ten years are integrally tied to economic shifts throughout Sierra Leone that have made diamond digging an increasingly attractive alternative to farming, government employment, or other kinds of wage employment. This refocusing has occurred not only because of the lure of quick riches but also because of the unpredictability of other sources of income and the increasingly limited possibilities for economic advancement outside the diamond arena. As the country faces shortages of foreign exchange, rising inflation, and other economic ills, the financial and transportation infrastructures have deteriorated. Businesses are unable to stock the foreign goods that previously filled their shelves, the government is unwilling or unable to pay its employees regularly, and farmers are unable to move produce to markets. Between 1982 and 1984, it was common for school teachers to have to wait several months for their wages. By 1989, some teachers had not been paid for twelve months, and many of the country's schools went on strike from November 1988 to April 1989 in protest. Teachers are only one group of trained professionals who are increasingly unable to survive within their field of choice. As a result of such economic instability, many individuals are left with only two options—agriculture or diamonds (assuming they can lease land in the productive areas).

Agriculture as anything more than a subsistence activity (i.e., securing enough food for oneself and one's family for the year), however, is currently as unpredictable as diamonds. The lack of dependable transportation and its exorbitant cost when it is available mean that an individual with produce to sell, whether it is rice, coffee, or cocoa, will quite likely be unable to transport it to market and still make a profit. In short, if one aspires to a standard of living above that available to subsistence farmers, one's only real alternative is getting involved in the diamond industry. Although the specifics of the refocusing toward diamonds are beyond the scope of this book, this brief description is important because it sheds light on some of the choices that are increasingly a part of the lives of rural farmers in eastern Kono.

EASTERN KONO AND KAINKORDU

There are fourteen separate chiefdoms in the Kono area, each with its own headquarter town. Paramount chiefs are responsible for settling land, marital, and other kinds of disputes within and between chiefdoms. Most of my research was carried out in Soa Chiefdom. The chiefdom headquarters is Kainkordu, which is midway between Koidu and the Guinea border. While the distance from Koidu to Kainkordu is only twenty miles, the trip can take from several hours to two days, depending on the condition of roads and vehicles. During the dry season in 1982 and 1983, several trucks made daily trips from Koidu to Kainkordu, then travelled twenty miles further to Kamiendo and the Guinea border, and returned to Koidu the same day. In 1988 during the rainy season only one truck a day passed through Kainkordu, and I was told that even during the dry season trucks were no longer a reliable method of transport. The deteriorating road conditions and the lack of foreign exchange at the national level, which would enable the import of spare parts for vehicles, were the major reasons given for this slowdown. When the trucks are running, they carry people, dried fish, kerosene, and other marketable goods into rural areas, and they return loaded with produce for the markets of Koidu or Freetown (Figs. 2, 3 and 4).

Some trucks are also involved in smuggling goods between Guinea and Sierra Leone. People can sometimes get higher prices for agricultural produce and goods, such as kerosene or petrol, in Guinea, but some also find that it is easier to transport a crop into Guinea than to Koidu. By 1988, a government produce buying agent was stationed in Manjama, three miles from Kainkordu, to buy produce, thereby relieving farmers of the financial burden of transporting their crops to Koidu. Even with this incentive, some farmers found it more profitable to continue selling their crops across the border in Guinea.

Some of the drivers own their trucks and some lease them from wealthy Kono or Lebanese in Koidu. The drivers and the lorry boys who maintain the trucks and land rovers are looked up to as important people by many, but these occupations have a negative side as well. Lorry workers are usually not the kind of men people want their daughters to marry. Because anyone who does not farm is considered somewhat shiftless and irresponsible, those who opt to work on the trucks lose a degree of respect. In addition, because they travel so much, lorry workers are assumed to have sexual liaisons with many women. While these kinds of liaisons themselves are not necessarily considered immoral, they are certainly demanding on a man financially. While the drivers and lorry boys may make a lot of money, they also spend a lot of it on the road. People also view the drivers as hard or greedy because they rarely make concessions or lessen fares for anyone, even in emergencies. At some time in their lives, this "hard heartedness" and lack of generosity inevitably comes back to haunt them. Thus, people are not surprised to hear that a driver has ruined his truck, been in a bad accident, or felt catastrophe in some other way (Fig. 5).

The drivers and lorry boys are also known as masters of ingenuity in a place where spare parts are almost nonexistent. During one of my waits in the lorry park, I noticed a makeshift spring arrangement in which the actual springs for a front tire had separated and had been repaired by tying them together with lengths of rubber from a salvaged tire. When a truck breaks down away from an urban center, the driver and lorry boys have to rely on their own ingenuity and stash of spare parts (Fig. 6).

Only after people are assured that a vehicle in the lorry park is ready for travel will they agree to have their goods loaded. Otherwise they fear that, if once committed, they will find that the truck really cannot make the trip after all. The passengers take their places as best as they can, usually four in the front seat and ten or fifteen others sprawled on top of the load in back. Several times during the journey drivers have to ask their passengers to get down and walk—up steep hills, over makeshift bridges, and in other places that are either too dangerous or too steep for a fully loaded vehicle. Passengers probably walk two to three miles of the twenty-mile trip. The fact that people remember when Datsun and Toyota taxis (the sedan or economy models) could make the trip between Koidu and Kainkordu is further evidence of the rapid deterioration of services in the Kono area.[5] By 1988, many people were opting to walk the entire twenty miles between Koidu and Kainkordu rather than putting up with the unpredictability and high cost of the trucks but, because the hills make it an all-day trek, anyone with a good-sized load to carry will usually take a chance on the trucks (Fig. 7).

The eastern Kono attribute what they see as the major problems in the area—the lack of access to markets and adequate medical care—to the poor road conditions. The twenty-mile trip over difficult terrain also makes full participation in the diamond industry difficult for anyone unable or unwilling to migrate to the Koidu area.

The proximity of the diamond mining industry around Koidu has had a tremendous effect on the demography of Kainkordu and the eastern Kono area in general. Most men have at one time or another been involved with mining. It is my impression that Kainkordu now has a dearth of young, able-bodied men because many of them migrate to the diamond fields for at least part of the year. This has left the population of the chiefdom made up primarily of older men, women, and young children. When the migrants flock back to town in the dry season, they are dependant on their in-laws and families for food. The small amounts of cash that they might have to contribute is often not enough to offset the presence of extra mouths to feed, and tensions can run very high. Most women, however, opt for participation in small-scale local marketing as a means to earn cash (Fig. 8). A few women have attempted to move into larger-scale marketing, buying agricultural products in Kainkordu and selling them in Koidu, then returning with goods to sell in local markets around Kainkordu. The increasing transportation costs and the difficulty of getting transportation have made this a more difficult option over the last few years.

The main outlet for women is the weekly Sunday market in Manjama, located three miles from Kainkordu. There, some Kono women sell salt, onions, *magii* cubes (a kind of bouillon cube), palm oil, peanut paste, produce, kerosene, and prepared foods, such as beans, *gari* cakes (a cake made from fried cassava), and fried potatoes. Other merchants sell an array of additional products. Mende women market dried, and sometimes fresh, fish; Mandingo men sell tobacco and, sometimes, pharmaceuticals; other men who come from Koidu sell used clothing, *gara* (dyed cloth), enamelware basins or metal cooking pots. One area of the market is set aside for wholesale produce that will be bought by merchants from Koidu. The market as a whole is both an economic opportunity as well as a social occasion. People from towns and villages in the area travel to Manjama not only to buy and sell, but also to gossip and see their friends and family members.

Rural Kono live in nucleated settlements and people travel daily to their surrounding farmlands. As the chiefdom headquarters, Kainkordu is one of the oldest towns in the area. It was settled during "warrior times," a period predating 1900 and colonial rule when war chiefs battled for territory and property (i.e., women, slaves, and crops). During this period towns were built on hilltops to allow sentries a view of attackers as they approached. Consequently, older towns in the area are difficult to reach, and their position on hills means they are well above the water table. Because water pumping systems are expensive and drilling is difficult, even when the equipment can be brought to the site, women and children in many older Kono towns must walk some distance downhill to obtain spring water and trudge uphill carrying a full bucket of water on their heads. Water is not such a major problem in recently settled towns since they tend to be located in low-lying areas. Many individuals have left their family hilltop homes and resettled in towns that have sprouted up in more convenient low-lying areas. Because the old warrior towns tend also to be political centers, the migration has potentially redistributed or diluted the political power of chiefdom and town elders. Kainkordu is also a center for education in the chiefdom. When the school teachers are being paid by the government, primary students for miles around descend on Kainkordu daily for lessons. The two-roomed schoolhouse accommodates all six primary grades. It was originally set up by Catholic missionaries and is still overseen by the Catholic mission in Koidu, but the government now pays the salaries of the five teachers and the headmaster.

Today, the buildings in Kainkordu flank the road, although remnants of houses arranged in compounds can still be seen as one moves away from the road. In 1988, there were 113 houses and a population of about 1,100 in Kainkordu (the population varies greatly between the dry and wet seasons). The size of rural settlements, however, varies from several houses in the smallest villages to over one hundred in chiefdom head-quarter towns. Larger towns are divided into *fondon* (quarters or neighborhoods of agnatically related males, their affines and clients or supporters). In these larger towns an individual's allegiance is not solely toward the town but is split between the *fondon*, the domestic unit (*sinyuenu*), and the sublineage, which may extend beyond the boundaries of the *sinyuenu*. Kainkordu has four quarters: *chewaiyo fono*, the area around the paramount chief's compound (it is also called the place that "if they do not call you there, you will not go"); Kundama *fono*, the

Kpakiwa family's part of town, named for the village of Kundama where the Kpakiwas came from; Kamadu *fono*, home to the people of Kamadu; and *nyande fono*, home to the people who do not eat dog. Each quarter is headed by a family elder, and the town chief presides over the elders of the quarters. The town chief often consults with the paramount chief (who controls the chiefdom), but each leader has specific responsibilities (these will be discussed later in the volume). Kono towns further away from the road are smaller, sometimes made up of only one family.

Most Kono houses prior to the 1930s and 1940s were round constructions (*chi chi*) with a lattice-work frame filled in with mud and faced with a layer of clay, conical thatched roofs, and a single front entryway. The interior of these houses could be divided into several rooms with mud walls or mat framing. Parsons (1964:4) describes one of these houses as follows:

> The interior of the house is simple and compact. The walls are plain
> mud daubed and yet covered with cobwebs and smoke. The one-
> room house has booths covered with mats to make separate sleeping
> compartments for the members of the family. Each booth is open and
> the front flap is rolled, letting light and fresh air in. The floor of
> each booth is a six-inch layer of hard packed earth upon which a mat
> is placed for a bed.

This type of housing is rapidly disappearing. Of the 113 houses in Kainkordu in 1988, only four were round. None of the round houses had earthen sleeping platforms, and none used mats to divide sleeping quarters for the occupants. Instead, wooden beds were used and internal space was divided by mud walls.

The circular structures have been supplanted by rectangular adobe block houses. Some of these have been faced with clay, some with cement, and all of them have *pan* (corrugated iron) roofs. Parsons (1964:3) reports that during his tenure in Sierra Leone in the 1930s the government was encouraging the construction of multi-roomed oblong houses with gabled, metal, or *pan* roofs, windows in each room, and a front and back door. Today, most of the houses in Kainkordu are of this type, although not all have front and back doors. Several versions of this contemporary house are shown in Figures 9 and 10.

Many of the newer houses also have store fronts. During rumors of a possible diamond boom in the 1940s, many builders constructed houses with storefronts in the hope of taking advantage of the boom. The store had a wide door that opened onto the front, a counter placed slightly behind this opening, and an array of goods displayed on the shelves and walls behind. Only three of these stores are still operating; all of them are run by Kuranko and Mandingo merchants who sell candles, kerosine, onions, *magii* cubes, medicines, mosquito coils, matches, cigarettes, tobacco, and other small items. In the houses that no longer use these rooms as store fronts the rooms are used as sleeping quarters or storage rooms.

All rectangular houses have verandas. During the day, people sit in the shade of the veranda, and women may cook there if they do not have a cooking house. Women may also sell produce or cooked food, such as beans, boiled cassava, or fried potatoes, on their verandas during the day. During the evening, people gather there to recount the day's events. The veranda is also the setting for much of the social interaction of a household, especially when it includes interaction with those not actually living in the house. A paramount chief, for example, often will greet people on his veranda rather than invite them into his personal rooms. In this way, much social interaction, whether it is of a political nature or a conversation with a friend, is public.

In most houses the first space entered is known in Krio as "the parlor" (Figs. 11 and 12). To my knowledge, there is not a Kono word for this area. In most houses this is a relatively empty space, with perhaps a table and/or a few chairs lined up against the walls. The parlor may also be used to store cooking vessels that are carried outside when meal preparations begin. In some houses the parlor itself is used for cooking, especially during the rainy season. In wealthier houses parlor furniture is more elaborate. The chairs are upholstered, photographs and pictures are hung on the walls, and other possessions are displayed.

Beyond the parlor are the occupants' rooms. These rooms contain personal possessions, usually a bed and, perhaps, a chair and a table. Again, there may be photographs or pictures on the walls. Even in this room, however, most personal possessions are hidden away. A woman's personal possessions may include fabric that is being saved for a special occasion, spun cotton ready to be woven into cloth, kerosene, foodstuffs such as palm oil (which is relatively difficult to get during certain times of the year), and the items that a woman may need for her next pregnancy or an impending birth (e.g., diaper pins, vaseline, infant's clothing, beads, and toys). Medicines, amulets, and other possessions that may be secret are also stored here. While the Kono participate in elaborate exchange networks (as will be described in Chapters 3 and 5), they have a tendency to hide personal wealth or items that others may request as payment for previously rendered services or loans. By secreting their personal possessions, they find that it is easier to counter the requests that others make for loans of money, clothing, jewelry, or other goods. It is for this reason as well that most daytime visiting takes place in relatively public areas, which display only those goods that most households have.

Along with a primary school, Kainkordu has a government medical dispensary and a midwife. Those who want more education or extensive medical care are required to go at least as far as Koidu.[6] Today, the infant mortality rate in Kainkordu is approximately 40 percent within the first year of life. The lack of adequate medical care, transportation, and clean water are major factors in this death rate.

The Kono year is divided into two distinct halves. The rainy season (March to September) is the time of agricultural labor. Families leave their homes in town early in the morning and walk to their farms, which may be several miles away, and return to town at dusk or later. Cooking, bathing, and all other household chores are done at the farms along with agricultural tasks. Beginning in March or April, farmers plant both savannah and hill areas with the principal crop, upland rice (*kwee*), using the techniques of shifting cultivation. This entails clearing a new area of forest each year. A few farmers also cultivate swamp rice, which was introduced in the 1930s. In addition to rice, other vegetable crops, such as cassava, potatoes, corn, beans, tomatoes, pumpkins, and okra, are planted. Some of the wealthiest families are involved in cash cropping—growing coffee, cocoa, or ground nuts for sale.

The rainy season is also the hungry season. By July or August many families have exhausted the previous year's supply of rice and they begin looking forward to the harvest, which starts as early as late August or September and continues into December. By late September or early October when the rains are decreasing, people say the dry season has begun.

After the rice harvest most families have several months without heavy agricultural labor. During this period young people are initiated into Poro and Sande societies,[7] families plan post-burial ceremonies (*dii boenu*) to send those who have died to the ancestors, older men weave outdoors, and women often organize communal fishing expeditions. In December and January the cold, dry winds of the *harmattan* blow into the area. Many people develop colds, runny noses, bronchial infections, and outbreaks of measles are common. During the dry season when most people stay in town every day, the tensions of close living are more likely to evolve into feuds and fights than at any other time of the year. Once the social events of the dry season are over, there is relatively little to keep townspeople occupied. By February and March it is hot, dusty, dry, almost oppressive. People's patience and tempers become short, and there is a building sense of waiting for something to happen, in much the same way that tension builds up before a thunderstorm. Finally the rains break and life changes gears as the rhythm of agricultural work once again takes over people's lives.

In general, the lives of most rural Kono are governed by the agricultural labor that is required in a subsistence economy, the recurrent cycling between rainy and dry season activities, and, to varying degrees, the economic policies of the national government. Within these boundaries people are engaged in the process of constructing meaningful, satisfying, and productive lives as outside influences and reinterpretations of what it means to be Kono (*Konomoenu*) are meshed in the actions of everyday life. In this process change occurs not only in the material aspects of life, but also in the ideas of what constitutes moral or appropriate behavior. How such changes occur and the direction they are taking in the Kono area provide the subjects of the rest of this volume.

I

STRUCTURE INTO ACTION

3

IDENTITY IN TIME

In the continuous interplay between past and present it is often difficult to distinguish new from old, tradition from innovation, and cause from effect because the past is used to interpret present events and present events are used to reinterpret the past. What can be seen are patterns that crosscut domains of experience. Such patterns link past with present and provide the resources for thinking about and shaping the future. As social scientists, we talk about these linkages as structures or structural properties, envisioning them as principles that are likely to endure, although possibly in ever-changing and contested forms, until they are no longer effective at sorting out and guiding individuals through the maze of behaviors they are called upon to interpret. According to Giddens (1976), it is important to see such structures as the product of human action, not as unchanging constants or rules. Structural properties provide the background against which individuals evaluate their own behavior, as well as the behavior of others. They provide models for behavior and, in doing so, form the basis for expectations. It is a given that various structures or structural properties sometimes, even often, come into conflict. It is within such conflicts that individuals are forced to choose among an array of possibilities in ways that have intended, as well as unintended, consequences for identity, reputation, and status. Embedded within such choices are multiple and sometimes conflicting goals, as evidenced in, for example, the tensions between the actions expected of individuals because of their social roles or positions and the actions that individuals determine to be in their own best interests.

This chapter looks at elements of Kono history, social organization, and identity in order to explore some of the patterns, principles, and structural properties that shape Kono action and aesthetic criticism. My focus will be on how ideas of history, rules of descent, and aspects of the domestic domain intersect to produce identity, affect, and sentiment. Such intersections structure action and identity in ways that provide individuals with a set of behavioral alternatives.

Throughout this discussion it is important to keep in mind that there are two dimensions that shape the actions of individuals. The first can be described as an ideological definition of personhood in which individuals behave according to the rules and norms that society imposes and expects. In many ways, ideas of the culturally objectified person provide the framework against which questions of morality and appropriate behavior are judged. The second dimension of individual identity is related to the ways in which individuals subjectively apprehend culturally objectified rules and norms as they respond to the realities of everyday life and attempt to match individual interests to the expectations of others.[1]

To begin with, one of the primary dimensions of Kono identity is construed in terms of time, as this is manifested in patrilineal affiliations. As will be seen, time and one's place in it is a question of interpretation. People are only who they say they are if others believe it and act accordingly. Embedded within the emphasis on the interpretation of patrilineal affiliation is the possibility of manipulating identity through action. The points at which interpretation and manipulation are allowed into determinations of identity tend to be reproduced over time. These nodes of ambiguity and possible contestation have to do with the intersection of two primary sources of identity—that assigned through the patrilineal affiliations associated with legitimate birth and those achieved through the manipulation of matrifilial ties.

HISTORY AND DESCENT

A discussion of Kono history provides a foundation for understanding the interpretive nature of identity in time and the nature of the identities assigned through patrilineal affiliations. In contrast to other Mande areas where bards or *griots* play the role of historian through recitations of epics that recount generations of ancestors, the Kono have no bards and tend to collapse most ancestry beyond the grandparental generation into a category of relatively undifferentiated persons known only as ancestors (*bemba*). Because knowledge of Kono history stretches no more than three or four generations at the most, it would be tempting to say that Kono historical time is comparatively shallow. This, however, is a misperception, since the Kono have a sense of permanence about themselves. For the most part, the Kono do not conceptualize their past by knowledge of individual names and biographies nor do they spend much time speculating about the past. Undoubtedly this orientation to time is a key factor in allowing the possibility of manipulating identity through interpretations of relationships to ancestors.

In most families the actions of great grandfathers, especially those who were warriors, may be remembered, but little else is. This is not surprising given the number of migrations and absence of stability in the area during at least the last 500 years. A common response to questions about the past or the origin of a particular custom or technique is "We found it that way," or "I don't know about that time, I was not there." This suggests, in part, an experiential dimension to knowledge in the Kono world view. It also suggests that people are oriented more toward present time than toward historical time. For the Kono, how one construes the past gives shape to social relationships in the present. At the same time, the relationships one wishes to claim or develop in the present become extensions of how one presents or interprets the past. For example, as Rosen (1973:32) writes " . . . holders of the village Chieftaincy are unable to actually demonstrate a genealogical connection to the founding lineage; rather, they asserted this connection by virtue of their hold over the Chieftaincy." This manipulation of identities and history is not restricted to holders of village chieftaincies but also extends to all claims to public office and inheritance. People interpret the past in terms of what is available to them and what they aspire to in the present. These interpretations, if accepted by others, validate a person's rights to what they achieve in the present and allow evaluations of personal style and charisma to enter into the construction of identity.

Kono today say their ancestors came from the east—from Guinea. But exactly when the migration (or migrations) occurred or how far east the original Kono homeland actually was do not seem to be relevant in today's world. A few elderly people say their families came from a region near a mountain in Guinea where the Lelli people lived and then go on to tell about the Lelli's extraordinary prowess in such tasks as spinning and farming.[2]

There are also stories that the Kono and Vai (an ethnic group now living in the coastal areas of southern Sierra Leone and northern Liberia) migrated from Guinea as a single group. When they reached what is today the Kono area, the Vai broke off and went on to the sea in search of salt, telling the Kono to wait for them until they returned. Eventually the Vai reached the coast, as their current location shows, but they never returned to their inland companions. To support this theory, most Kono will remind the listener that *ma kono* means "wait for me."

Studies in historical linguistics suggest that the Vai reached the seacoast more than 500 years ago. In the mid-sixteenth century, leaders of the Mane invasion of Sierra Leone probably spoke a version of Vai. It has been suggested that speakers of Kono, Vai, and Dama, which may all derive from one language, formed a trading corridor that stretched from the coast of central Liberia to the headwaters of the Niger River. Then, in the mid-seventeenth century, the corridor was split by southwestern Mande speakers, the forerunners of today's Mende speakers, as they moved west from the Mande heartland (Hill 1971; Jones 1981:177–78). The theories of early connections between the Kono, the Vai, and others in the region are further supported by a complex of cultural traits that Kono share with Mende and other west-central Atlantic groups. These include economies based primarily on rice production, a sense of complementarity between men and women, and a system of ranked lineages, with founding lineages being the most powerful (d'Azevedo 1962).

Kono also share linguistic and cultural affinities with their Kuranko neighbors, but these have yet to be fully explored. Both groups seem to have migrated from the Mande heartland, although this may have occurred at different times and along different routes, in order to reach their present locations. See Jackson (1977) for a brief discussion of Kuranko migrations to northeastern Sierra Leone.

What little is known about Kono history has been reconstructed from oral histories. It begins around 1850. The later part of the nineteenth and the beginning of the twentieth centuries were characterized as a period of upheaval and fragmentation when power and control over pockets of territory continually changed hands. Today the period is described as a time when warriors (*chekugba*) and their supporters fought for control of land, rice, women, and slaves. Stories of the magical and deadly deeds of great warriors, such as Nyagwa (a Mende) and Gbendawah, and tales of battles for individual towns make up most of what is known as Kono history today. In an interview, a chiefdom elder described warrior times as follows:

> So, if someone conquers an area, he will take all the people from that place and carry them to his own town. All the property will also be carried away. The leader of a war who sees his enemy coming with war will escape, but, if his enemy conquers, he will return and make another war to collect his people and property and bring them home. If he brings his enemy's people as captive, but he can not control them, he will have to kill them. This is the way it was done.
>
> K.H: How did a warrior become powerful?
>
> There were many ways. If another warrior was in Koardu and he brought his people here to attack I would escape. I would turn myself into a leopard. If you cut the leopard with a knife, he would not bleed. If you fired a gun, the bullet wouldn't touch him. He would have the leaves they used to work with [leaves here refers to medicines made from leaves and other substances that a warrior might use to achieve supernatural ends]. If it came to war he would train his people to hide as he did. If they are trained and they go to attack, he will remain at Kainkordu waiting for them. All he has to do is support them, train them, and send them to fight. When they return, the people have to hand everything over to him. He is the one who will know what to do with it, how to distribute it. The leaders of the warriors are now the chiefs.
>
> K.H. The chiefs and warriors use the same medicines?
>
> Yes. But every group has their own. This chief has his own and this has his own. Only by testing will they know which are the most powerful. Some warriors used to change into birds when they saw the enemy. The enemy would never see him. He would teach his followers to do the same. Those without such powers were captured.

Kono individuals rose to positions of leadership by proving their strength in ways similar to those that Wylie (1969:297) describes for the Mende.

> To become an Ndormahei (Chief) a man had to get power by war and by proving himself as the first among the warboys. He could then get farms and wealth, because all feared him and respected him,

and his warriors protected him. If he got it by inheritance, he had to
prove it this way [through war].[3]

It is uncertain how far in the past abilities at war served as one of the
primary criteria for leadership. It has been suggested that during the
nineteenth century Mende social and political organization shifted from
a pattern of dispersed settlements to a more centralized system of power
in which numerous villages came under the control of a single warrior. A
similar shift probably took place in the Kono area. As Wylie (1969:297)
describes it, this change occurred because of the increased frequency and
intensity of warfare:

> [s]trong leadership and harsh measures were necessary and the an-
> cient ways of keeping social control could no longer meet the
> demands. Mende social organization was based upon sanctions pro-
> vided through kinship. Social controls were traditionally designed to
> deal only with the most local disputes. Violence was handled on the
> local level, but, when it became a matter of hundreds of square miles,
> the system proved inadequate. The result was a rapid transforma-
> tion . . . Kinship and lineage groupings with their outwardly simplis-
> tic forms began slowly to give way to the beginnings of a centralized
> "political" system.

New towns employing new defensive measures were established. The
use of slaves also intensified, especially in the households of the warrior
chiefs. Such individuals established their empires with a single town and
expanded as they conquered surrounding areas. According to Wylie
(1969:298), expansion occurred "partly by conquest and partly by the
consent of outlying villages, which needed and welcomed the protection
of strong leadership."

Similar shifts toward more centralized political organization undoubtedly occurred in the Kono area as well. Although kinship remained
important, allegiance to a warrior chief was more a matter of protection
than loyalty to specific individuals or family ties. Rosen (1973:30) writes
that a primary unit of nineteenth-century Kono social organization was
a collection of villages united under a single warrior. These nucleated villages were composed of agnatically related males and their wives (as
mentioned in Chapter 2, the Kono are polygynous). Villages were composed of tightly packed houses and were often enclosed by a stockade or

fence. Village members had to travel outside the village confines to work on their farms during the day. While villages tended to consist of patrilineally related males, the exact membership fluctuated according to the fortunes of the war chief.

During this period of flux and upheaval, the epitome of a powerful Kono man was a successful warrior, a man capable of controlling people and resources. Positions of power and leadership were achieved through the manipulation of patron-client relationships, often along kinship lines, in which clients exchanged allegiance for resources and privileges. Leaders remained in power only as long as they could guarantee resources and protection for their clients (Rosen 1973:32). A leader's death or a series of territorial losses, for example, would inevitably lead to realignments. The important factor in leadership, then, was that clients had a degree of power over leaders in that the protection and resources the leader provided were primarily the product of the labors and support of clients. While patrons redistributed these resources, they had to do so in ways that met the varying needs, as well as the expectations, of supporters. If they did not, clients were likely to transfer their support to a new patron. The resources traded within these patron-client relationships included rice and other foodstuffs, wives, and slaves, labor, and support during war campaigns that were designed to capture more resources. In this context, power was a relatively fluid and shifting phenomenon.

There is no question that outsiders played a major role in the growing instability and fragmentation of this period. The social and political institutions that have been recorded for the last half of the nineteenth century probably had their roots in the slave trade that began by the eighth century, first with early kingdoms of the western Sudan and later with Europe and the New World. It is possible to suggest, based on stories of warrior times that are told today, that warriors were involved with the selling or trading of some of their captives. Atherton (1979:42) also suggests that the slave trade with European powers, which began in the mid-fifteenth century, filled a gap left when the the Sudanic empires in the interior disintegrated at about the same time. As this change occurred, people's attention shifted westward toward the coast and toward the economic and political possibilities of the European slave trade. Interviews with elderly Kono in 1988 revealed that during warrior times captives were sometimes sold or traded to dealers who marched their human prisoners to the west coast for sale. An accurate estimate of the extent of the slave trade and its effect on local institutions is difficult to determine, but it was certainly a contributing factor in the upheavals and fluctuations of warrior times.

The years of conflict were also fueled by British and French exploration and territorial competition. Each power sought to control as much land as possible before the boundary between French (Guinea) and British (Sierra Leone) interests was established in 1895. Rosen (1973:54–55) writes that "[t]his entire period in Kono history was characterized by the general fragmentation of larger Kono Chiefdoms while smaller groups, under local chiefs, sought any sort of political alliance that would insure some safety."

Finally, the upheavals were further inflamed by Mende war chiefs who used the Kono as a buffer against Sofa incursions into Mendeland in the late 1800s (Matturi 1973). The Sofa consisted of an army of mounted soldiers, led by Samori, who rose to power in the area around the Upper Niger in the 1870s (Fyfe 1962:114). To avoid both the Sofa and Mende raiding parties, large numbers of Kono fled into the Kuranko area, leaving behind farms and any possessions they could not carry. According to Abraham (1973:44), most of the Kono stayed away from their homeland for about a decade. This story of migration is also supported by the official reports of Governor Cardew, the British-appointed governor, who described the Kono area as devastated and depopulated when he toured the region in 1900 (Abraham 1973).

As colonial rule became more established, the British placed more emphasis on the exploitation of non-human commodities. Between the passage of the Anti-Slave Trade Act in 1806 and the end of the slave trade sometime in the early 1860s, the British military made the slave trade increasingly difficult. The British feared that disturbances brought about by the slave trade in the hinterland of Sierra Leone would eventually hamper trade and commerce in the Crown colony along the coast (Fyfe 1962). By mid-century the colony's ports were filled with groundnuts, timber, palm oil, and other export goods for shipment to Europe. In 1896, the hinterland, which included the Kono area, was recognized as part of the British Protectorate. In keeping with British colonial policy elsewhere, local rule was primarily in the hands of local leaders who were, in turn, controlled by a small group of British civil servants (Rosen 1973:55).

The British appointed specific land chiefs (controllers of particular regions) as paramount chiefs in 1896. This resulted in shifting authority and power from a non-hereditary and fluid system to an hereditary system in which power and resources were concentrated in the hands of a relatively few individuals and their families.[4]

In addition, the British instituted a system of town chiefs who were responsible for the day-to-day affairs of their own particular town or village. Each paramount chief, then, had numerous town chiefs below him. When disputes between towns arose, they were settled by the paramount chief. In the Kono area three chieftaincies were recognized—Soa, Sando, and Nimi Koro. At a later time these three were subdivided into fifteen chiefdoms, one of which was transferred to the Mende area. As a result, there are fourteen Kono chiefdoms today.

According to Rosen (1973:60), as the British became more entrenched in the area, the chiefs were increasingly free of the traditional checks on their chiefly powers. In other words, as paramount chiefs began to inherit their positions rather than fight for them as warriors had, they were less dependant on the patronage and support of their clients.

The shift from a fluid power structure based on force of personality and personal strength to a primarily hereditary hierarchy did not occur without opposition. In 1905, nine years after the British established the office of paramount chief, at least one Kono chiefdom erupted in civil war. The revolt was put down, further solidifying the shift to a consolidated power system based on family ties rather than on personal achievement. The new system had wide-ranging effects on the political, economic, and social organization of the area (Rosen 1973:59; see also Abraham 1973).

An argument can be made that aspects of pre-colonial methods for achieving identity and position, specifically manipulating or slanting chiefdom history, lineage affiliations, or familial ties to enhance one's position, have worked their way into the colonially inspired system of achievement through inheritance. This can be seen in the narratives that people use to describe the positions they hold within their own patrilineages and the relationships between the main patrilineages of an area. Individuals also continue to take advantage of their ability to shift alliances or allegiances in ways that can threaten the position of a patron or enhance personal interests. Although this has less effect on those holding nationally sanctioned offices than in pre-colonial times, it still remains an important threat in most patron-client relationships. Shifting allegiance is not only possible within one's own patriline but it is also a way of escaping the constraints of patrilineal affiliation by utilizing ties of matrifiliation.

Clan and Lineage Affiliation

According to Fortes (1970), such continuities over time can be seen as a function of the specific ways in which the domestic domain is bound to the political-jural domain. In the Kono descent system today, children fall under the jural authority of their father for the purposes of inheritance, succession, and citizenship, as long as the father has paid bridewealth for the child's mother. With the payment of bridewealth comes the recognition that any children of the relationship are the legal offspring of the woman's husband; it also links the child to the father's patrilineage and clan through a series of rights, obligations, and capacities. The structural significance of the descent system ensures that the rights and capacities so appropriated are legitimized by politico-jural sanctions rather than by purely moral, ritual, or affective concerns (Fortes 1969, 1970).

The defining feature of Kono clan affiliation in pre-colonial times and the factor that made social relations jurally binding were shared prohibitions (tana) against eating particular foods. These prohibitions continue to distinguish clan groups today. See Table 1 for a list of clan names and associated tana. In the Kono descent system, children inherit the tana of their fathers, but direct lines of descent cannot be traced to clan founders. Clan membership, then, is based on the assumption of shared descent, while patrilineages are made up of more immediate kin.

Today, most Kono men bring their wives to the villages of their own agnatically related kin when they are married. While members of the same clan cannot necessarily trace their descent to a common ancestor, members of the same lineage can. Lineages are also exogamous, while clans are not. Lineages are generally shallow, up to only three or four generations in depth. In no case are lineage founders considered synonymous with founders of the clan, and in most cases clan founders have been forgotten.[5]

Today, clan and patrilineage affiliations are used in relatively specific contexts. Clan affiliation can be used to demand hospitality in an area where one is not personally known. It is also used to ensure the right to reside in a particular town; this right is ritually marked shortly after birth by introducing the infant to his or her agnatic ancestors. This is done in two rituals that literally attach the child to the town. (These rituals will be described more fully in the section on space and identity.) At death, at the end of the life cycle, an individual should be returned to his

TABLE 1

Clan Names and Associated Tana from Soa Chiefdom

Clan Name	Tana	English
Kamaamoe[1]	*wootanati*[2]	chimpanzee
Gbensenemoe	*yambitanati*	bush yam
Kondemoe	*tehtanati*	birds, fowl
Nyanimoe	*faiitanati*	lizard, crocodile
Sandumoe	*kwiitanati*	leopard
Siyomoe	*kamatanati*	elephant
Manfundomoe	*wuutanati*	dog
Mongomoe	*chootanati*	tortoise and goat
Komamoe	*gbiitanati*	pumpkin
Pengusamoe	*kwenyatanati*	ground pig
Dunbiamoe	*santanati*	catfish

[1]*kamma moe* (*moe*=person)
[2]*woo tana ti* (*woo*=chimpanzee, *tana*=taboo, *ti*=owner)

or her natal village or town. If an individual dies in another place and the body cannot be transported to the natal home, a stone from the burial site is carried back to the deceased's birthplace and placed on a false grave. This substitute grave is treated as the actual burial place during subsequent rituals in which descendants ask the ancestors for assistance. Ancestors, then, are symbolically tied to their descendants by virtue of the spaces that they share. The living also validate social relationships on the basis of mutual attachments to specific locations, such as a town; such attachments work, to some degree, to stem the tendencies of sublineages to break off from larger patrilineages.

A man also has rights to farmland by virtue of membership in a patrilineage. Women may also obtain farmland through patrilineal affiliations, although this is unusual and will be discussed further in Chapter 8. While the paramount chief legally owns the land in his chiefdom, lineage elders hold historically validated *de facto* rights to tracts of farmland. Kono lineages act as corporate groups to disperse land to their male members. Although ideologically all male lineage members are entitled to land that was cultivated by their ancestors, contemporary elders decide what land will be farmed and who is entitled to work the best land.

Lineages may also, at their discretion, disperse land to non-lineage members who have attached themselves as clients to particular elders in exchange for services or a percentage of the crop.[6]

Lineage elders who are descendants of the Gbensene, Sandunu, and Mongo clans control access to farmland in the area around Kainkordu. (Other clans predominate in other sections of the chiefdom, or in other Kono chiefdoms.) Ties to the clan founders and the relative status of sublineages are ritually validated in pilgrimages to *Kongweh Kor* (Under the Mountain), the site where Gbendawah, the first paramount chief of Soa, was transformed into a warrior.

As the legend goes, Gbendawah was called to Kongweh Kor in a dream by a spirit who promised that, if he wanted to be a warrior, he would find powerful medicine at the spot described in the dream. When Gbendawah found the place, he discovered a ring waiting for him. He was instructed on how to use the ring and was told to pass it down to future paramount chiefs when he died. Even today, stories are told about the ring's power. Not only did it protect and assist Gbendawah in battle by turning away bullets, knives, and other weapons, but it also is said to have given him the power to travel to distant places instantly. Gbendawah used his newfound powers to unite and strengthen the chiefdom.

When Gbendawah's descendants make a pilgrimage to the magical site, they engage in a day of feasting and dancing. The most important part of the festivities, however, consists of calling out the names of the founders of particular clans and lineages and of previous officeholders of the chiefdom. As the names are called out, the ancestors are praised and then asked to listen to their descendants. The feasting and dancing that accompany the pilgrimage are considered sacrifices (*sara*), actions dedicated to pleasing the ancestors. In return, the ancestors are expected to work to improve the lives of their descendants. In the Kono world, ancestors can both help and hinder their descendants. Sacrifices of palm wine, kola, and cloth are frequently left on ancestral graves by descendants in an attempt to encourage the ancestors to intercede and influence events on their behalf. While sacrifices are no guarantee that the intercession will be benevolent, failure to perform sacrifices at an appropriate time can sometimes result in ruin.

During the yearly pilgrimage to *Kongwe Kor* the names of the chiefdom's ancestors are called out in order of importance.[7] As a result, the names of those deemed important are remembered (although it is quite likely that they, too, have changed over time). But the way in which living individuals or sublineages connect to these ruling ancestors remains slightly ambiguous and open to manipulation. Claims of ancestral associations are transformed into land tenure decisions in which competition is usually strongest for tracts closest to a village or town. Decisions on land assignments are based on genealogical closeness to elders, with elders' brothers being given preference over elders' sons, and eldest sons being given preference over younger sons. If disputes arise between sublineages, the paramount chief will be called in to interpret the genealogical claims of lineage elders.

In land tenure decisions the position of nonmembers of the patrilineage (for example, strangers in a town, town members who have been away for a considerable period of time, or the child of a female member of the lineage) depends, normally, on what the client has to offer a potential patron in return. A man with few assets and little power may fare badly in the decision-making process, while a man with several wives or daughters or with influence in the national political arena may fare better than the real sons of the patrilineage.

The flexibility allowed in these decisions can be seen in the contrasts between two cases. In the first, a middle-aged native of the town and chiefdom returned after several years in Europe where he had been pursuing professional training. He returned at the beginning of the rainy season, at a time when most of the desirable agricultural tracts had already been allotted for the year, and people had already started clearing the brush from forest and swamp areas prior to planting the yearly rice crop. The returning official requested a relatively large swamp area close to the town for his wives and other family members to farm while he went to the capital city to work. To many people's surprise—and anger—he was given the land. In actual fact, the land had already been promised to several other families who had begun work on it. When the arguments and discussions began, at least one other individual also started to work in the contested area with the hope that, in the confusion, he would also receive permission to farm there. Because the returning official was a man of influence, a central figure in one of the three clans of the area, and, more importantly, someone whom the paramount chief hoped would help develop the chiefdom, his request was given precedence over the rights of others, and he received some of the finest land in the chiefdom.

By contrast, the fate of an aging Kuranko man who had been living in the town for at least ten years when I met him was not as positive. At the time I met him he had several Kono wives but very few assets and little influence. He asked for and was given farmland, but, as he complained, the land was so far from town that by the time he and his wives reached it the workday was half over. As a rule of thumb, a farm that is a 30-minute walk away is considered prime; most people would think twice about agreeing to farmland that was more than a 45-minute walk from town. This land decision turned out to be the beginning of a downward spiral from which the Kuranko man has, as yet, been unable to recover. At least one of his wives deserted him for a younger man, which further limited his production capacity. Rumors of impotence began and then became quite public. Another wife was caught stealing rice from a neighbor's rice barn. This was not wholly unexpected as the Kono have a saying that an impotent man is unable to control his wives or have any real effect on most situations (a reference to the fact that he had not been able to arrange for good farmland). The wife accused of thievery finally left town and moved in with another man, further humiliating her husband and curtailing his ability to grow rice successfully. In 1988 he still had one wife but had been reduced to working for others for small amounts of cash.

Land decisions, then, are made by evaluating the rights of patrilineage members in conjunction with what specific individuals have to offer those who are in positions of power. Individuals not recognized as being lineage members are at a distinct disadvantage, especially as they get older and have fewer resources to offer.

Historically, those who are younger sons or who, for a variety of reasons, appear to have little chance of success typically receive the most distant land. These individuals are most likely to move to unclaimed farmland, attract clients of their own, and eventually establish new settlements. Alternatively, they might be forced to attach themselves as clients to elders of other lineages, especially those of their mother's patrilineage, in the hope of improving their situation. What is apparent here, particularly in the case of younger sons, is what a number of scholars (for example, Karp 1978b and Moore 1978) have termed a lack of fit between the ideological and the behavioral dimensions of a descent system. While all the sons of a patrilineage are supposed to receive land, actual allotments may be impossible. This leads not only to dissatisfaction but also to movement away from the patrilineage on the part of those who find themselves at the bottom of the distribution system. It is at such points that individuals are forced to make choices. In doing so, they gauge their expectations against reality and their personal goals against what others expect of them. While shifting allegiance away from patrilineal ties necessarily weakens those ties, such decisions are made only after careful evaluations of patrilineal possibilities and predictions of the potential that matrifilial or other ties hold. Some individuals are not willing to gamble with their reputation or economic situation in this way and opt to remain hangers-on in their own patrilineage. As with all such predictions, these decisions are sometimes based more on hope than on actual reality, as I discuss below.

The lack of fit between the ideal and the possible in land tenure decisions opens the way for interpreting the strength of an individual's claims to resources on the basis of personal style and charisma and of personal interests. Choice and other forms of evaluation enter the picture and encourage individuals to present themselves in particular ways and to perform or lay claim to these chosen roles in ways that have important consequences for the construction of identity, as well as of history. In a related way, the interpretive possibilities embedded in land tenure decisions allow personal interests to play a part in interpreting another's claims to land rights, as can be seen in the willingness of several elders to grant land to someone returning from school in Europe because of what the individual might be able to do for the chiefdom rather than because of his position in the chiefdom hierarchy.

At one level, lineage membership orients an individual within an array of political and jural institutions that are validated by history and tend to endure over time.[8] A *tana*, for example, cannot be ignored. There are antidotes that people can take if they unknowingly eat their *tana*, but even with the antidote, they are likely to become ill. Likewise, Kono fathers provide their children with some of the attributes that Fortes (1970:104) calls a "normal jural person"—citizenship, inheritance, and succession. Inheritance is part of a legal system that recognizes specific jurally sanctioned rights regardless of the emotional or affective relationships between the individuals involved (Fortes 1970:115).

In addition to their use in land tenure decisions, lineage affiliations provide the right to run for political office (this has been the case since the British established hereditary chieftaincies in the 1890s). Village and chiefdom leadership positions are held by individuals who claim descent from village and chiefdom founders (those leaders who were installed by the British). In Soa Chiefdom, for example, the office of paramount chief is held by a member of the Gbensene clan. *Gbensenemoenu* (Gbensene people) are all descendants of Gbendawah, the land chief recognized by the British as the first paramount chief of Soa Chiefdom in the late nineteenth century. The office of paramount chief is now traded between the descendants of two of Gbendawah's sons, Foyoh and Gbenda. Although not all individuals in the chiefdom can trace their ancestry directly to chiefdom founders, individuals aspiring to political office are required to do so.

Interpreting History and Affiliations

As in land tenure decisions, however, there is the possibility of manipulating history and biographies in ways that allow for the reinterpretation and use of lineage ties for personal advantage. It is clear that the ability to reinterpret or reframe historical events, and one's place in them, becomes a resource in itself. The right to hold political office, then, is still somewhat related to such factors as strength of personality, personal style, and the ability to manipulate resources in much the same way as these factors were important in warrior times. Variations in the historical accounts of Soa Chiefdom demonstrate the nodes at which reinterpretations of history and lineage relations tend to occur, although to some degree these points are structurally determined.

What follows below are several stories of the origins of the major patrilineages of Soa Chiefdom. Each version presents the major contenders for political office in a particular way, including or excluding possible candidates for the chieftaincy in ways that can be interpreted as more or less advantageous to particular sets of individuals. In one version the founder of Soa Chiefdom, Foyoh, had a slave named Gbenda. He was so pleased with this slave that he adopted him and made him his son. Since then, there has been an agreement that the Foyoh and Gbenda families will trade off the chieftainship (both are of the *tana* Gbensene).

In a second version Gbenda was the first settler of Kainkordu, the chiefdom headquarters. He had several sons. One was named Kanda; another was named Foyoh, which means someone of big stature; the third was named Gbenda after his father. When the chief Gbenda died, the son named Kanda became chief, but for some reason his descendants moved to another area of Kono. The reason for this move remains ambiguous. When Kanda either died or left the chiefdom, his brother Foyoh became chief. It was then decided that, because Foyoh and Gbenda were brothers, their descendants would alternate the chieftainship. The circulation of this story today allows the descendants of Kanda to continue to present a candidate for paramount chief, and at each election they do so in order to maintain this right.

In a third version the first paramount chief was named Gbendawa, the second was his brother Kanda, and the third was Gbendawah's son, Foyoh. Gbendawah's sister was taken to Gbane, a neighboring chiefdom, as a slave during warrior times. She was later rescued, along with a son she had by someone from Gbane. The son's name was Kpakiwa. This son was made chiefdom speaker (basically an assistant paramount chief). When Gbendawa died, Kanda became chief, and when Kanda died, Foyoh was made chief. Kpakiwa tried to fight this in order to become chief himself, but he was unsuccessful. In return, Foyoh locked him up for a year but later released him and returned the speakership to him.

In a fourth version Kanda and Gbenda were not related at all. In 1896 when the British took control of the Sierra Leone hinterland, Kono was divided into three chiefdoms—Soa, Sando, and Nimi Koro. A powerful warrior was selected to control each area. At that time Gbenda controlled the area that became Soa Chiefdom. The British notified the chiefs to gather to be installed as permanent heads of the regions they controlled. Each was to be given a staff of office as a sign of their right to rule. Thinking this might be a trap, Gbenda sent Kanda to represent him, and Kanda was given the staff of office. At the gathering Kanda told the British that he was head of Soa Chiefdom. When he returned to Soa, the staff of office was taken from him by Gbenda. Since that day Kanda's descendants have always had the right to stand for election to paramount chief, but none have been elected.[9]

These versions of the chiefdom's history demonstrate the range of variation possible in historical interpretation and present various ways of framing events in support of particular interests. Thus, while aspects of identity are established through political and legal structures, claims to particular identities can, to some degree, be manipulated and remain open to interpretation.

It is not accidental that the point at which most of the historical accounts diverge from one another is the relationship between the sons of Gbendawah. Even today, the relationship between brothers is problematic. This was evident, for example, in the way a young secondary student presented his position within his patrilineage to me. He began by saying that his mother had given birth to seven children and he was the only remaining son. He also said that his mother was the first wife of one of the elders of the community, which in turn meant that, as the only surviving son of a first wife, he had certain expectations of someday advancing to a leadership position within his family, as well as in the chiefdom. What he neglected to tell me was that his mother had actually been married to the elder's brother and that, when his real father died, his mother had "pointed" to the man he was now claiming to be his father to support her. At a man's death his wives are given some choice in selecting the member of their husband's patrilineage who will become responsible for them. (Widow inheritance will be discussed in greater detail later.) This new wife had been selected by the elder to manage his household and his younger wives. The inheritance of any titles, however, would most likely fall to the elder's real sons unless the stepson happened to become powerful enough on his own to make his version of history the accepted one.

Embedded within the very structures that relate brothers, half-brothers, and stepbrothers to each other are potently disruptive forces, such as jealousy and potential loss of inheritance, that can split a lineage apart. As I show in the section on the fission of domestic units, a contributing factor in lineage fission is the mother's position in the domestic domain. Fortes (1958:6–7) writes that the political-jural and domestic domains are linked in an intricate dialectic such that "fission in the domestic group can be regarded as the model and starting point of segmentation in the lineage" at the same time as "differentiation and fission in the domestic group are reciprocally determined by norms and rules derived from the external [political-jural] domain." In other words, relations within the domestic unit affect the relations of individuals to patrilineages; at the same time, the patrilineage, through laws of inheritance and other jural constraints, produces distinctions within the domestic domain.

Conflicts in claims to rights and inheritance among brothers (full, half, or step) illustrate the weak links in lineage alliances and the boundaries to certain levels of affection and emotion. It is at such critical points that households are likely to divide and new sublineages emerge. Because residence in smaller towns and villages is also lineage-based (as opposed to larger towns where multiple lineages exist), conflict between brothers is also the point at which villages are likely to split and new villages are established. While the source of distinctions among siblings originates in the domestic domain (in the form of different mothers), it is sanctioned by rules of descent in the political-jural domain (Fortes 1970:109).

DESCENT AND THE DOMESTIC DOMAIN: THE DEVELOPMENTAL CYCLE OF DOMESTIC GROUPS

While the Kono utilize patrilineal ties to assign specific jurally sanctioned rights and capacities to individuals, connections to a father and his lineage provide only that part of an individual's identity that deals with citizenship, inheritance, and succession. Access to the rights and capacities established by patrilineal ties rests on the interpretation of an individual's place in historical time. The recognition that the establishment of these kinds of identities is an interpretive process is critical for understanding the roles that charisma and personal style play in establishing identity.

In contrast, matrifilial ties are used to manipulate the identity resources available in contemporary time and to judge which affiliations are most likely to bring the best results for the individual. Thus, matrifilial ties, while less apparent than patrilineal ties, are an equally important facet of identity. Fortes (1969:264), for example, writes that "[f]iliation . . . signifies the presumed perpetuation in each person of both his parents in respect of those capacities they are each entitled to bring into the filio-parental relationship by ideological, jural, and moral authorization." According to Fortes (1970:115), in a segmentary patrilineal descent system, matrifilial ties endow a child with attributes without which it cannot be a normal jural person. While these attributes stem from relations within the domestic domain, their transfer to a woman's children derives, to some degree, from the jural rule that women never completely forfeit their membership in natal lineages (Fortes 1970:100.) While filiation is always complementary, it is custom that prescribes and social structure that decrees "the form this complementarity will take in a given society" (Fortes 1969:257).[10] In Kono society matrifiliation provides what might be called the individuating dimensions of Kono identity.

Marriage

I begin my consideration of the aspects of identity provided by the domestic domain by describing marriage, the nature of domestic relations, and the developmental cycle of the domestic group. As I noted previously, the Kono are polygynous, although only the most wealthy men will actually take on the responsibility of multiple wives. Approximately 15 percent of the adult married men in Kainkordu in 1984 had more than one wife. A much larger percentage have cohabited with more than one wife at some time in their lives, but because Kono marriage tends to be transitory, very few men live with more than one wife for a major part of their adult lives.[11]

While a man's first marriage does not necessarily signal the creation of a totally separate residential unit, it does lead the way toward the establishment of a new domestic unit. A young man may initially bring his new wife into his father's household, but it is understood that the couple will eventually move into their own domestic space. In some smaller towns it is relatively common for a young unmarried man to construct a small house (*kamin chene*) within his father's compound, sometimes several years before he marries. In that way he begins separating himself from parental control, even though he probably still works in his father's rice fields and eats his meals with his father's family. When he marries, he will bring his wife to this house, and eventually the couple will begin farming for themselves. Only young men who are married can begin to ask elders for access to lineage-controlled farmland.

The normal pattern for a man with several wives is to construct one large house (*chenba*) where the wives cook and sleep. Each wife will have her own room and firestones (meaning they will cook separately if they can). The wealthy husband lives in a smaller house (*kamin chene*) and invites the wife he is currently sleeping with to join him there. Often this is the first house he builds, and the *chenba* will be built only as he takes on more wives. The households of less wealthy men who are able to marry only one wife, then, usually include only a single house.

In the compound of a wealthy middle-aged man of a founding lineage, one is likely to find several dwellings that house his wives, their children, one or two younger brothers, and their wives and children. An elderly parent of the husband may also live in the compound. It is less likely that a parent of one of his wives would reside in the compound because of the sometimes negative influence husbands perceive their mothers-in-law to have over their wives.

Marriage is a problematic relationship, especially in its earlier stages. In warrior times, villages of agnatically related kin were the focal point of loyalty and allegiance. Under these circumstances villages had to "turn outward to find wives from other hostile villages. This one fact meant that every village contained elements which were potentially subversive to its political integrity" (Rosen 1973:161). The Kono have a proverb *chenge si ne a ma ka ni an fiya gbanban si na* ("the stone that rolls is never equal to the stone that is steady"), which means that no matter how they behave, strangers, including wives, cannot be the same as someone born in the town.

As outsiders, Kono wives are suspect because of the allegiances they maintain to their own patrilineages. While women move to their husband's home at marriage (usually between the ages of fifteen and twenty for a first marriage), they usually return to their mother's home for the birth of their children, sometimes staying for as long as a year and a half. They also return to their natal homes in the case of divorce or when they are widowed in old age. Thus, they have a vested interest in maintaining relationships with and fostering the welfare of their own patrilines. Suspicion, then, is one of the rarely inescapable facets of relationships between affines, especially in relatively new marriages. As time goes on and a marriage endures, suspicion and doubts lessen, although they can reemerge at any time.

The uncertain relations between affines are formalized through the presentations for marriage, or in Krio, "tying kola." Paying brideprice also opens the way for a specific complex of rights and duties, formulas for behavior that, if upheld by both parties, guarantee peaceful, if not amicable, relations between the families concerned. The negotiations and gift giving can be long and extended, requiring a number of visits between a prospective husband and his future in-laws. It is no surprise, given the importance of marriage negotiations for later social relationships, that the most important individual in the presentations is the *tendu*. Selected by the groom's family, the *tendu* is responsible for remembering exactly what gifts the husband's family presents to the wife's family; he is also responsible for remembering at what stage the arrangements are in at any point in time (they can sometimes drag out for six months or more).

In the initial stages of negotiations, the *tendu* is given a small amount of kola to present to the bride's parents to announce that a man is interested in marrying her. At this point both families' histories are examined to determine if sexual relationships between the potential husband and wife are possible. A man is prohibited from marrying or having sexual relationships with his wife's older sister or mother, his wife's mother's co-wife or sister, the daughter of his mother's brother, or his brother's daughter. In addition, he is prohibited from marrying a woman who is the daughter or older sister of any woman he may have had sexual relationships with in the past. For example, I witnessed the cancellation of marriage negotiations between a man and a much younger woman because the man had had a brief affair with the young woman's mother's half-sister when they had both been young. The acceptance of an initial gift of kola by the woman's family signals that past relationships will not interfere with the union and that the parents of the bride agree to the marriage.

At this point kola is also presented to the *bain den moe,* a term that literally means mother's brother's child person and refers to the bride's mother's brothers and their descendants. Throughout their lives, a man and his sister's daughters have a relationship that is jokingly referred to as a marriage. Presenting kola to the *bain den moe* releases the woman from the fictitious marriage with her mother's brothers, although it does not terminate the close relationship. A woman's *bain den moe* also watch over their sister's children, even though the payment of bride-wealth for the mother establishes her children's rightful place as members of their father's patrilineage. Fortes (1970:105) called this payment of bridewealth "the distribution of jural control over a woman's off-spring." A child's patrilineal line is known as *fa den moe,* literally father's child person, and refers to the father, the father's father, the father's brothers, and their descendants and ancestors. While the child is legally part of his or her father's patrilineage, the tie to *bain den moe* remains important. Any life crisis ritual or other major event in the life of the child must be sanctioned by the *bain den moe.* This tie continues even after the death of the actual mother's brother of the child. By the time the child matures to old age and dies, it is no longer the mother's brothers who actually sanction the burial but their descendants. Only at the death of the children of a marriage will the affinal relationships established at marriage be dissolved.[12]

The bride's mother is also given kola to ensure that she cooperates with the arrangements and provides her daughter with sound advice, which means advice that coincides with the interests of the new husband. Women retain influence over their daughters long after marriage. There are songs and stories about uncooperative mothers-in-law who advise their daughters to leave a husband (for example, see the lyrics in the weaving songs presented in Chapter 5). I return to this point shortly.

Next, cloth is given to the bride's mother and brothers. The gift of cloth to the mother is to replace clothes soiled by the bride when her mother carried her as an infant. The gift to the bride's brothers signifies the beginning of a relationship between the groom's patrilineage and the *bain den moe* of any children of the marriage being negotiated (the brothers of the wife-to-be will become the *bain den moe* of her children).

The second-to-last step in the exchange process is the gift of money or a pot (*boda*) to the bride's parents. At that point the bride is asked if she will accept the suitor. If she answers yes, he is told to return to his home and the family will bring the daughter.

While the amount given at each stage of negotiations varies depending on the wealth of the individuals involved, the gifts essentially open new kinds of social relationships and close off others. For example, the gifts signal the beginning of a relationship of respectful distance between mother and son-in-law; they also sever any claims a mother's brother might have had on the bride, however in jest. Relationships between a man and his wife's mother and elder sisters (*bien musu*) and relationships between a man and his wife's father and elder brothers (*bien gai*) are characterized by constraint and respect to the extent that they are not even supposed to shake hands.

Marriage institutes a more relaxed relationship between a man and his wife's younger sisters and brothers (*nimoti*). In what can be characterized as a joking relationship between a man and his younger in-laws, a man can even marry his wife's younger sister. Men who do so say that marrying a wife's younger sister is easier than marrying another woman because the wives are already close and there is more harmony and less jealousy in the household. The *nimoti* (the younger brothers and sisters of one's spouse) also play an important role in specific ritual contexts. A wife uses the same terms as her husband for her new in-laws (*bien musu, bien gai,* and *nimoti*). For her, too, *bien musu* and *bien gai* are treated with the utmost respect, while her relations with *nimoti* are more relaxed.

In the past it was common for the initial stage of marriage arrangements to begin when the girl was still a baby or quite small. These were often made by the intended groom's mother or, in the case of a man who was already married, by his senior wife. Husbands were often considerably older than their new wives. Today this rarely happens. In explaining this change, people say that these arrangements were too costly. The prospective groom was called on to contribute a great deal of money before the girl actually reached marriageable age. This money was used for medicines for her illnesses, contributions for her membership in Sande, and other needs. On the other hand, some people say that marriage used to be simple. One elderly woman described it this way:

> So a woman has a baby daughter. When a man sees the daughter,
> you tell her mother she is going to be my wife. When he goes to the
> bush [forest] and finds palm oil, he has to take it to the mother.
> Then, if he has palm wine, he has to take some of it to the mother. If
> the mother has work to be done, he has to go and do the work.
> When the girl is to join society, her family has to inform the man,
> and the mother has to say that the man loves her daughter. After that
> they will go into the marriage until the end of their lives. So it used
> to be.

In the past it was also common for a man whose family lacked the resources to arrange a marriage to work for his in-laws for several years in order to be given a daughter. Another variation, still occasionally practiced today, is when a wealthy man brings a girl from a family of few resources into his household when she is very young. The marriage is not consummated until after her initiation into Sande, but in the intervening years she works in the household, assisting her future co-wives with their tasks in exchange for her upkeep and the payment of her initiation fees.

As cash becomes more prevalent in rural Kono areas, it is increasingly substituted for the cloth, ceramics, and other goods of bridewealth. As this happens, the potential for deceit between future affines increases. I recorded one case in which an elderly man "tied kola" for a young girl the year before she was to be initiated. The brideprice had included the initiation fees (in cash). When time came for her initiation the next year, he was told that the money he had paid was gone and he would have to pay again. The old man had no recourse but to repay the fees. If he decided not to pay, he would end up marrying an uninitiated girl, something that was totally unacceptable to him. If he stopped the marriage arrangements, he would lose the money he had already invested. He finally repaid the fees, and the family proceeded with the initiation and then the marriage.

Older people see today's marriage arrangements as markedly different from what they experienced. Where once mothers or senior wives began the marriage arrangements for their sons or their husbands, respectively, thus giving them some choice in the composition of a man's household, it is fairly common today for the prospective bride and groom to choose each other. This is especially the case among those who have had some secondary schooling or who have moved away from their families and natal homes. In the words of the elderly woman cited above:

> Now, if your child has reached the age of joining society, she will say this is my man. She will bring him home and say this will be her husband. So when they have married, if they make a quarrel or make a palaver, so the family must come and return the man's money, and the girl goes to another man. And that is how marriage is today.

In many cases today, couples also cohabit either without beginning the process of paying bridewealth or without completing the marriage payments. In these cases, children of the union belong to the patrilineage of the mother, not the father, although they maintain the food prohibitions of their biological fathers.[13]

In public, marital relationships are marked by constraint and respect. The formalities established between affines by brideprice extend to the married couple as well. Wives and husbands, for example, do not touch in public, even to shake hands in greeting. This reserve extends to attitudes toward domestic space. Although male and female domestic space is not formally marked, passage from one to the other is not easily made, especially in the early stages of marriage. Males enter female space hesitantly, and, likewise, women enter their husband's rooms only for certain reasons, for example, to leave food for him or to spend the night with him. However, a woman will often search out a child or other intermediary to send messages or food to her husband.

In the past, marriage established relationships of complementarity between husbands and wives in several ways. In terms of the identity of their children, men provided the attributes that legally and jurally sanctioned their offspring's social position. Women provided two sets of attributes. The first had to do with the way in which a mother's position within a polygynous household transferred to her son's likelihood of inheriting resources or position from his father. Second, women provided access to alternative relationships that might augment an individual's chances to be successful. These aspects of complementarity continue in marriages today in similar forms and will be discussed in more detail later. In terms of labor and household production, complementarity entails the notion that husbands and wives each have specific tasks to perform and neither could survive without the labor of the other. During the early stages of marriage, women provide children and farm labor for their husband's patriline; in return, a husband meets the subsistence needs of his wife and children and feeds her relatives when they visit. Legally, a woman who does not meet her obligations can be divorced and sent back to her family with a demand that the brideprice be returned. A man who is unwilling to meet his obligations is likely to find his wife uncooperative during the next year's growing season. While a woman's withdrawal from the labor force has no legal consequences, it is usually serious enough to give her an opportunity to air her grievances to her husband and his family. In extreme cases of abuse, a wife's family can legally demand the return of their daughter. This usually entails a return of the brideprice, although this is often left to the discretion of the paramount chief. Complementarity is important throughout the life span of a marriage, but it takes different forms as the marital unit ages and changes shape. The complementarity in marital relationships can be seen as constraining, limiting the activities of each side, but it continues to be important to the ways in which power and control are exercised in marital relationships. Each spouse is required to make concessions and meet the needs of the other, and each side has an avenue for redress if an imbalance is created.

Complementarity in itself is an important theme in Kono social life. Its manifestation vis-a-vis marital relations begins when Kono girls and adolescents start to learn how to demonstrate respect for themselves and their productive powers. For example, young women are warned to meet their marital obligations but, at the same time, to demand that their husbands meet theirs. In general, they are trained to be constantly wary of anyone who might take advantage of them. Even in the sexual alliances that women might have before marriage or in sexual relationships with lovers after marriage, there is an expectation that men will provide gifts or other goods in return for sexual favors. In turn, however, married women constantly complain of the drain on their husband's resources that his extramarital alliances cause. The emphasis on balance tends to instill young women with a stridency and animosity towards men that might be tempered or enhanced over a lifetime, depending on how their relationships with men take shape.

A critical sign that a woman may be getting into trouble in her marriage is her failure to exhibit the formality and distance expected between wives and husbands in public. Such breeches are interpreted in terms of misplaced emotions, specifically love. Among the Kono, it is common knowledge that women who care about a husband too much are likely to begin to overlook his failure to meet his obligations to her and her family. Such a woman is thought not only to be damaging herself but also failing to respect her own patriline. Men, on the other hand, are not cautioned in similar ways, presumably because they are perceived as less likely to waver from their allegiances to a patrilineage.

The ideal marital relationship is one in which balance is maintained by each side (both husband and wife, as well as their families). The countless stories of women who fail to demand the respect that is their due always end in disaster, and the women are always blamed for the imbalance. Take the case of Mani, a relatively low-ranking member of an important lineage, who brought his wife to Kainkordu from another chiefdom without her family's consent and before he had completed the brideprice payments. People described the woman as very beautiful but pointed out that her one fault was that she loved Mani too much. Mani was not strong and could not work very hard, and thus he was unable to support her. Although the woman was not accustomed to hard agricultural labor, she still made a cassava garden. She did all the labor herself, except for the very heaviest jobs, for which she had to hire young men. She and Mani subsisted on the cassava and sometimes she sold some of it to buy rice, the staple of the Kono diet. But without Mani's help, she could not cultivate a rice farm. After working for several years, the woman became ill. People were not surprised because she was not used to hard labor. Mani had no money to get medicine for her and was heard to say that if she was going to get sick, it would be better that she just died. Occasionally Mani would beat her because she could no longer work and feed them. Finally, the man's family took pity on her and provided money for medical treatment. She got better and worked for several more years but then became ill again, this time to the point where she could no longer walk. The family decided that this time it was up to Mani to help his wife, even though he still had no resources. Their response might have been different if she had had children. The woman went without medicine, and the beatings started again. Finally she died. No one from her family attended the funeral, and they sent nothing to help with the funeral expenses.

After her death, someone dreamed that the woman would not leave Mani alone until he had joined her in death because she loved him so much. Several years later, Mani had the first of a series of illnesses. His own family, convinced he would die because of the influence of his wife, refused to help him get medical treatment. After Mani consulted a diviner who said there was nothing he could do to break the woman's influence, Mani's family withdrew all support, even locking him out of their house. Mani was reduced to spending his last days and nights moaning in pain on the veranda of his relatives' house.

This is a case in which marital responsibilities were not met, and the woman allowed the relationship to continue against the advice of her family. Women whose husbands refuse to meet their marital obligations can usually return to their families. But because Mani had not completed the bridewealth payments, the woman's brothers had no legal recourse other than to ask their sister to come home. According to Kono interpretations, the disaster that confronted both families could have been avoided if the wife had only refused to compromise herself. In short, the fault was hers.

Because women are perceived as strangers and marital partners are constantly on the lookout for betrayal, emotional support and security are not qualities that most Kono individuals search for when they marry. Instead, young women (as well as their families, since many marriages are still arranged today) search for a husband who is already financially well off or, alternatively, who is well placed in his lineage, under the assumption that such placement will guarantee him access to farmland and other resources. In addition, they look for a man who will be able to give them children. This is one reason younger women tend to be reluctant to marry men much older than themselves; they believe that older men are more unlikely to be able to father children. If a man already has wives, a woman will be interested in how they are treated: Does he beat them when he is in a bad mood? Does he show them respect in public? Does he treat their families with respect? One young mother who had not been married with kola explained why she refused to become the second wife of a relatively wealthy man. In her terms, the suitor was not a good man because he was weak and had gone into small-scale trading rather than into farming. By weak, she implied that his first wife controlled him and would probably be given to controlling the new wife as well. Other young women talked about not wanting to marry (even though they already had children) because the men who had asked for them were unpredictable. Furthermore, they did not want to move too far from their mothers.

Men, on the other hand, especially those without many resources, look for women who are able to do farm work. As one young man put it, he goes to his farm all the time (he was helping his sister with her farm at the time) because he doesn't like to sit in town all day; if he married, his wife would have to be the same. In the words of another man, "men can't cooperate enough to make farms so they marry a lot of women because you need a lot of hands to have a successful farm. If men could cooperate enough to help each other, there would be no need to marry." Men also look for someone who can give them children. As in many other parts of Africa, a wife's inability to produce offspring is commonly grounds for divorce. One relatively well-off young man told me he had finally decided to marry his girlfriend because she was pregnant. As he put it, "it really isn't the wife at all that is important, but the child is." All of these discussions about marriage reflect a degree of distrust and uncertainty about potential mates and a general reluctance to leave the certainties of current situations for a new set of responsibilities.

While an emotional closeness between spouses might develop in some marriages over time, it is not a prerequisite of marriage. Instead, most young women get their primary emotional support from their relationships with other women (their mothers, sisters, and other female relatives, and their female friends). These are the people whom they trust, whom they will confide in and gossip with, and with whom they are at ease socially. Young men, likewise, gain emotional support from their age mates, or *togbai* (those who join Poro society at the same time), and from other male friends and relatives. Even in marriages in which spouses have chosen each other, distrust appears after a year or two because of such factors as the financial drain of extramarital affairs, the interference or dependency of a wife's family, and the tendency for each spouse to hide resources from the other.

Only as a marriage survives and a couple ages, particularly after a man can no longer take new wives and the worries of childbearing are over, is it common to see people investing a degree of emotional attachment in their marriage. Usually this occurs when a man has only one wife or when an elderly man is left with only one wife either through death or divorce. Because resources are usually minimal at this time of life, they must be devoted to survival (rather than to treat girlfriends or support relatives). Thus, years of habit and coexistence, as well as a diminishing set of alternatives, wear down the tendency to distrust a spouse, but this happens only over time.

As exemplified in the case of Mani, marriage is more than a relationship between two individuals. It also implies a relationship between two sets of relatives. In the past, marriages were arranged between families, and this is still the case to some degree today. Brideprice is still paid by a groom's family to the bride's family, solidifying the relationship and the rights and obligations between wife and husband as well as between their respective kin groups. Bridewealth also legitimizes children of the union and solidifies their incorporation into the husband's descent group.

Although in the past wives and their children were seen as investments, today there are increasing opportunities for investment elsewhere. As a result, bridewealth is often viewed as a mechanism that makes a man liable for an unending number of obligations to his wife's family. He must feed his in-laws when they come to visit, even for extended periods of time, and he is required to give them gifts at certain junctures. In the past, excess resources were frequently depleted by a wife's relatives (people guard against this today, but it is still one of the major tensions of contemporary life). The distribution of such accumulations enhanced an individual's prestige and set the stage for reciprocal exchanges that could be utilized in times of distress. It is also important to note that the storage time of most accumulable resources was relatively short (rice, for example, lasts for less than a year before pests and mildew destroy it).

Today, however, young men constantly complain that it is too expensive to even consider "tying kola" (paying bridewealth) for a wife. They point out that the problem is not with the initial presentations but with the unpredictability of future expectations. People speak as if this is a new phenomenon. Although men historically invested in wives, today they are more reluctant to do so because other alternatives are available that do not necessarily have the potential for depleting excess resources in unpredictable ways. Instead, they are taking advantage of the cash economy by using cash resources to invest in other kinds of opportunities (education, small-scale marketing, or other ways of entering wage employment). By doing so, they are pulling away from both the initial costs of marriage and from the financial obligations to in-laws that marriage implies. My impression is that these changes reflect a shift from the accumulation and dispersion of perishable resources to the accumulation of nonperishable capital (specifically, rice and cash). While it is advantageous for in-laws to equate perishable and nonperishable forms of capital, it is disadvantageous for sons-in-law to allow them to do so. As in-laws increasingly define sons-in-law as stingy and disrespectful and sons-in-law see their in-laws as too demanding and overstepping their rights, conflict is inevitable.

My evidence for suggesting that bridewealth marriages are declining is that between 1982 and 1984 I recorded only three marriages being negotiated in Kainkordu, a town of about 1,200. When asked about this, young men, as well as older men and young women, said they were hesitant to enter into marriages. Young men were afraid that they would be unable to meet the expectations of a wife and her family. Many felt that the expectations required of them were too high and that trying to meet them would lessen their ability to advance. Several young men spoke of trying to establish "a foundation" before marriage, referring to a pool of resources, accumulated either through wage labor or inheritance, that would allow them to continue to accumulate enough resources to meet marital expectations. On the other hand, young women generally felt that men were disrespectful to them and, moreover, tried to take advantage of them by expecting their labor and children but were unwilling to support them or be respectful to their families. Such cautionary attitudes may signal only a delay in entering marriages but, because many of the young men who find themselves in precarious positions within their families become migrant workers, it is likely that a certain percentage of them will never marry, although they may father children or marry non-Kono women and thus have a different set of responsibilities.

To return to a point raised earlier, marriage does not end a woman's relationship with her natal family. By maintaining ties to her patrilineage, she retains a certain degree of power in her husband's household because she is not totally dependant on her husband's family. She is also able to provide her children with a set of rights and obligations that augment their identities beyond those established by patrilineal ties.

The tension that this engenders is manifested most clearly in men's relationships with their mothers-in-law. While a man is supposed to treat his mother-in-law with the highest degree of respect, his primary complaint is about the influence mothers wield over their daughters. This can be seen in the following case. A Soa woman named Fiya married Tamba, a Kono man from a neighboring chiefdom. Tamba was living in Soa to maintain the coffee plantation that he and his father had started when he was a teenager. One year when Tamba became very sick, Fiya brought him food every day and the two fell in love. After Tamba recovered, he approached Fiya's family and the marriage was negotiated. Although Tamba's father had a house in Kainkordu, it was rather rundown, and so

Fiya and Tamba lived in her stepfather's house, along with her mother, sisters, and other relatives. After several years of marriage and the birth of several children, the marriage began to fray. Fiya accused Tamba of having affairs and of spending money on himself rather than putting it into their marriage or their children; Tamba accused Fiya of many small offenses, such as failing to cook for him until late in the day. This meant that he was unable to offer anyone food during the day and that by the time his own food was prepared, Tamba had already eaten at one of his friend's house. The small problems reached a crisis state when Tamba accused Fiya of stealing some of the coffee that he had asked her to dry and beat (coffee has to be dried and cleaned before it can be sold). Because Fiya was convinced that Tamba had more resources than he was letting on, she felt her small theft was justified to give her a fair share of her husband's wealth.

As with many men who have trouble with their wives, Tamba was advised that he had to do something to appease his mother-in-law or his relationship with Fiya would continue to be painful and problematic. Finally, Tamba learned that his mother-in-law was upset with him because several years earlier he had torn one of her *lappas* (skirts) in anger and had failed to replace it. Tamba and his mother-in-law discussed their problems in front of several female elders, and it was arranged that Tamba would present his mother-in-law with a small amount of money and kola nuts to beg her to cool her heart towards him. She responded that his gesture was good and well-intentioned but that she still had no clothes and that he would have to eventually replace the torn cloth. He agreed and things improved between he and his wife for a while. But because Tamba did not replace the cloth, his mother-in-law became impatient, and the trouble started again. Finally after Tamba lost the coffee plantation (the reasons for this will be discussed later in this chapter), he and Fiya were forced to move to a neighboring chiefdom where he had been born. Since that time, Tamba told me, his mother-in-law has been unable to interfere in his marriage, and his troubles with Fiya have stopped.

Children

Once a woman begins to bear children, her relationship with her husband, as well as with his family, enters a new stage. Although she is still suspect as an outsider, she is at least recognized as a valuable asset because she has helped the patrilineage to increase its size. While a young wife without children has little to keep her in her husband's house if a quarrel erupts, she is much less likely to leave if her husband demands, as is his right, that she leave her children to be raised by his family. It is at this point that some of the tensions between husbands and wives begin to shift. For example, women are less opposed to their husband's infidelities, as long as they do not affect their access to resources. Children, then, are a desired part of life. Although I did not ask specifically how many children women hoped to have, it was my impression that most women were content when they were relatively sure that five or six of their children would survive. Given the infant mortality rate in the area, this meant that most women try to have eight or nine children in the hope that five or six will survive to adulthood.

A woman's position in her natal lineage is also enhanced when she begins bearing children because she passes certain rights to her children. Children provide an enduring link between a woman's husband's lineage and her own. As noted earlier, children are born into a position that brings together the interests of clan and patrilineage affiliations, or *fa den moe*, (the child's father, his brothers, their descendants and ancestors) with the interests of *bain den moe* (literally mother's child person, referring to the child's mother's brothers, their descendants, and ancestors). The birth of a child strengthens the relationship between affines that began with the payment of bridewealth for the child's mother. The relationship started at marriage will be terminated only after the child has gone through adolescence, adulthood, and finally death. A major part of burial rituals and post-burial ceremonies consists of an exchange of goods that finally settles the accounts between these two groups in regard to the deceased.

The complementarity embedded within the obligations of *fa den moe* and *bain den moe* towards the child mirrors the complementarity between Kono wives and their husbands. Not surprisingly, Kono children experience the complementarity between their father's relatives and their mother's relatives in emotional terms. The affect and sentiments engendered within the domestic domain are tempered by rights and obligations stemming from the political-jural domain. This is especially the case in the relationship between a father and his children. The emotional relationship of a child to his or her father and *fa den moe* is complicated. It is tinged with respect and formality in situations that are related to political and jural affairs but with sentiments of affection and love in the domestic domain. Mediating the two can be difficult, and young children must learn to distinguish between the two domains. As a result, emotional attachments to fathers tend to be deep, as evidenced by the respect and awe that even old men use when talking about their long-dead fathers. While the feeling is deep, it is for the most part not expressed or acted upon. It is, for example, very unusual to see public displays of affection between middle-aged fathers and their sons or daughters after the children have entered adolescence. Even small talk is avoided. In situations of relatively scarce resources, when most sons know their chances of inheriting either resources or position are slight because of their birth-order position, the pressure to succeed, to influence, and to curry favor is intense. Anxiety, tension, and anger are words that crop up in a young unmarried man's discussion of his relationship with both his father and mother. One young man, who I will call Aiah, described himself as similar to a cutting grass (a large rodent notorious for stealing rice) trapped in a hole and unable to get out. He had too many obligations to his family (both his *fa den moe* and his mother), which prevented him from doing anything for himself. He felt intense pressure to guard his *fa den moe's* interests in the community and to help with the support of his mother and sisters. Aiah's father, who had been wealthy, died while Aiah was still considered a child. The father's plantations and other wealth had passed to his brothers, Aiah's uncles. This left Aiah virtually penniless and at the beck and call of his *fa den moe*, for whom he worked very hard. He had no idea, however, if his work would ever be rewarded through inheritance or if his *fa den moe* would be willing to pay bridewealth for him. At one point Aiah discussed suicide as a possible alternative to the constant expectations he faced from his father's relatives, his mother, and his sisters.

The father-child relationship is full of conflict for fathers as well. Often they find themselves favoring younger sons over their first-born. As a man ages and his obligations to provide sons and daughters to ensure the continuity of his lineage are met, his relationship with his youngest children often becomes more relaxed. In a large family the emotional ties between a man and his youngest children tend to be more intense than those between a man and his oldest sons. As I discuss later, this occasionally leads to clashes between sentiment and the jural reality of inheritance laws. This is what happened in the case of Fiya and Tamba. Tamba's father was able to plant a coffee plantation in Kainkordu because his mother had been born there (this was a case of utilizing a mother's patrilineal affiliations to establish rights to land). While Tamba came to Kainkordu to help his father with the plantation, his senior half-brother stayed away. By the time his father died, Tamba was thirty-five or forty years old, the trees had matured, and the coffee plantation was starting to produce. At that point the older half-brother let it be known that, even though Tamba had helped his father develop the plantation and despite the fact that his father had promised the plantation to Tamba, by customary law it should revert to him. The chiefdom and lineage elders agreed, and Tamba's inheritance was taken from him. Because this had been his biggest asset, Tamba decided it would be better for him and his wife to return to his father's chiefdom and ask for land from his father's brothers there.

The emotional quality of relationships between children and their *bain den moe* is in direct contrast to that between most fathers and their children. It is informal and relaxed, with affection, teasing, and admiration openly displayed. In the case of the young man who talked about suicide, his mother's brother was a tremendous help by arranging for employment. At a father's death a son may inherit his father's property, but during a mother's brother's lifetime a niece or nephew feels free to steal or borrow the property of their classificatory *mbain* (mother's brother). The Kono say that the relationship is "as if the mother's brother owns the sister's child, and the child owns the uncle's property." Jackson (1974) suggested that in Kuranko marriages a husband, upon receiving a wife from her brothers, becomes overindebted to her brothers. Children of the union, then, who belong to the husband's patriline, are given the right to take back from their mother's brothers what has already been paid. The Kono conceptualize the relationship in terms of brothers owning their sisters. It is the brothers who give a woman (and most importantly her ability to bear children) to her husband's patrilineage and, therefore, give children to the patrilineage as well. The metaphor of ownership is especially strong in terms of the mother's brother and sister's daughter, the fictitious "husband and wife" bond, as was demonstrated by the suitor's compensation of his new wife's *mbain* during bridewealth payments.

As most husbands will tell you, however, the mother's brother's control of the niece does not end with her marriage but remains constant throughout her life and continues with descendants of the mother's brother. For example, a husband must ask his wife's mother's brothers to beg the wife's ancestors for assistance if the wife has been unable to conceive or if she becomes seriously ill. Essentially, the *bain den moe* guard the interests of their *bain den*. If an individual does not have a mother's brother, their mother's father's brother will be substituted. Any woman unable to name their *bain den moe* is considered a slave, at the mercy of the patrilineage into which she is born.

The extent of the freedom between *bain den moe* and a sister's child can be seen in the following description. I joined three daughters of one of the town's elders late one August as they walked from their home to a place where they could get transport to return to school in Koidu. In all, it was a distance of about ten miles. The sisters stopped at several towns and villages along the way, ostensibly to greet their relatives. Several of these relatives turned out to be *bain den moe*, and at each of these houses the performance was the same. There was much joking and laughter, and the sisters entered the rooms of the male relative as if the rooms were their own. In one house they borrowed the antiperspirant spray that was visible on a shelf and checked for cooked rice in the covered dishes sitting on the table. The uncle was soundly reprimanded when they found the dishes empty. In another house one of the sisters begged her mother's brother for the blanket on his bed; in another they asked for, and received, a sum of money to help with their transportation costs.

On the other hand, a sister's son or daughter has certain obligations towards a *bain den moe*. The mother's brother can ask his sister's child to do anything for him, from going to buy cigarettes to changing his or her marriage plans, and the niece or nephew cannot really refuse. A niece or nephew must also be present at the burial and post-burial ceremonies of their *bain den moe* to help ease their way into the world of the ancestors.

Clearly, individuals' relationships to their *bain den moe* provide them with both an emotional outlet and access to resources outside the patrilineal line. The particularities of an individual's relationship to their mother and their *bain den moe* is also one of the major mechanisms that distinguishes half-siblings within the domestic domain. In distinctions between siblings, mothers provide the feature that designates between full siblings and half-siblings. While full siblings share the same mother and father, they also share the same identities by virtue of sharing the same sets of *fa den moe* and *bain den moe*. In most cases, half-siblings (children of the same fathers but different mothers) operate between different sets of *fa den moe* and *bain den moe*. This implies different sets of social relationships, different sets of opportunities, and different ways of defining themselves, as each mother (except in cases where co-wives are sisters) provides her children and their patrilineage with new sets of opportunities.[14]

Fissioning of Domestic Units

In general, during the period between marriage and the end of childbearing, a domestic unit is usually made up of a young Kono man and his wife or wives. Although they may maintain close ties with the domestic unit of the man's father, the demands of time and energy made by their own immediate family cause them to turn toward internal interests and concerns and away from those of the man's father.

A domestic unit begins the process of splitting up when the children are initiated into the rights and responsibilities associated with membership in Sande (or Bundu) or Poro. For female children, initiation signals their identification with other girls, usually between the ages of nine and twelve or thirteen, who are outside the domestic unit. Shortly after initiation many girls will marry. For boys, initiation into Poro marks new rights and responsibilities in lineage affairs. In general for both girls and boys, initiation signals new elements of identity, interests, rights, and obligations.

By the time a Kono domestic group stops expanding and the sons and daughters begin leaving for their own marriages, the head of the household is engaged in activities designed to enhance his position within the community. One important way of doing this is by manipulating patron-client relationships. Although traditional warriors have disappeared, the model of a man consolidating power through patron-client relationships remains in the form of the "big man" (*gbako*). Today, politicians are viewed as the warriors (*chekugba*) of the past. Patron-client relationships are pyramidal, with a single individual as client to more powerful men but also patron to those who are less powerful than himself. The Kono word for power, *gbaseia,* when used as an adjective, refers to someone who has the same capacities as a warrior—an individual who is capable of attracting admiration and thus support. As in warrior times, admiration is rooted in practicality. People are admired and liked for their ability to do things for others—their ability to provide extra rice in times of famine, to guarantee votes during a political election, or to provide wives and potentially children for another man's patriline. Admiration is related to the ability to transform resources and situations into favorable opportunities for oneself and one's clients. The extent to which one rises within the pyramid is determined by one's access to resources and skill in their manipulation.

While patron-client relationships occurred primarily along kinship lines in pre-colonial times, they are less likely to do so today. This is partially the result of the increasing importance of a cash economy. As I discussed earlier, cash is seen as similar to rice or any other resource. It is exchanged in the same way as other resources are within a patron-client relationship to increase social status. It is also subject to the same demands from those in need as are other resources. The dilemmas here are obvious. Previously, both survival and power were dependent on crop yields, lineage connections, and the fertility of wives—all unpredictable resources that could not be accumulated beyond certain limits. For example, rice can only be stored for a certain period of time before it is destroyed by pests and mildew; the richest man can only deal with so many wives in his household; a man can farm only so much land in shifting cultivation. Within this system resources, and thus power and authority, could be lost as quickly as they were gained, and most people experienced lean years as well as good years. In good years one "lent" to others; in bad years one survived by collecting on the loans and favors that had been dispensed during previous years.

With the possibility of a steady cash income that could be accumulated and stored over time, the nature of reciprocal exchanges has changed. Individuals with resources are expected to continue giving to those in need until the resources are depleted, but a family's expectations of a trader, bureaucrat, miner, teacher, or other wage earner always exceed the actual amounts earned. This has been complicated in recent years by the Sierra Leone government's inability to pay its employees on a regular basis. For most young men (few women have yet to be fully involved in the cash economy), remaining in the kin-based system of reciprocity usually means bankruptcy, either economically or in terms of the social networks that family ties provide. To avoid this, young men of moderate means who do not belong to chiefly lineages are likely to attempt to distance themselves from their lineages and other family responsibilities. For example, teachers today often seek posts away from their homes, using distance to mute the constant requests for assistance. Often the individual is forced to choose between duty and personal interest.

Members of chiefly lineages, particularly elder brothers, however, tend to be less likely to follow this pattern. By accepting familial obligations they forego the immediate personal gains available in a cash economy in favor of future aspirations to the chieftaincy. These individuals recognize both the necessity of having family support to meet their aspirations and the likelihood of inheriting the resources and position necessary for meeting such aspirations.

To succeed in this contemporary cash system, men attach themselves as clients to powerful individuals in the diamond company, to foreign missionaries who control the school system, to representatives of the bureaucracy in Freetown, or to those controlling the transport and marketing of crops. In these relationships men continue to utilize the modes of behavior found in primarily kin-based patron-client relationships, but the interactions take place within a much enlarged arena. What has changed are the previous emphasis on kinship within the relationship and the nature of the resources that pass through the relationship. In addition to land allocation, crops, and marriage ties, cash and new kinds of services are also acceptable tender. Men, then, are moving into new domains and often using different kinds of resources, but, for the most part, they are retaining patterns of behavior borrowed from the past.

There are several patterns for the dispersal of households as children begin leaving their parent's homes. For men, fission is most likely to occur along the lines that distinguish step-siblings from half-siblings, half-siblings from full-siblings, and adopted siblings from siblings by birth. As this happens, tensions between sons over inheritance and rights intensify. Inheritance of moveable goods (kola, coffee or cocoa trees, personal objects, and houses) passes from a man to his brother if his sons are still considered jural minors, or from a father to senior sons. If the deceased's brother inherits over the deceased's sons, it is difficult for the sons to regain the wealth when they become recognized as adults. The rules guiding inheritance rights between the youngest son of a senior wife and the youngest son of a junior wife are less clearcut, with relative age tending to be the deciding factor. The likelihood of inheritance plays a significant role in divisions of the domestic unit. On the whole, however, the tendency is for junior sons of junior wives to leave their father's house in search of other opportunities. More senior sons may leave later as their father ages and their own position becomes more apparent. The points at which fission occurs, then, are based on a young man's gauging of his likelihood of inheriting wealth and on his sense of personal ambition. Younger sons who perceive themselves as likely to be disinherited by the father, denied access to lineage farming lands, or given land at some distance from their natal homes tend to leave.

A second point of fission is likely to occur with stepsons, the sons of widows who are brought into their father's brothers compound when their father dies.[15] Here, again, the conflict between ideological and behavioral dimensions emerges. Although a father's brother is legally supposed to substitute for the father, when resources get scarce the dead man's sons are the most likely to be disinherited. This was demonstrated in the case of the young man whose widowed mother had been brought into the household of a lineage elder to manage the wives of the household. In his narrative the young man neglected to tell me that his biological father had actually been the chief's brother and that his mother had been inherited by the chief only after her husband died. By ignoring this fact, the young man hoped that he would improve his chances for inheriting from the chief. In fact, this did not happen. The stepfather continued to invest in his own sons while he left the stepson to fend for himself. Eventually, the young man's mother died, and he became even more cut off from the resources of his stepfather's household. Because he had some secondary education, he was reluctant to return to subsistence farming, even if he had been able to obtain land from his lineage. In time, he left both the compound of his stepfather and the town. In 1984 I heard that he was drifting outside the Kono area looking for work. In 1988 I was told he had been arrested for theft in the Mende area.

This story is not unusual. It is important to realize that it varies from what might have happened in pre-colonial times only in the nature of the alternatives available to the young man. In the past, the young man would probably have attached himself to his mother's brother or an agnatically distant man in his own patrilineage, or even the wider clan. There he would have worked for his patron in exchange for food and, perhaps, eventually for a wife and farmland of his own. If he had been married at the time of his father's death, he would have tried to acquire farmland from his patrilineage. If this had been some distance from his home, he might have moved nearer his land and eventually established a new village. Today's young men have a wider range of options to choose from, but movement away from the rights and obligations of the natal home to explore those options is still the primary way of bettering one's position.

The student's history also suggests that contemporary solutions are being sought to problems of inheritance in ways that reproduce patterns of fission that existed in the past. There is a remarkable similarity between the student's life history and the various histories of the chiefdom presented in the section on history and descent. In accounts of descent the problematic or disguised nodes are the relationships between brothers, the relationships between fathers and sons, and the relationships between stepfathers and stepsons. These are the ambiguous points in the descent system that men manipulate to present themselves in the best possible light. In these representations of history, men with a certain personal style, as well as access to resources, fare better than their less endowed brothers. In the story of the student presented here the young man was not able to change people's minds about what he was entitled to.

The patterns for the dispersal of daughters are very different. Women leave their natal compounds at marriage to move to their husband's homes. They return, sometimes for as long as a year and a half, for the birth of a child, especially a first child.[16] At this point a woman may decide not to return to her husband, providing her brothers agree to repay any bridewealth that has been paid. Usually this is only a possibility if the husband has been disrespectful of his in-laws or if the wife has been physically abused. Even in these cases, however, the wife's brothers can refuse to repay the bridewealth, in which case the wife is obligated to return. Alternatively, the woman's husband may decide not to ask for the wife's return (although the child will always belong to the husband's patrilineage, provided he has paid bridewealth). In such cases the woman's brothers will be told why the wife is no longer wanted, usually because of infertility or problems within the household. The brothers will be asked to repay the bridewealth, and, if they refuse, the husband may take the matter to the paramount chief. Women retain important connections to their own patrilines throughout their lives and often return to their natal homes when their husbands die. In rare cases women will marry men from their natal homes. Powerful leaders of the Sande society, for example, may try to arrange such marriages for their eldest daughters. These women are often related to the leading patrilineage of the community. In this way power tends to remain consolidated within ruling patrilines. Bledsoe (1980) describes a similar case for the Kpelle.

Household shifts are probably less patterned and clearcut today than in the past because there are more options, particularly for men. Movement away from patrilineal ties is predicated on economic concerns, such as employment in nearby diamond fields or outside schooling, rather than on traditional signs of adulthood (marriage and independent farming). Today, migration to the diamond industry for wage labor is a major draw for those who believe they might be disinherited. Senior as well as junior sons are likely to be lured away from subsistence farming to wage employment outside the community. Today, wealthy families are also likely to send senior sons to Koidu or Freetown for higher education. Junior sons of these families are likely to remain home and learn to farm. As in the case of Tamba, these sons labor for their fathers, even though jural rules dictate that in all likelihood they will not inherit their father's property. When senior sons return, they often find themselves in the midst of controversy centering around the fact that they inherit resources, such as rights to farmland or plantations, that have been worked and sometimes expanded by other family members. On the other hand, less well-off families are likely to send a son to school only after their farms have been established. This means that senior sons tend to stay on the farm while junior sons go on to higher education. Here, the tensions between brothers are amplified because of the respect given a junior son for his education.

The contradictions embedded in both of these scenarios have yet to be worked out in customary law and everyday practice. Each scenario, however, reproduces the points at which tensions within domestic units have erupted in the past—relations between brothers—but the fact that two patterns related to economic differences seem to be emerging suggests that Kono society, in addition to being divided along lineage lines, will in the future be increasingly divided along economic lines as well.[17]

The case of the young student who turned to thievery also points to the lag time between practical reality and ideas about advancement through education. Until very recently, a university degree or even a few years of secondary education virtually guaranteed social advancement, a steady salary, and a degree of respect that largely stemmed from the association of literacy with Europeans. In 1948, Little (1948:15–16) described the way in which literate people were viewed:

> In the eyes of the illiterate man, a "civilized" individual is a "book man," "one who knows book," that is, one who can read. In a more general and quite neutral sense it also means some one who practices European ways or someone who has given up farming and who earns his living in some other way than on the land . . . In literate eyes it denotes a person who practices European ways—but with the very strong implication that such ways are the "right ways" . . .

Today, however, with a deteriorating economy and an overabundance of educated people, it is clear that a university degree no longer guarantees success. The illusion of education as an alternative, however, remains, and young men as well as young women will struggle very hard to attain schooling beyond the primary level. Those whose families will not support them in these endeavors fervently look for other patrons. Sometimes these are found in the adolescent's mother's family. Some students arrange to work for one of the Lebanese families in Koidu in exchange for room, board, and school fees. Others target Peace Corps volunteers, missionaries, and other foreigners with requests for school fees and living expenses.

Individuals who are successful in primary school and then advance to the secondary schools in Koidu and in other major towns, even if only for a few years, consider themselves too educated to return to farming and what they consider the boredom and poverty of "village life." Many young, educated Sierra Leoneans find themselves in what can only be described as an inescapable trap. For example, the disinherited son of the widow discussed above was unable to approach his patrilineage to request farmland because he was not married. His lineage was not interested enough in him to provide his bridewealth. While some young men in similar positions opt to do wage labor on farms to support themselves and save some money, the young man's education and the associations of superiority it carried with it made such labor an intolerable option, even though the nature of the young man's education did not qualify him for any particular employment.[18]

Young women are as eager to participate in the educational process as young men. Young women use education as a stepping stone to employment or marriage to a prosperous man. Here, too, there are problems for those whose families cannot support them. Rumors about school girls and prostitution are rampant, partly because any woman not under direct control of her family or husband is thought to be engaging in illicit sex and partly because many young girls use sex as a way of surviving. The money, clothing, or small gifts that men are expected to exchange for sex will not totally support a student but they will certainly help with her expenses.

Middle and Old Age

As a family's reproductive years come to an end and children begin leaving the household, the number of wives in a polygynous household tends to dwindle. Either through divorce and remarriage, death, or other circumstances a man's wives drift away from a household until only one or, at most, two remain. At this point, because a man has fewer resources to provide to his lineage and a smaller voice in decisions made in the political realm, the bond between a man and his wife or wives can take on a sentimentality that is impossible during earlier years. There are few excess resources to argue about, and, as physical capacities decrease, survival becomes a major factor.

Elderly men who no longer have the strength to farm or the ability to control resources often find themselves indebted to their children for support. In what is a very gradual process, older men are replaced in the lineage hierarchy by sons, whose energetic search for resources during early adulthood and middle age attracts clients and supporters. For chiefdom elders, such replacement is only finalized when they become incapacitated or die, but for those with few resources, it happens when they can no longer farm and when their children, wives, or clients drift away. According to an elderly successful trader, it is important to prolong the point at which one asks for help because such a request signals a decline from which there is little escape:

> They [jealous people in the town] started to poison me with rum and then food. So I was sick from that time. When I was sick, the women [his wives] started to take my money. Everyone came to take my money. At the time my children were going to school. I was admitted to the hospital and left to go mad. My wives left me, and my money was finished so my children couldn't finish school. Finally, I got out of the hospital and I was able to plant coffee and cocoa. When the cocoa started to yield, I got ten or twenty pans per year, but now it only gives me one bag. Up to now I have not had to ask any of my family to help me or to tell them I have no food to eat. I have one wife. She has stayed with me a long time and has been a good wife. If you have not done anything bad to anyone but someone thinks bad of you that person will die and you will stay. All of those who planned bad for me have died now, and I am left.

There is a time in a man's life when he can no longer contribute to the lives of others, when he can no longer fill the role of patron by distributing the resources accumulated over a lifetime. As patron becomes client, wives tend to drift to new husbands or back to their natal homes. Children who are not established in their own right or who are not in a position to move into their father's role as family head will search for other avenues to success.

The period between being a powerful patron and death is also the point at which men are most likely to be accused of witchcraft. As suggested in the man's narrative above, illness or other setbacks can accelerate the rate of decline in status. Illness or other setbacks in old age can also accelerate the onset of rumors of witchcraft. In the early 1980s, for example, a dry season brush fire decimated a chiefdom elder's coffee plantations. For days the elder, visibly distraught, wandered through the town. He was disheveled and his speech was incoherent. Not long after I left Sierra Leone in 1984, I heard rumors that all of his wives had left him. While he was still respected in the town, it was clear that his position was slipping. When I returned in 1988, I was told that he had died and that, in fact, he had been discovered to be a witch. The proof of his witchcraft lay in the fact that several children in town had died, seemingly without cause. Witches are typically known to eat children, trading the lives of children near them for skills or resources that will raise their social status. (This will be discussed further in Chapters 4 and 5.) As often happens when children in a community begin to die, the town called in a witch-finder whose powers allowed him to battle and capture the witches of the town. Although such performances occur in dreams, trances, or other nonpublic contexts, people learn the identity of the guilty individual because he or she falls sick shortly after the event and dies. The elder in question died within weeks of the witch-finder's performances, and everyone was convinced that this was a sign of his attempts to regain his previous prosperity and power through illicit means.

This might appear to be an isolated case. But in the town of Kainkordu, with a population of about 1,200 individuals, I know of no death of an elderly individual that has been attributed to natural causes over the last eight years. The deaths of men and women who are no longer actively contributing to their households are followed by accusations and rumors of witchcraft.

As suggested by the narrative of the man who has yet to ask his children for food or money, there is pleasure in longevity and self sufficiency. Longevity is, in some ways, the sign of a good life. Once an individual is no longer able to support himself or herself, however, what had been the virtue of longevity is transformed into the curse of witchcraft.

Just as men face a series of choices about affiliation and about the best way to meet their goals, women, too, face a series of choices. These usually begin in middle age, a time when a woman's children are almost grown up and she must begin to worry about what will happen to her in old age. The lives of elderly women are similar to those of men, except that older widows (those past childbearing age who are no longer of value to their husband's patrilineage) or women whose husbands have become elderly usually return to their natal homes, taking up residence in or near the homes of their brothers, their brother's descendants, or the descendants of their *bain den moe*. Sometimes such women are given small plots of lineage-controlled land to cultivate rice swamps or gardens until they are no longer able to work. A few women who have trained as potters or indigo dyers are able to do enough work to feed themselves. Those not so lucky eventually become dependant on the kindness of those around them.

Certain women, however, can rise to positions of considerable power and authority. Such positions are only available through the ties they have maintained to their own patrilineages. When these women return to their homes, they share in the power of their patrilineages and are likely to become powerful Sande leaders in their natal homes. (See Bledsoe 1980 for a discussion of similar avenues to power and authority among Mende women.) Some of these women are given access to relatively large parcels of land for cultivating rice. The only women seemingly capable of farming successfully in the eastern area of my research were older widows with younger family members attached to the household who were capable of doing heavy labor and were paid with food each day and a portion of the crop at harvest time. Equally important, these women had usually married men from their own natal homes, or they had returned to their natal homes and their own patrilineages when their spouses died. These older women also had access to the labor of a wide network of women through their position as Sande elders. It is not unusual for Sande elders to claim the labor of younger members as part of a tribute payment. It is also important to note that these older women were not involved specifically in cash cropping but, instead, raised rice for their household's need and sold only surplus rice or used it for community needs. Once these exceptional women are no longer able to farm or play an active role in the Sande hierarchy, their lives begin to resemble those of other elderly men and women and they fall prey to the same rumors of witchcraft and antisocial behavior.

Death and Burial

At the ceremonies associated with death and burial, the link between the individual's *fa den moe* and *bain den moe,* established at the marriage of the deceased's parents, is finally severed. During post-burial ceremonies, the dissolution of affinal relations is marked ritually and taken very seriously. It occurs at post-burial ceremonies called *diiboe* (to pull the cry) and *beeboe* (to give) that are held several months to several years after an actual burial. Without this ceremony, a deceased woman or man cannot join the ancestors but is forced to walk on earth until she or he can stir up enough trouble to force the descendants of their *fa den moe* and *bain den moe* to bury them properly. During the *diiboe*, the *bain den moe* is officially told that his sister's child is dead. In most cases, they already know this because they have been summoned to participate in the ceremony, but until the ceremonies are actually held the public declaration of death is not accepted by the *bain den moe*. This is also an added incentive for the *fa den moe* to hold the sometimes expensive ceremony; claims by the *bain den moe* on the *fa den moe* can continue until the deceased is officially buried.

When first told of his sister's child's death, the *bain den moe* denies the fact, as if he thinks the *fa den moe* is trying to trick him. The *fa den moe* finally presents the *bain den moe* with red kola to show that the child is indeed dead.[19] The argument continues back and forth several times, and finally the *bain den moe* accepts the fact that the death has occurred and that the affines are telling the truth.

On the night before the *diiboe*, both *fa den moe* and *bain den moe* approach the deceased's grave. The *fa den moe* calls the ancestors and tells them their son or daughter will soon be among them and that the morrow will be their last day in the town. The dead individual is also told to stay nearby on the next day because the family will be arranging for him or her to join the ancestors. At the graveside the *bain den moe* repeats the words of the *fa den moe* and leaves white kola on the grave.

Before the *diiboe* can begin the next day, the *fa den moe* must bring the *bain den moe* a clay pot (*boda*) in which to wash. The *bain den moe* washes his feet with water from the pot and rubs them with oil. Food is brought and, after he has eaten, he presents the *fa den moe* with gunpowder. The *fa den moe* arranges for a hunter to fire a series of shots, clearing the road in front of the deceased as they move toward the ancestors. When the shooting is finished, the *nimoti* (younger siblings of the deceased's spouse) begin a wailing cry that is picked up by other relatives who have gathered around the grave.

The *bee boe* is held on the same day or the next day. In a series of exchanges the accounts between the *fa den moe* and *bain den moe* are officially settled. The *bain den moe* is seated inside a house, usually the house inhabited by the deceased, and the *fa den moe* sits outside. (The significance of inside and outside will be discussed in Chapter 4.) Both groups are fed and then the negotiations begin. They speak to each other through the open doorway, beginning with the *bain den moe* who asks why they were called to town. The *fa den moe* again tell their guests that their *bain den* (sister's child) is sick. The *bain den moe* answers that his *bain den* is not sick. On the third interchange, the *fa den moe* announce the news that the *bain den* is actually dead. Those surrounding the exchange offer their condolences and the *bain den moe* asks what caused the death. The *tendu,* who has been invited to mediate between the two parties, explains the nature of the illness. The *fa den moe* ask the *bain den moe* to bury the person. The *bain den moe* present their burial contributions, which include a country cloth blanket that represents the clothing worn by the deceased, a mat that symbolizes the bed of the deceased, and a small amount of money. In the past, rice would have been used in the place of money. Essentially, these articles represent the necessities provided by the *fa den moe* for the deceased while he or she was alive.

The *fa den moe* accept the contributions and then the *bain den moe* ask for money because of what the deceased did for the *fa den moe* during his or her life. The *fa den moe* appoint a group of people to decide what the appropriate amount should be. The group includes representatives of both *fa den moe* and *bain den moe,* as well as the *tendu,* who is responsible for recounting the brideprice that led to the legitimate birth of the deceased. Once a decision is reached, the *bain den moe* receive a refund and a little extra cash as an added goodbye present. In this way the deceased's life is reviewed, and inordinate expenses accrued by either side (e.g., expensive illnesses or barrenness in a woman) or unexpected gifts or talents that benefitted the *fa den moe* are recognized. If either side appears to have lost out in the original bridewealth transactions of the deceased's parents, the loss is compensated for, more in terms of recognition than in the actual repayment of costs.

The last duty of the *bain den moe* is to bless the deceased's grandchildren in order to ensure the continuity of the patrilineage to which they lost their child so many years before. With this final act of cooperation, the *bain den moe* demonstrate they harbor no ill will toward the *fa den moe,* and the relationship that existed between the *fa den moe* and the *bain den moe* finally comes to an end.

CONCLUSIONS

The preceding discussion has shown the nature of rural Kono social organization and the ways in which jural, behavioral, and ideological dimensions intersect and shape interest, obligation, and sentiment. Identity has several dimensions. One is assigned through the political and legal structures associated with patrilineal and clan affiliations. These structures provide the individual with rights to land, inheritance, and political office. There are, however, critical points at which lineages tend to split and allegiances and affiliations are likely to shift. Thus, identity is somewhat fluid and manipulable, and individuals have a variety of choices to make about the affiliations that are most likely to benefit them. Structural features of the descent system allow for this degree of identity manipulation so that individuals attempt to frame historical events in ways that present them in the most advantageous light. Chief among these features is a lack of specificity in relationships between brothers, which stems from the fact that, although male siblings are viewed as equals, in reality certain siblings are judged more worthy than others. Fathers as well as patrilineage elders tend to favor real sons over stepsons.

Mothers provide a second dimension of identity, one that allows distinctions between siblings and provides a set of alternative affiliations that can be used to enhance status. These affiliations stem from a woman's continuing association after marriage with her patrilineal kin, especially her brothers who become her children's *bain den moe*. Relations with *bain den moe* and other kin from the mother's patriline may provide economic options for both men and women. As will be seen in the next chapter, these alternatives tend to be risky. Attaching oneself to a patron from a mother's family necessarily limits one's interactions with patrilineal kin.

There are several features that, because they are repeated in multiple contexts, can be discussed in terms of principles or structural properties—those patterns that, as the product of human action, are likely to be reproduced over time and to shape ideas about what constitutes appropriate action. The complementarity and balance that forms an important part of a husband/wife relationship, for example, is mirrored in the complementary relationship between *bain den moe* and *fa den moe*. I would argue that this complementarity constructs a split in emotional attitudes that contrasts right and obligation with affection and sentiment. This is reflected in the formal and relatively severe relations with one's father and *fa den moe*, as opposed to the warm and affection-filled ties with one's *bain den moe*. The structures of descent and marriage systems, then, can also structure emotions and, to a certain degree, action.

A third dimension of identity stems from the individual's own ability to manipulate ambiguities and loopholes in the descent system to his or her best advantage. These abilities rest on another principle that is found in the multiple domains of Kono life—a pairing of clarity and obscurity. (For a discussion of a similar principle in Bamana life, see McNaughton 1979 and Arnoldi 1986.) This pairing leaves an opening in Kono social life for a degree of ambiguity. By leaving certain relationships ambiguous, a degree of fluctuation and manipulation enters into questions of identity, and personal action in the form of personal style and charisma can be as important as genealogical reckoning. Social positions are only made clear through the acceptance of one's claims to identity by others. I argue later in this volume that this too implies complementarity because, in general, one's identity can only be established and maintained when others accept those claims to identity, essentially making them real. A degree of manipulation allows charismatic or ambitious individuals to be more successful than their identity at birth might otherwise signal. Such success often depends more on getting others to believe one's claims to identity than on strict adherence to biological or temporal realities. Ambiguity in the divisions between brothers or the ideological notion that the father's brother is equal to the father have historically opened the way for the manipulation of kinship ties in ways that provide potential avenues to better social positions. By accepting the possibility of manipulating identity, one must also accept that Kono social structure has points that are ambiguous and opens the door for the interpretation of claims to identity. As I show in Chapter 8, there is a political aspect to interpretation that is fundamental to understanding Kono aesthetic judgments and the processes by which change occurs.

The means of achieving identity discussed here suggest another principle or structural property—that people and their connections to others are known and judged through their public actions. The emphasis on and attention to action informs Kono social relationships, production processes, and ways of conceptualizing the world. More importantly, the emphasis on action and its interpretation provides a critical avenue through which the experiential or subjectively apprehended aspects of personhood can affect ideologically derived or culturally objectified dimensions of the person in the form of judgments of action. Furthermore, the emphasis on action and its evaluation ensures that evaluating others plays a central role in shaping definitions of appropriate action in the future. In the process of continual adjustment that changing evaluations provide, the pull towards the values, habits, and familiarities of the past is being challenged by the realities and choices inherent in contemporary situations. Some of those habits and values are being transformed to meet the needs of everyday life, and it is at this level that questions of aesthetic criticism and judgments of appropriate behavior become relevant.

4

MANAGING SUBJECTIVITY

While the rules of kinship and descent provide individuals with a set of possibilities that they can manipulate to establish certain aspects of identity, awareness of the rules and emotions related to or engendered within the confines of the descent and domestic domains and the ways in which they can be manipulated do not provide the full picture of how individuals establish identity. Other factors impinge upon or inhibit the claims to identity that individuals might make by manipulating the ambiguities of descent rules or the alliances available through matrifilial ties. This brings us to the point of discussing Kono notions of personhood and the ways in which individuals seek to comply with norms and expectations while, at the same time, they seek to meet their own goals, needs, and interests. The norms of personhood are internalized in ways that suggest individuals are constantly moving between subjectively apprehended and culturally defined notions of personhood. From one position, it is possible to achieve status, goals, and individual success. From the other, it is possible to be recognized as a good or moral person. These two positions, however, are often in conflict, with actions directed toward one end working against those directed toward the other.

This approach to the pragmatics of establishing identity borrows from Fortes's (1973:287) description of the two dimensions of personhood—the objective and subjective:

> Looking at it from the objective side, the distinctive qualities, capacities and roles with which society endows a person enable the person to be known to be, and also to show himself to be the person he is supposed to be. Looked at from the subjective side, it is a question of how the individual, as actor, knows himself to be—or not to be—the person he is expected to be in a given situation and status.[1]

Male versus female, young versus old, and membership in one lineage as opposed to another are some of the assigned categories that impose limits and expectations on the actions of Kono individuals. Complying with the limits and expectations is one way of being recognized as a good or successful person. Compliance, however, is not always an easy task. It is often clouded by tensions between who an individual is supposed to be and who they actually turn out to be. At times compliance with social norms comes into direct conflict with the aspirations, needs, and idiosyncracies inherent in individuals. According to Fortes (1973:287), such tensions are an innate part of social life: "[t]he individual is not a passive bearer of personhood; he must appropriate the qualities and capacities, and the norms governing its expression to himself." Jackson and Karp (1990:28) have expanded upon this idea:

> Formalized notions of personhood are not to be construed as descriptive of a static, preordained, social world; they are instrumentalities which people actively use in constructing and reconstructing a world which adjusts values and goals inherited from the past to the problems and exigencies which comprise their social existence in the here and now.

Everyday life, then, is problematic as individuals reconcile who they think they should be with who they want to be.

While all societies have ways of harnessing individual interests to ensure willing compliance in the reproduction of social forms, such methods are culture-specific and layered with questions of how value is constructed. For the Kono, the limits to using the systemic ambiguities embedded in descent and domestic relations come in varied and probably ever-changing forms but, essentially, they are shaped in two ways. The first set of constraints is related to rituals that attach people to particular places. In this case, constraint comes from what others know of an individual's genealogy and history. The second set of constraints is much more complicated. It is related to the ways in which emotion, affect, and the cultural ideals of personhood are internalized, in other words, the ways in which the expectations of others shape emotion, affect, and ideas of correct action. Much of the turmoil at this level takes place in attitudes toward and treatment of the body.

IDENTITY IN SPACE

In contrast to identity in the temporal plane, which is somewhat fluid and dependant upon how individuals present themselves, identity as it is established along spatial lines is somewhat more limiting or concrete. It relies on an assortment of ritual actions that actually locate individuals in particular spaces by giving them rights, as well as obligations, to others who share those spaces. Where someone is born, where they join Sande or Poro, where their ancestors are buried, and where they themselves will be buried work to limit the claims to identity and the rights and statuses available through the descent and kinship system. Rituals associating the individual with particular places are performed at critical junctures. These ritual acts tie individuals to particular places and to the ancestors associated with those places. In addition to legitimizing rights to resources, such public demonstrations function in ways that supersede future personal claims by making it difficult for others to forget essential parts of an individual's genealogy.

The active association of an individual with particular spaces begins shortly after birth when the umbilical cord is tied and cut about two inches from the knot. A few days after birth the excess skin dries up, falls off, and is given to the child's father to bury. He buries it at his patrilineal home, which guarantees the child certain rights in the town and in the father's lineage. If the father has not tied kola for the child's mother, the ritual will be carried out by the mother's brother and the child will become a member of his or her mother's town and lineage. If the legal father is not the biological father, the task of burial still falls to the legal father and the child's legal identity belongs to his patriline. When the child is older (usually before joining Poro or Sande), he or she will be told where the burial occurred. Because the burial site can be used to curse the individual in future years, its whereabouts is not made public.

In a second ritual of attachment, the child is taken to a central location in his or her father's town known as the *tamba tina*. Rosen (1973:37) writes that "... no child born to any village could hope to have good health and fortune unless this introduction was formally made." In this context, *tamba* translates as spear, *tina* as place. Together they refer to the primary allegiance owed to this particular locale by those of the town, the place they must defend. Rosen (1973:37) also writes that the spear of the town's founder is often buried within the *tamba tina*. This visit also links the child with its patrilineal ancestors in spatial and active terms. Other ritual occasions, such as a child's initiation into Poro or Sande, are also marked by visits to the *tamba tina*.

A third location that has consequences for identity is the place where an individual joins an initiation society, usually Sande or Poro (female and male, respectively). There is a degree of flexibility in the location where girls are initiated into Sande. Their options are to join in the town where they were born (under the guise of patrilineal affiliation), to join the Sande branch that their mother joined, or to join the branch in which the mother's patrilineage holds power. In some cases these options might overlap. My impression is that daughters of lineage elders tend to join where their fathers are powerful and daughters of less important individuals join where their mothers joined or where their mother's patrilineage is powerful. Daughters of women already powerful in Sande will join where their mothers are most active. In some cases, then, initiation associates adolescent girls with the home of their matri-kin and provides an array of associations much wider than those available through patrilineal ties alone. Young boys join Poro in their patrilineal homes or areas in which they have patrilineal relatives, which further strengthens ties to their patrilineal kin. One of the first questions that young people often ask when they first meet is where they were initiated. In this way location, in addition to family name, becomes a way of categorizing and identifying others.

In the Kono area today most children must be initiated into Poro or Sande in order to be considered a full adult member of Kono society. Poro was apparently adopted from the Mende in the late nineteenth century. At that time Mende warriors from the south were attacking Kono villages regularly. Because the raids continued for so long, many Kono migrated north to the Kuranko area and eventually organized into Poro to keep their activities secret from the Kuranko (see Matturi 1973 and Abraham 1973). According to Matturi (1973:208):

> After they [the Kono] had stayed there [in the Kuranko area] for
> some years they began to have a longing for their homeland, and also

they felt that any further stay with the Kuranko would in the end change their children into Kurankos, which feeling they disliked, and so they made a plan and the plan was this—they initiated the Poro Society. The Kurankos are not Poro men, so the Konos were safe to discuss their secrets in the Poro Bush, and thus they were able through their Poro boys to remove their property secretly as they felt if they did this in open daylight it would doubtless cause friction between them and their host tribe, which would almost certainly bring about warfare between them. When they felt that the best of their property had been moved away by the Poro boys, one day the remainder of the tribe suddenly left the Kuranko country.

Until very recently there were only two categories of men who did not join Poro. The first were men of the sanduu clan whose *tana* is leopard. This *tana* is located primarily in the areas around the towns of Tombu and Kurandor. Legend has it that during warrior times these men were told by their fathers that if they joined Poro they would become crazy. Instead, these men joined Bii, an initiation society reserved primarily for Muslims today.[2] In 1980, after an elder of one of these areas grew tired of the laughing and jibes he received because he had not joined Poro (he was also left out of one of the most important contexts for decision-making in the chiefdom), he joined Poro and disproved the legend. Since that time, I was told, the Bii bush[3] around Kurandor has been burned down and other men from that area have also joined Poro.

The second category of men who still do not join Poro are Mandingo and Kuranko men living in the Kono area. They are usually Muslim and are likely to join Bii. Bii is a men's circumcision society that may have originally been tied to Poro, possibly as the first stage of initiation into Poro. There seems to be less connection between Bii and Poro now. Non-Muslim men who were initiated into Bii in the late 1950s claim that Bii was the first step in Poro. (Poro initiation is apparently made up of several levels; as a man advances in levels, he becomes privy to new sets of knowledge and power.) According to Parsons (1964), however, even in the 1930s and 1940s Bii was primarily for Muslims. The only explanation I was given for the separation of these societies was that families were unwilling to spend the money for initiation into both groups, so it is possible to be initiated directly into Poro today.

Someone who has already been initiated into Poro will not join Bii. A Poro member, however, can enter the Bii bush, but a Bii member cannot enter the Poro bush. Furthermore, Poro members refer to Bii

derogatorily as "a woman's society." Parsons (1964:143), whose research in the Kono area was conducted in the 1930s and 1940s, writes:

> The Bili training has prepared [the man] biologically for parenthood,
> yet it does not add the *bui* [medicine] to his life, which is a part of the
> work of the Poro. The Bili member, therefore, does not have the powers
> of a full man, for he has not received that from the Poro society.[4]

Muslims are still active in Bii in the Kainkordu area today. I witnessed
public portions of the Bii initiation ceremony in 1983, the first held there
in twelve years. While Poro initiations are held annually, Bii initiations
are held much more sporadically.

I know very little about another initiation society in the Kono area
that is called Do (pronounced dō, and which translates "to join"), except
that the medicine associated with it, which is called *yaa* or lion, sometimes appears at the funerals of chiefdom elders. Do is a society that is
specific to Soa chiefdom and may have been present before Poro was
introduced. Other chiefdoms also have societies associated specifically
with them. Sumoe, for example, is found in Sando, another Kono chiefdom. Sumoe members are known for their skills at healing both physical and spiritual ills. Members of Sumoe may be called for from all over
the Kono area to practice. Men as well as women can become members.
Yombo, another initiation society, is specific to Faiama Chiefdom and is
known for its masked figures and its distinctive performances.[5]

Exactly when and how Sande entered the Kono area is even more uncertain than Poro's origins. It is the only association for women in Soa
and its initiations are held yearly (as opposed to some parts of the Central West Atlantic region where Sande and Poro will alternate times
when each is in session).

Initiation is the first step in becoming a full-fledged member of society. Failure to be initiated condemns an individual to a lifetime as a jural
minor. Initiation is one of the few times in an individual's life when he or
she becomes the center of a family's attention, commanding donations of
goods and labor from both father's and mother's kin to make the event
a success. See Figure 13. Its success, however, belongs to both the individual and the family since the associated festivities provide an opportunity for family units to demonstrate their wealth and prestige to the
community. A child enters Poro or Sande somewhere between the ages of
eight and fifteen. At this time the interests of *fa den moe* and *bain den*

moe once again coalesce around the individual in the form of a set of mutual responsibilities. The *fa den moe* must notify the *bain den moe* of the impending ceremonies and the *bain den moe* must agree to allow the initiation of their child. Failing to make such notification is a serious insult. There are stories of uncles who have entered bush areas to remove their nephews from the Poro camp because they had not been notified. The *bain den moe* is responsible for providing some of the goods, such as rice, meat, palm oil, and clothing, associated with initiation.

Aside from family and marital relationships, the bonds between those initiated at the same time form the strongest ties an individual will establish with others in the community. Boys who join Poro at the same time are called *togbai,* and they are sworn to a lifetime of cooperation and mutual support.

In Kono today not all of the towns or villages have Poro bushes. Instead, the paramount chief designates the place where initiations will take place each year. Boys are often initiated away from their homes, thereby developing intense ties to non-agnates. The fact that the paramount chief makes the designation suggests that he has a degree of control over Poro that may not be present in other areas. D'Azevedo (1962), for example, noted the strict separation between the secular power of chiefs and the sacred dimension of power held by Poro in the Mende area.

Girls who join Sande at the same time develop similar relationships of mutual support. Even though they marry and participate in Sande in the town of their husbands, they will often maintain important ties to their natal or their mother's homes and to a network of women their own age through Sande activities.

In order to understand the ways in which spatial distance can constrain action, it is necessary to consider a fourth principle that is found in multiple domains of Kono life (I have previously discussed complementarity, clarity and obscurity, and the emphasis on action). Spatial distance or being away from one's home is in some ways equated with being away from the controlling influence of kin or other social relations. This is related to a principle that I describe as containment or bounding. Things that are either dangerous or need protection are physically contained. Individuals away from the social attachments that birth, marriage, or initiation provide are unbounded or uncontained because distance, in most cases, mutes the possibility of complementary relationships or of being known by one's actions. In general, the identities providing dimensions of space limit the range in which individuals can operate. As individuals move further and further from their home they can no longer be controlled by the constraints of jural obligations. At the same time they become less able to utilize the advantages that patrilineal or matrifilial ties provide. Here, too, individuals are given a degree of choice, but the choices are not without consequences. In the ever-expanding geography of the twentieth-century Kono world, individuals who leave their natal homes for at least a part of their life define themselves as being in one of two situations. Some feel they have freed themselves from the constraints and demands that accrue when relatives are close by. Others define themselves as being cut off from the identities and resources normally available to them through ties to place. For example, as distance increases and the ability to honor ancestors at critical junctures becomes more remote, they are less and less likely receive any ancestral assistance in their daily affairs. At the same time, they find it more and more difficult to leave the small graveside gifts that might encourage ancestral assistance. Some individuals are unwilling to take the chance of cutting such valuable ties. Others, whose ancestral ties are already weakened by low status or other factors, are more willing to move should such an action hold the possibility of advancement. These individuals will, in all likelihood, be forgotten by their lineage, unless they go to great efforts to maintain contact, send resources back, or otherwise demonstrate that they still consider themselves part of the lineage. Also those who leave often find themselves without the familial contacts that would allow them to advance. The patterns of containment and complementarity are deeply rooted. To be contained is to be controlled by responsibilities to others and to maintain relations of complementarity. To be away from one's home is to be outside these relationships and outside the controlling influence of others.

The final arbiter in the complex calculus of Kono identity is what happens to the individual in death. Death, too, is marked in spatial terms. After death there is a period of time when the deceased's spirit remains near the place of death waiting for family members to send it to the ancestral home. Because powerful spirits left to wander too long get impatient, ancestors who have not been properly buried, or who have not been permanently located in space, are capable of wrecking havoc upon their descendants. Descendants must decide who should be buried properly and who can be left to wander without causing trouble. The dead, then, depend on their descendants to keep their names alive through graveside sacrifices, notifications at important life-cycle events, and pleas for assistance. Such acts also encourage ancestors to refrain from causing havoc in their descendants' lives. Those who die in or near their homes are likely to be able to interfere with or assist their descendants simply because of proximity; thus, descendants have more of an incentive to perform the sometimes costly post-burial ceremonies described in Chapter 3 for those who die close to home.

For those who die away from home, the process is more complicated. If individuals die away from the place where their umbilical cord was buried, they will usually, by necessity, be buried where they died. Those who die far away but whose reputations are known back home may be ritually incorporated into the ancestral community. For these individuals, a stone from the actual grave will be carried back to the natal home to serve as the foundation of a false grave, and efforts will be made to hold the post-burial ceremonies. This site will serve as the real grave and will be used for sacrifices and other occasions for which the descendants wish to contact their ancestors. Decisions about post-burial ceremonies are complicated. Descendants try to gauge the potential danger that deceased individuals might be able to cause before deciding to invest resources in rituals that place them in the ancestral world and open future communication between them and their descendants. If individuals are thought not to be very powerful, the descendants will not trouble with them. There is, however, always the chance that these decisions will underestimate someone, which can cause grave harm to the immediate descendants as well as to the lineage as a whole.

The foregoing discussion suggests that there are two facets to considering space and its effect on identity. The first has to do with locations in space and the second has to do with the knowledge that others have of these specific locations and their meanings. In terms of locations in space, Kono individuals are publicly tied to particular spaces at specific points in their life trajectories by ritual acts. Birth, initiation, marriage (especially for women), and death are the most important. In terms of knowledge of others, as individuals pass through the ceremonies associated with each phase of life, they establish an interpretive framework through which others will know them. This framework necessarily limits what an individual might claim as his or her own identity in the future. Some individuals, after assessing their possibilities in their natal homes, opt to distance themselves from the identities available there. By doing so, they free themselves from the constraints of natal identity (specifically, the expectations of others), but they also cut themselves off from any resources that might be available through links to natal homes. Without distinguishing themselves in some way, these individuals are likely to be forgotten in their natal homes, and the rituals that associate the dead with the ancestral realm will probably not be done for them.

Kono individuals negotiate and manipulate subjective identity and sense of self in coordination with the personal knowledge and culturally objectified expectations that others have of them. Most often, knowledge and expectation are held by those who are close by. Only those who distance themselves from lineage or natally based affiliations free themselves from these constraints. It is not enough, then, to state one's status or reputation; others must accept such statements and act accordingly in order for identity to be established and for the rights and obligations inherent in particular identities to be acted upon. Identity, then, is established only in relationships of complementarity; it implies both a claim and an acceptance by others in ways that make individual action somewhat ineffective.

PERSONHOOD

The second set of constraints on action comes directly from the tensions associated with the struggle between self expression and social expectation. In most societies the impetus to be recognized as a "good person" is very strong. The Kono are no exception. The actions of individuals are directed toward the pursuit of ideal personhood as they try to live up to the social roles they inhabit. One of the highest compliments that someone can receive is "they have good character" (*a sone nyi*), which essentially means they behave according to the rules and norms. When individuals feel they are not living up to other's expectations, they may suffer a great deal of pain, as happened to the young man who discussed suicide in Chapter 3. Just beneath the surface of cooperation that much of Kono social life implies lies the potential for chaos and uncertainty as individuals endeavor to control or come to terms with the tensions and conflicts engendered by the clash of objectively imposed and subjectively developed ideas of who they are.

In Kono experience approval or disapproval of others is manifested in action. A woman who is angry at her husband will withdraw her labor from his rice farm, just as a client who feels he is being cheated by his patron will look for another patron. It is no surprise, then, that most

Kono activities or production processes are, on the whole, cooperative enterprises, enterprises that require a degree of complementarity for success. Rice production, marriage arrangements, initiation into Poro or Sande, and even birth and death are activities that require the coordination of various categories of persons. Successful rice production, for example, depends on the skillful coordination of labor, as well as a man's ability to obtain land through lineage elders. Cooperation is also a fundamental part of cloth production. While women grow cotton and spin it into thread, only men can weave it. Neither men nor women can perform the job of the other and there are negative sanctions against those who attempt to do so. The complementarity embedded in most labor processes ensures a degree of compliance to social norms in that someone who is disrespectful, stingy, or otherwise unpopular will have difficulty finding laborers for farming or dancers willing to help with a son's initiation into Poro.

As with other Mande groups, a central problem of Kono social life is the maintenance of a balance between individuality or individual intention and personhood or expectations (Arnoldi 1986; Bird and Kendall 1980; Jackson 1977). Bird and Kendall (1980:15) describe the tensions engendered in such conflicts among the Bamana: "They [the Bamana] know that they depend upon the individual who resists the pull of the established social order, just as they depend upon the individuals who do not resist; they know that they require the individual who will change things, even if these changes are potentially destructive."

In addition to the constraints that others place on an individual's claims to identity, Kono social life and socialization practices work to channel individualization into socially acceptable norms with a multiplicity of techniques that include naming practices, proverbs, and theories of emotion and the body. In this way the Kono emphasis on connections to others serves as an ideological underpinning to most activities and leads to an actual channeling of how people think about themselves and what they are capable of doing. Proverbs and their use in daily life, for example, illustrate how important connections to others are. The Kono say, for example, *gbo fiya ambe kwe si* ("two hands scratch the back"), which means nothing is accomplished by one person alone, or *moe i buo anso moe kama i ni kooson* ("you have to put your hand on someone's shoulder before you can stand"), which means someone always has to help you or teach you. A person, then, is unable to understand anything alone.

TABLE 2
Kono Birth Order Names

Birth No.	Boy	Girl
1	Sahr	Sia
2	Tamba	Kumba
3	Aiah	Finda
4	Komba	Yai
5	Kai	Bondu
6	Safia	Fiya
7	Mani[1]	Mani[2]

[1]If Mani has already been used to name a daughter, the name Kogba will be used. Kogba is laughingly translated as "after the harvest."
[2]If Mani has already been used for a son, Mafoo will be used to name the seventh daughter.

The emphasis on connections to others, compliance with notions of personhood, and deemphasis of the individual are fostered in multiple ways, each of which reinforces the others in ways that work essentially to mask characteristics of individual personalities. Naming practices are only one of the ways in which an orientation towards objective roles is internalized during socialization and made visible to the outsider. The Kono practice birth-order naming. A child is given a name depending on its sex and how many children its mother has already given birth to. A first daughter is given the name Sia, the second is named Kumba. A first son is given the name Sahr, the second is named Tamba, and so on (Table 2).

In a polygynous household there may be three or four daughters named Sia and several sons named Sahr, and so on down the list of names for each sex. Only if the end of the list is reached will the mother and father begin choosing names. In most cases the name of a child who dies will not be reused. Only in exceptional circumstances or in the case of older individuals who have established some kind of personal identity within the community are nicknames given that allow an individual's characteristics to emerge as a part of identity.

The implications of the naming system are far-reaching. In everyday conversation it forces people to use qualifiers in order to identify who they are referring to. The name Sia is not enough to distinguish a particular individual. The qualifiers invoked are usually family names or birth locations; Sia becomes Sia Gbenda (Gbenda is a family name) or Sia Fenbudu (Fenbudu is a town name). Another common alternative is to include Sia's relationship to the speaker, as in "Sia, my sister," or "Sia, my friend." If speakers have no particular personal relationship with the subject, they will identify which Sia by referring to her relatives, as in "Sia, Bondu's daughter." Individuals, then, are described and made known through their relationships to others rather than through recognition of idiosyncratic personality traits or others' experiences of them. The use of Kono names, then, continually submerges individual identity within the identity of others, it limits the emergence of personal characteristics of action as a means of identifying others, and it fosters a tendency towards defining others in terms of their social relationships within the community. Likewise, this naming system channels perceptions of the self towards identification with aspects of personhood rather than individual identity. Being the first daughter (Sia) or son (Sahr) entails different obligations and expectations from those attached to someone named Safia or Mani.

In what might be seen as exceptions to the emphasis on personhood, nicknames are individualized and they make distinctions among people based on aspects of their identity. Instead of allowing individual identity to show through and be appreciated, however, one can argue that nicknames are used to set certain individuals apart from social norms. For example, the nickname *Tumoe* (fishing net) is sometimes given to a child whose birth has been very difficult. During the birth, the mother was advised to dismantle a fishing net and lay on it. The metaphor of trapping the child, as one would trap fish, refers to the difficulty of the birth, as well as to the possibility of future difficulty with the child. In another example, the daughter of a woman who had already lost three or four daughters at birth was given several names in an attempt to stop the cycle of death. The child was given her birth-order name as well as a boy's name, Tamba, in the hope of confusing the witch who was thought to have eaten the woman's previous female children. In addition to the boy's name, the daughter was also nicknamed *Kokwe* (Maybe)—maybe the child would stay or maybe she would leave—another ploy to confuse witches into thinking the parents were not particularly concerned about this child, when, in fact, exactly the opposite was the case. I suggest that these nicknames mark certain children at birth in ways that alter both their obligations and people's expectations of them. This process, however, is achieved in a patterned way, suggesting that there are categories that extraordinary individuals are put into, roles they are given, if you will, that are as predetermined as the roles and obligations engendered by the naming system.

Powerful adults may also take on nicknames, which suggests that individuals of a certain stature can begin to construct their identities in unique ways, providing their supporters accept these constructions. This can be seen in the following case of a chiefdom elder. As he rose in stature within his lineage, jealous competitors started the rumor that he was actually the illegitimate son of a Temne man. If this was true, it could be used to invalidate any claims he might make to lineage authority. Rather than suffer the insults in private, the man took matters into his own hands and incorporated "Temne" into his name. In a defiant reversal of the original challenge he showed that his claims to power were so genuine they could not be minimized by rumor or innuendo. Both his followers and detractors were impressed by his daring, and the man continued along the road to becoming a powerful individual. This is an example of an extremely powerful man who was able to manipulate the naming system and maintain some control over his own identity in a way that allowed personal ambition to override the social constraints on the expression of individual intention.

While names are usually invariant, the character of individuals remains indeterminate. The naming system itself works against this indeterminacy to structure action according to social norms. Nicknames, as well, provide only a modicum of distinction, since they are more often than not categories of otherness that certain individuals are channelled into. Exceptions do occur, but such exceptions are only the privilege of a very small minority of the most powerful individuals.

It is clear that most Kono consider the naming system to be one of the central features of Kono identity. The naming system was one of the first things described to me when I arrived in the Kono area. Descriptions of what it meant to be Kono, whether in casual conversation or in directed interviews, invariably yielded a discussion of the naming system. Without a doubt it was the single most frequently mentioned characteristic of what it meant to be Kono or how the Kono distinguish themselves from surrounding ethnic groups.

The manner in which Kono infants are named further demonstrates the efforts taken to reduce the indeterminacy of individualized or subjective appropriations of social norms. Kono infants are named during small household ceremonies that show the extent to which individual personalities and capacities are shaped by the expectations of others. Seven days after birth, a child who is in good health is taken out of the house for the first time by a small group of family members for the naming ceremony. The child's parents invite an adult who they consider to be of good character and who is the same sex as the child to perform the ceremony. Usually this adult has the same birth-order name as the infant. During the ceremony the adult spits into the face of the child and gives it advice on how best to proceed in life. In this process the name, as well as the character and even the physical traits of the adult, pass into the child. Along with character traits, the social identities of the name-giver and the child become mixed. The name-giver becomes the sister or brother of the child, sharing in the familial relationships of the child. When the child is older, he or she addresses the name-giver as "*n kor*" (my older sibling). Thus, the name-giver becomes the child of the infant's parents, and the infant adopts the relationships of the name-giver, even to the extent of becoming the mother or father of any of the name-giver's children.

Children also inherit traits from their ancestors. Virtually every trait that the child develops is attributed, not to the uniqueness of the child, but to influences on the child from other people. Children are watched for the appearance of traits that their families expect them to display; they are even encouraged to develop the positive traits that the carefully arranged naming ceremony is expected to invest in the child. In the same vein, any unexplained traits that a child exhibits are attributed to unknown or unnoticed characteristics of either an ancestor or the name-giver or to the influence of a forgotten ancestor.

The important thing to emphasize here, however, is that the source of identity, personality, and physical characteristics of an individual is usually external—for example, the traits of others in the child rather than unique aspects of the child's personality and physique. Instead of celebrating individual identity, naming practices foster identity through others and temper perceptions of the extent to which individuals can actively shape their lives and environments.

INDIVIDUALITY

Individuality, however, does emerge. In fact, managing individuality in socially accepted ways is one of the major tensions or concerns throughout an individual's life. Kono individuals have a sense of self, as well as a degree of tolerance for the idiosyncratic in human behavior. The fact that the Kono recognize the importance of difference is evident in such proverbs as *fen dondwe mu kugboa che foo am ba a te,* which can be translated as "all things have one behind but it is cut in two," or "the behind is all one part but it is divided into two," meaning that we are all human beings but we are not all of the same mind or character.

There are two dimensions to Kono individuality. The first has to do with public display, as in the actions of the chiefdom elder who publicly took the nickname that was meant as an insult. The outcome of action in the public dimension ends in personal gain through public recognition and appreciation of difference. Such public demonstrations are contained or socially controlled because they are in full view (see the early part of this chapter). The use of the idiom of containment means that actions can be controlled. For example, actions can be upheld or ridiculed by others, which means that others remain in control of identity and reputation. Before any difference or expression of individuality can be recognized, it must be publicly demonstrated and appreciated. As in the earlier description of warriors and power (see the beginning of Chapter 3), power must be tested before it can be recognized. This emphasis on public display is found in other Mande groups as well (Arnoldi 1986; McNaughton 1979).

The Kono conceive of this distinction as well. The Kono term for public or outside is *baama.* To go outside implies subjecting oneself and one's acts to the scrutiny and judgments of others. The Kono say that you will never achieve anything without first going out of your door mouth (doorway). This can lead to the enhancement or ruin of one's reputation, and there are a series of rituals that can be undertaken in doorways to protect and guide one's actions in the public sphere. Thus, only by placing oneself in the public eye and by opening oneself to the challenges of others can claims to status, position, or reputation be validated. The importance of recognizing such individuality publicly relates to exposing and thus controlling it in order to channel individuals into the social roles they are expected to fill.

The second dimension of individuality is much more private and dangerous. The outcome of action in this dimension is personal gain at the expense of the community. Public action is contrasted with hidden action, with being inside or being away from the watchful eyes of the community. Individuals who spend too much time out of the public eye are suspected of antisocial behavior. People wonder what they could possibly be doing by themselves for so much of the time. Witchcraft, for example, is conceived of as a lonely and secret activity, and those individuals who continually spend time alone become immediately suspect, as in the case of the elderly man described in Chapter 3. Kono students often complained about this to me, lamenting that it was impossible to study while visiting their relatives because they could never get away. They were discouraged from sitting in their rooms in order to read, even for a short period of time. Even very sick people spend a large part of their days out on the veranda in public view, saying that only those near death stay inside. I should add here that it is not only inside spaces that are dangerous. Walking in the forest alone, unless one is hunting, is equally suspect. The key point is that it is dangerous to be out of the public eye, to be in spaces where one's actions cannot be seen and thus cannot be used in the construction and validation of identity or reputation.

One of the few exceptions to the emphasis on being out-of-doors occurs during a woman's confinement after giving birth. A woman and her newborn remain indoors until the infant's umbilical cord falls off, usually a period of about seven days. During this time, the woman's room is kept relatively dark and warm, to some extent recreating the atmosphere of the womb for the newborn, who is only gradually introduced to human life. This confinement protects the infant not only from drafts and illness but also from exposure to the dangers of the world, especially the work of jealous witches who are known to "eat" children. During seclusion the mother's room becomes a public space to some extent. Other women come and go freely, although they must still announce their presence before entering both the main door of the house and the bedroom. The mother and child are, in fact, rarely left alone. This visiting transforms a private space into a public space for the duration of confinement, and the infant is protected through containment within the house.

EMOTIONS AND THE BODY

The location of emotions within the body and the prescribed methods for dealing with them demonstrate further some of the ways that individual intention is downplayed and Kono individuals learn to behave appropriately. In fact, I would argue that the enculturated body is one of the primary sites for the struggle between culturally objectified norms and subjectively apprehended definitions of self, as Jackson and Karp (1990) have suggested. Such struggles come in two forms. First, evaluations of what people do to bring subjective goals into line (by supporting or denying particular actions) with cultural goals. The importance of complementarity for establishing identity is critical here. Second, individuals' experiences of their own bodies are both culturally based and idiosyncratic. While people learn about affect and emotion through culture, cultural control of that knowledge can never be certain. In fact, as the seat of emotion, the Kono body is, in some ways, conceptualized similarly to the interior of a house or the private realm. In Kono conceptions, the body (gboo) is the container of individuality and identity. This can be seen, in part, in the description of the name-giving ceremony in which bodily fluids, such as spit, provide a mechanism for transferring the characteristics of an admired person to an infant. An individual with no anger or animosity is said to have "a cool heart" (faa chima), and someone who is enjoying an occasion will remark that "their stomach is sweet" (n gbuo dia). On the other hand, an angry or disappointed person will say that "their heart has spoiled" (n faa a yonda), or that "their heart has been cut" (n faa a te). If a situation is hopeless or an individual is at such a loss that they don't know what to do, they might say "my mouth is dry" (N da o gba), meaning that they have no words left to speak on the particular subject, that there is nothing inside to let out. Death, as well, is announced in terms that suggest that the essence of an individual in life is encapsulated within the body. At death the essence escapes. The words A nii bo ("her soul has left or gone out") are pronounced over the deathbed and the mouth of the deceased is shut if it has fallen open.

Since the body is conceived of as the seat of individual intention, it is not surprising to hear people speak about the personal effort it takes to keep antisocial emotions hidden from view. If such emotions are let out, they may disturb the balance of social life or expose rifts that the ideals of complementarity are unable to hold together. A common way to begin a complaint against someone is "I can no longer keep it inside," indicating that an individual recognizes that what they are letting out is somehow not supposed to emerge.

While emotions are supposed to be contained and controlled within the body, it is inevitable that occasionally they build up to a breaking point and explode in often violent and destructive ways in the public arena. In fact, when emotions do break out they are often uncontrollable, testimony to the fact that people spend a great deal of energy trying to contain them. People speak of these outbursts as a weakening of the bodily shell that normally contains emotions and a failure of the individual to control themselves or behave appropriately. When one of these outbursts begins it is not unusual for someone to fall into a state of uncontrolled rage, striking out at anything or anyone within reach. This is illustrated in the following case. A man whose family I had come to know quite well returned from a short trip to Koidu. While away, he had heard rumors that his youngest wife had been having an affair with a young man. He returned to Kainkordu in the evening, greeted his family and others around town, and waited for his wives to come back from the farm. When they returned, it was almost dark. Because they had not expected him, they had not brought enough food for him from the farm. (During the peak agricultural season, women cook the main meal of the day on the farm and bring the leftovers back to town to be eaten before going to bed that night.) There was obviously not enough food for the whole family, and the husband expected a full meal, which would take at least an hour to prepare. The women were exhausted from the day's work and refused to cook for him because he had not sent word he was coming. A dispute started between the husband and his younger wife. As his family later described it, he was unable to control himself. They started arguing about the food, and suddenly the husband started screaming about her extramarital affair and threatening to kill her. By that time everyone nearby knew a fight was going on. When the husband hit his wife, she ran screaming from the house, and he ran after her. As he left the house, he met his brothers who had hurried to his doorstep to stop the argument. One of his brothers stepped behind him and encircled him with his arms. The husband spun around, lifted his brother off his feet, and threw him to the ground. By that time the wife had disappeared, giving her husband time to cool down to the point that other family members could surround him and block any further efforts to go after the woman. As he calmed down, his family was able to lead him back into his house. The wife stayed elsewhere in town that night. The next day both the wife and the husband agreed to seek the advice of a mediator, and both disagreements (the alleged affair and the wives' refusal to cook for their husband) were settled in such a way that each side could return to the union without losing face.

In this case, family members moved in to control the antisocial behavior of their relative. The disruption was considered antisocial because of the degree of his rage and because there are culturally appropriate ways of dealing with a wife's failure to cook for a husband or extramarital affairs. By allowing the rage to consume him the husband turned his back on accepted sociocultural norms. In effect, the man's family helped him to return to his normal social role by physically surrounding him, putting a barrier between him and onlookers, and denying his self expression. This suggests that other people can serve as substitutes when an individual's own body can no longer contain emotion. In such cases, individuality is further thwarted in that the uncontrolled behavior of the adult is attributed to external factors. Essentially, such outbursts are explained as the result of a curse or witchcraft or the inheritance of a particular fault. Individuals are rarely, if ever, held accountable for their own actions.

There are many other contexts in which bodies and containers are metaphorically linked. For example, the womb is conceived of as a container. A woman who wishes to stop bearing children for a time will place medicinal leaves in a clay pot, which she then turns upside down and hides. Next, a rope is tied around her waist. The woman will not become pregnant until the rope is cut or the pot is turned right side up so that it serves as a container again.

In another context, the Kono body is conceived of as a pot that is filled with emotions and learning as a child matures. If a boy dies during initiation into Poro, as occasionally happens, his mother will not hear of the death until several weeks or months later when all the boys are brought back from the place of initiation to town. On that day the returning boys, led by Poro elders, will gather on the doorstep of the dead boy's mother. An elder will announce that the pot (meaning the son) the woman gave to Poro was flawed. At that point the elder holds a ceramic vessel above his head and smashes it on the woman's doorstep.

The body, then, is a container for knowledge and emotion. It can be used to hide negative emotions that indicate individuality, individualized expression, or experiences that are not condoned by others. Anger, hatred, greed, desire, and other indications of an individual's feelings are supposed to be hidden and, when they cannot be, the body's containing function is thought to have failed. To be a good individual is to be constantly vigilant about how individual intention is displayed. The fact that negative emotions exist at all only reiterates the extent of their power

and danger and, in turn, fundamentally denies individuals the social per-
fection they actively seek.

CONTROLLING INDIVIDUALITY

In addition to emotional outbursts, anything that can be construed as abnormal or out-of-the-ordinary behavior can be conceived of as an expression of individuality. This is the case when one is speaking of thievery or
madness or of such seemingly valued behaviors as singing, being a chief,
hunting, producing a particularly good rice crop, or other activities that
can be perceived as deviations from normal identity and fall into the
realm of individualized identity, ambition, and reputation. When expressions of individual identity or intention emerge, they tend to be problematic, ambiguous, or paradoxical, and often all three at the same time.
Every attempt is made to control individuality by exposing it in ways that
allow it to be contained and open to public view and, thus, subverted.

Expressions of individuality that can be controlled are celebrated, as
can be seen in the appreciation and respect given to some chiefs, singers,
hunters, and other specialists. While these individuals are normally personally ambitious, even to the point of delving into witchcraft to achieve
or enhance their powers, they have channelled their ambitions in socially
approved ways by moving into roles that are still complementary in nature. In other words, all of these specialists require, to some degree, the
approval of others to be recognized or to achieve renown for their actions. This guarantees that the larger social group maintains some measure of control over their actions. Chiefs, for example, are very aware of
the degree of power held by clients in patron-client relationships. Singers,
too, are public figures whose actions are constrained by the performance
framework itself, as well as by the negative sanctions associated with being a singer. (I return to these two points shortly.)

As with emotional outbursts, deviations from normal social roles are
attributed to factors external to the individual. These include inheritance, as in a hunter inheriting his skills from his father, an ancestor, or
a namesake; witchcraft; curses; and other forces over which the individual has no control. Likewise, the actions of specialists are usually attributed to forces outside their control. For example, a chief's bad decisions
might not be blamed entirely on him but, instead, might be attributed to
curses or witchcraft that may have clouded his judgment. The actions of

singers, who are often outspoken critics of the status quo, are also perceived as outside their own control. The singer's sometimes acidic condemnations are attributed to forces behind them. Even the actions of witches are not necessarily attributed to them, but to forces external to them. Likewise, thieves may not be blamed for their actions, although the negative sanctions associated with being a thief tend to dissuade most people from thievery. The reputation of being a thief follows an individual to his grave; it affects the way he is treated by others and is likely to be passed on to any children as well.

By explaining out-of-the-ordinary social roles or behavior as the effect of curses, the work of witches, or the inheritance of special skills, individuals are once again relieved of a degree of responsibility for their actions. The Kono tendency to remove responsibility from the individual in this way should not suggest, however, that sanctions against deviant behavior do not exist. It is here that special roles become problematic. The life of a singer, for example, is not to be envied. The sanctions against becoming a singer are so harsh that few would try to do this work by choice. Singers told me that one way of getting back at a man is to use a curse that will turn his wife into a singer because of the grief and suffering this will cause. Because they often travel to towns where they have been hired, singers have more freedom of movement than most women who stay relatively close to their husband's or their mother's homes. As a result, they tend to be known as loose or uncontrolled women. Furthermore, because singers also fortify themselves for their long, sometimes all-night, performances with large amounts of alcohol, over a period of time they are expected to become alcoholic or damage their voices.

Those women who have become singers without a curse are believed to delve in witchcraft to obtain the medicines and powers necessary for a singing career. In the process of becoming well-known, they often trade the norms of family life, sometimes even children, for the prestige, power, and money of a singing career. A singer's voice, however, usually lasts for only five or six years. As it begins to spoil, people say that they cannot hear the words clearly. To have a really fine voice, a singer must treat it with medicines, which eventually become ineffective. Once her powers desert her, she will find it difficult to cope with a return to "normal" life.

Even individuals who are extraordinarily successful in their work are subject to the sanctions exercised against those whose individuality might lead to social imbalances if it remained unchecked. This is exemplified in a brief life history of the individual whose comments on old age appeared in Chapter 3. Aiah was a junior member of an important lineage. When I met him, he was quite elderly, probably seventy or more. His father had trained him to be a farmer, so when diamond mining came to Kono he did not get involved with it. When he saw how people were making money by selling their farm goods, he began to invest in crops like tobacco and kola. With the profits, he began to travel to neighboring chiefdoms to buy tobacco and kola from the farmers there and carried them to markets to sell. Then he began travelling farther away— to Segbwema (in the Mende area) to buy dried fish to sell in Kono. With money from the fish he bought rice to sell in Segbwema. With money from the rice, he bought mentholatums and other small things to bring back to Kono to sell. One day a Syrian trader asked him if he had palm kernels in his home. They agreed to an arrangement in which the Syrian would lend Aiah his vehicle, Aiah would buy palm kernels up-country and transport them to the nearest road, and the Syrian would buy them and send his vehicle to pick them up. So Aiah went back to his home and began to buy bushels of palm kernels and the Syrian arranged for their transportation. This continued for about a year and Aiah became very wealthy. He finally bought his own vehicle (one of the first in Soa, and the first of three he eventually owned). As Aiah explained it, he went about his business trading but most of the authorities of the chiefdom started to hate him because of his success. In addition to buying the trucks, Aiah had ten wives and he was able to send six of his children to school. He began contributing to the election campaigns for chiefdom offices, which probably had an effect on the outcome of several elections. Then someone started to poison him (this probably occurred in the middle or late 1940s), and he has been sick ever since. When he became sick, his wives started to steal from him. Aiah was admitted to a hospital where he was left to die. His wives left him and his money was all spent. When he got out of the hospital, he returned to his home, and now he lives on the proceeds of his coffee and cocoa. Although he manages to get by, he lives much below the standard he once knew. As he puts it, his house used to be in the center of the village (meaning he was a powerful man), but he has had to move.

As this history illustrates, those who are too successful must be able to deal with the anger and jealousy of others. Being successful (or outside) implies being able to handle the challenges of others. Such challenges can come from the economic sphere, or, as in the case of Aiah, from the supernatural sphere in the form of illnesses or spells that a more powerful individual might be able to inflict. Success can be a sign that someone is working with witches, but, in a system in which power must be challenged to be validated, it can also be a magnet for the challenges of others. In Aiah's case, his powers did not match those of his challengers, and he has paid the cost by being brought down to the economic level of most of his village mates.

Without a doubt, the most dangerous and subversive avenue to individual ambition and success is witchcraft. It is the most private and, thus, the most ambiguous, serious, and antisocial way of achieving one's ambitions or goals. Engaging in the private activities of witchcraft is equated metaphorically with aspects of being nonhuman and, in most cases, requires transforming oneself into a snake, animal, or other nonhuman form to accomplish one's tasks. Such images of the forest and its use by antisocial forces set up a contrast between the predictability of the socialized world and the unpredictability and danger of the forest in ways that allude to the methods by which individual agents can escape the social constraints that frame appropriate behavior (for a Kuranko example of similar principles, see Jackson 1990).

Witchcraft and its use as an avenue for advancement is further complicated by the fact that there are at least two ways of obtaining a witch. An individual can be fed a witch, without knowing it. This makes wives and female relatives particularly suspect, and people are careful about where and what they eat. Alternatively, an individual can actively seek out a witch. One way of doing this is through "witch markets" where drops are placed in an individual's eyes to allow them to see and talk with powers they might appropriate. Deals between humans and witch forces are struck, much as they are negotiated in patron-client relationships. One of the most feared witch's demand is that it be allowed to eat children in the host's household, and so rumors of witchcraft surround houses where many infants or children have died. In return, a witch can offer successful crops, wealth, a singer's voice and creativity, a leader's authority and power, or any other desirable commodity or skill. Everyone knows, however, that these are not strict negotiations. Once the witch force enters a body there is no way of predicting if it will keep its side of the bargain. In other words, witches are outside the realm in which the principles of complementarity and balance apply, and they may demand far more from their host than was originally agreed upon.

Even in witchcraft, the issue of individual intention remains obscure and distanced from individual responsibility. Linguistic forms, for example, demonstrate that witch activity is conceptualized as being external to the individual. Kono individuals speak of having witches or witch properties—*su fene am bi gboa* ("you have witch things in your hand or body"), or *sua ambi bua* ("you have a witch")—rather than "you are a witch," as one might in English.

Adding even more to this ambiguity is the fact that there is no way of telling if an individual has been fed a witch or if they have actively sought one out. An individual would never admit to having a witch, and the Kono say that even to see a witch or to comment upon "witch business" is tantamount to admitting to having a witch; thus, the histories of those suspected of witchcraft remain relatively obscure. Paradoxically, however, most individuals will admit to having witches at some point in their lives, and when most elderly people die they are somehow connected to witchcraft, largely because those whose relatives and friends have died end up spending so much of their time alone (see Chapter 3). Thus, knowledge of dealing with witchcraft and protecting against it is rampant, although it is somewhat tempered by the fear of publicly demonstrating too much knowledge. Determining the presence or absence of witchcraft, then, is often a question of interpretation, just as other aspects of identity are.

From this discussion it is clear that Kono individuals learn to rely on others and that coordinated activity is safer and usually more successful. Loners, if such a word could even be used to describe a Kono individual, and those too old or feeble to engage in coordinated activity, such as agricultural labor, are suspected of witchcraft. The fact that those who engage in witchcraft are thought to be transformed into animals reinforces the idea that acceptable human activity is coordinated, and those not engaged in coordinated activity are nonhuman and certainly antisocial.

There is another subtle way in which the actions of individuals are controlled. Once an individual is defined as out-of-the-ordinary in some way it is virtually impossible to remove that aspect of identity. The expectations attached to leadership, the rumors about a singer, or the negative view of a thief are almost impossible to shake off. If an individual succumbs to temptations such as theft or madness or a woman comes under the influence of powers that make it possible for her to sing professionally, there is the implication that once such forces have been actualized they become a permanent part of a person's identity and will shape that individual's life trajectory in unpredictable ways. There is no middle ground here. Because extraordinary capacities are attributed to external forces, there is little individuals can do to rid themselves of the effects of their presence once they appear. In short, the Kono have few mechanisms or techniques for changing or developing the self, once the steps towards individuation have been taken. Those that are available entail seeking out a *yawakgbasimoe* (diviner), a *chooma* (witch-finder), or a Muslim *mori* man (a Muslim diviner), who will intercede by pinpointing the cause of the deviant tendency and prescribe the way to alleviate its influence. Once again, in the prescriptions of these specialists, the construction of individual identity is taken from the individual's hands and placed in the hands of others.

As I noted above, most extraordinary behavior is attributed to curses, witchcraft, and heredity. Rarely is it made explicit which of these is operating on an individual. It is here that individual intention becomes ambiguous, open to interpretation, and, thus, brought back to the control of cultural norms. Heredity, as explained above, is obviously open to interpretation. Sometimes expected traits appear. Other times unexpected traits or actions are rationalized by naming previously unknown ancestors as culprits or villains who have suddenly entered the lives of their descendants for unknown reasons. Curses are the expression of secret angers or jealousies. They are usually made when an individual is driven by anger or jealousy to the point of consulting a specialist who is capable of delivering the sometimes deadly, but always destructive, curse and making it stick. Such anger can build if an individual is unwilling to let a dispute fade away after it is mediated by others, refuses to go through mediation to settle a dispute, or in any other way holds a grudge that he or she refuses to make public. Curses can kill, or they can change a person's character to make their life miserable, such as making someone a thief or singer. Curses can sometimes be lifted, but it is a difficult and expensive endeavor. Witchcraft, as already explained, is a private enterprise, one that few are willing to discuss openly.

The fact that excursions away from the public eye and group control are considered, in a general sense, to be particularly antisocial and threatening underscores the cooperative and moral nature of public activities and the dangers associated with individual or immoral action. The inability to distinguish whether antisocial or extraordinary behavior is the result of a curse, heredity, or witchcraft further limits the possibility of perceiving individuals as effective forces in their environments.

Fig. 2 *Lorry park in Koidu.*

Fig. 3 *A lorry as it passes through Kainkordu.*

Fig. 4 *Basin and clothing merchant at Manjama market.*

Fig. 5 *Vehicle loaded for the trip to Kainkordu.*

Fig. 6 *Driver and helpers working on a broken-down vehicle.*

Fig. 7 *Women with goods to sell on the way to Manjama market.*

Fig. 8 *Women selling produce and cooked foods at Manjama market.*

Fig. 9 *Houses in one of the small towns near Kainkordu.*

Fig. 10 *Newest house in Kainkordu.*

Fig. 11 *Row of older houses in Kainkordu.*

Fig. 12 *Parlor and doorway into private room.*

Fig. 13 *Two girls travelling through the chiefdom to notify their relatives they have completed Sande initiation.*

Fig. 14 Woman spinning on her veranda.

Fig. 15 Weaver warping a loom.

Fig. 16 *Chiefdom elder wearing chief's cloth.*

Fig. 17 *A singer and her entourage.*

This brings us back to the control of individuality through its definition as antisocial behavior.

CONCLUSIONS

At this point I continue the discussion of structural properties that I began in Chapter 3. In general, I am interested in trying to further tease out the patterns that crosscut domains of experience and, thus, serve as frameworks for action and for ideas about judging and evaluating action.

The first pattern is complementarity—between wives and their husbands, between affines, between patrons and clients, and within most forms of labor. In addition, claims to particular identities can only be validated by others. Those who place themselves outside complementary relationships are, in a sense, outside the boundaries of social control. As I showed in the discussion of space, boundedness is central to questions of identity. Identifying boundaries is an important technique for controlling emotion and individual intention. The fact that others can substitute when one's own skin fails and that witches as well as warriors can change their shape (see Chapter 3) suggests that the Kono conception of the body extends beyond the skin in certain cases. In public spaces, the individual is under the watchful eye of others, essentially in bounded space. In private spaces, whether the interior of a house, a forest path, or the negative emotions that well up inside the individual, the individual is in unbounded space, outside the watchful eye of the community, and subject to accusations of antisocial behavior. As will be seen in Chapter 5, much criticism of social life in general revolves around questions of containing individual intention in socially appropriate ways. Thus, chiefs, singers, and others with special skills are free to use their skills, even when this includes the powers of witchcraft, only as long as the community or public agree they are doing so for the public good. When this is no longer the interpretation, public support and appreciation are withdrawn.

This brings us to a related concept that has been implicit in the discussion of complementarity thus far—balance. Social relationships work best when they are in balance, essentially when each side upholds the expectations that the other side has of them. The fact that witch properties, once internalized, often demand more than was originally bargained for is a further indication of a witch's lack of humanness. A balanced relationship does not imply it is nonhierarchical; the balance stems from the fact that each party to the relationship has a degree of power within it. Often, but not always, balance is maintained through the threat of withdrawal by one party. Clients can withdraw their support from a patron, a wife can refuse to work on a husband's farm, or the *bain den moe* of a deceased woman can refuse to participate in the post-burial ceremonies, thereby guaranteeing that the woman will begin to cause trouble for her patriline.

The second principle—containment—is one of the ways in which balance and complementarity are maintained. Concepts of the body and of space limit individual action through the expectations that people will contain their emotions and desire to live within the confines of those who know them best (their relatives, Sande or Poro mates, and most importantly their ancestors). While living lives that are bounded or contained in such ways are highly problematic for most individuals, living in such a way holds the key to being recognized as a person of good and moral character.

The third principle—the relationship between clarity and obscurity—is less straightforward. Activities outside the public eye are obscure and thus dangerous, and yet ambiguity allows most evaluations of action to remain relatively subjective. The subjective nature of evaluation ensures that complementarity, in the guise of one's relationship with the person being judged, enters into the act of evaluation. It is probably the case that negative sanctions, such as rumors of witchcraft, enter into evaluations of another's reputation or moral character only when individuals are slighted in some way or when relationships become unbalanced.

The fourth principle is the emphasis on action—the attention actions are given in evaluation and the possibility of manipulating action to establish identity. In general, however, the emphasis on evaluating action also constrains individuality by bringing subjective goals into line with cultural ideals. Related to the emphasis on action is the notion of socially contained action. Those actions that take place in public view are contained by the threat of negative sanction. Ambiguous or private actions cannot be controlled by social sanctions. Thus, they are perceived as dangerous at best, and as antisocial and nonhuman at worst. This is the case whether the ambiguity stems from an individual being far from home or being involved in secret and hidden activities within a natal home. The use of the body to contain negative emotions suggests another side of containment, one that emphasizes the containment of things that are also dangerous. For example, a common method of controlling and exposing witches involves trapping them in old coke bottles or long-necked wicker baskets and then killing them. This duality (containment for control and containment for protection) will be explored more fully in Chapter 5.

These, then, are some of the structural properties that inform action in Kono life. They serve as lenses through which individuals make decisions about their own actions and the actions of others. They suggest the kind of minefield that individuals must make their way through as they attempt the impossible task of trying to live up to the expectations of others and still construct personally satisfying lives in which they are able to meet some of their own interests and goals. In the next chapter I more closely explore the ways in which actions in specific contexts of production reproduce and perpetuate, in various forms, the principles described here.

5

STRUCTURE INTO ACTION

The Aesthetics of Production

Just as contemporary Kono social organization is constructed in the sometimes rocky and contested terrain between structure and the contingencies of everyday life, aesthetic evaluation provides an arena for bringing together the habits and traditions of the past with the realities of people's current situations. In this chapter, I explore the ways in which the principles described in Chapters 3 and 4 are played out in other domains of life. For the Kono these structural properties include, but are in no way limited to, practices related to containment and the marking of entrances and exits, complementarity, the pairing of clarity and obscurity, and the importance of action. Tracing the idiomatic forms that manifest these structures will provide a clearer picture of the connections between domains of production and the ways in which habits of action provide a framework for evaluating action, solving problems, and conceptualizing future action. The idiomatic forms themselves, as well as evaluations of them, also provide a baseline from which to look at the role of aesthetics as a mediator between structure and action. I am particularly interested in exploring how these principles structure action that is defined as appropriate, and how struggles to produce events and experiences that are deemed appropriate or pleasurable tend to reproduce similar principles over time.

This approach raises the perceptual and constructive aspects of redundancy and brings us to a consideration of Giddens, structuration, and structural properties. Giddens (1979) transcended the distinction between synchronic and diachronic analysis by arguing that what functionalists and structuralists have variously called social structure should be understood as structural properties (the resources and rules used in the construction of action), which exist only paradigmatically. Paradigms, in this sense, consist of selections from, and arrangements of, the range of conceptual associations engendered by particular actions and are similar to Bateson's (1972a) use of redundancy. Particular paradigmatic arrangements of structural properties are "temporally 'present' only in their instantiation, in the constituting moments of social systems" (Giddens 1979:64). In other words, particular structural properties emerge at various times and in varying configurations. Structure, then, is potentially always in flux, always in the process of becoming.

It is my contention that the key to understanding the relationship between aesthetic evaluation and changes in structural properties has to do with redundancy and repetition. What I will argue is that positive aesthetic evaluation results from the repetition of idioms across domains of experience. The end products of this process are the structural properties that guide action, including evaluation. In a similar vein, Sieber (1985) suggests that the well-known phrase "I may not know what is art, but I know what I like" should actually read "I may not know what is art, but I like what I know." It is that sense of knowing that redundancy provides. Embodied within the act of doing a specific task, then, is a meshing or integration of other examples of similar tasks or habits in other domains. As actions resonate across domains, meaning, coherence, order, and power relations are constructed. In other words, the sets of resources and rules that constitute structure at any particular point in time are produced. When they do not resonate, or when accepted patterns are not adhered to, actions are evaluated in negative terms and are often associated with the immorality of antisocial beings.

My starting point is a description of three production contexts: agriculture, cloth, and dance. After looking at action in these three contexts, I compare the expressions of a variety of structural properties as they occur in a number of different domains. While it may be tempting for some to argue that production in one particular domain serves as a model for production in others, it is not my intention to give one domain primacy over others. Rather, my interest is in showing the way that patterns crosscuting various domains reinforce each other, and how these patterns lead to aesthetic responses or evaluations. From this perspective two things become apparent. The first is that similarities between domains do exist—that ideology, techniques of the body or ways of conceptualizing and managing the body, and social organization, for example, can be related across domains through the patterns that emerge when the actions in one domain are compared to the actions in other domains. The second is that the nature of similarities or patterns affect habits or predispositions for action long after their "functional" significance in any particular domain may have disappeared. In this way patterns rooted in past experience and habits of action have an impact on the choices made in contemporary life. Yet each example or performance of the pattern also accommodates the exigencies of everyday life. I will argue that these intersections or resonances are an important component of aesthetic response and that the process whereby agents actively trace connections among various domains must be understood to understand both aesthetics and change.

THE AGRICULTURAL SYSTEM

Rural Kono are still primarily subsistence agriculturalists. The principal crop for Kainkordu farmers is upland rice (*kwee*). Rice, palm oil, and vegetable sauces, which sometimes contain beef, fish, or chicken, provide the dietary staples. A Kono person who has not eaten rice in a given day will say that they have not eaten, regardless of the quantity of beans, potatoes, fruit, or other foods they may have consumed.

In the Kono agricultural system men are the landowners (see Chapter 3) and are responsible for initiating the agricultural cycle in any particular year. The Kono practice shifting cultivation, which means that the location of farms changes every year. Men also control the rice crop once it has been harvested. The possession of a farm is a sign that a man has reached a certain level of maturity. Women contribute labor to the rice farm; in exchange they are allowed access to the harvest to feed themselves, their children, and any relatives who might visit.

Secondary crops, such as corn (*nye*), beans (*swe*), small tomatoes, pumpkin (*bii*), okra (*bondwe*), millet, a leafy cabbage (*pii*), and cotton (*fande*), are intercropped with rice. Root crops, such as cassava (*tanga yamba*) and potato leaf, are planted in separate areas. Peanuts (*yaa*) are also cultivated in separate fields. Cash crops include coffee, cocoa, kola, and sometimes peanuts.

Land for cash cropping is also obtained through lineages. It passes as inheritance to the sons of the individual who planted the crop (or to his brothers if the sons are too young). When a lineage agrees to provide land for cash crops, it is done with the understanding that the land will remain in the hands of the individual farmer and his descendants until the plantation no longer bears crops. Coffee trees, for example, will yield for about fifty years and cocoa for thirty. Most men will be involved in cash cropping by the time they are middle aged, either as plantation owners themselves or as occasional laborers on someone else's plantation.

The proportion of household income that is derived from cash cropping varies with the acreage, transportation costs at harvest time, and the number of laborers hired during the year. A wife who works in her husband's cash crop plantation expects to receive either cash or a portion of the crop in return for her labor. This is in distinct contrast to labor in her husband's rice fields, which are considered a part of her marriage obligation and for which she receives no pay.

Women's attempts to obtain access to land for subsistence farming or cash cropping are restricted by an ideology that defines men as farmers and women as laborers (see Chapter 3 for a fuller discussion). In some areas these contrasting definitions have been legalized by the court system, as in Njaiama Nimi Koro (Nimi Koro is a Kono chiefdom closer to the diamond mines than Soa). Rosen (1981) has described a legal case in Njaiama Nimi Koro in which women tried to obtain legal rights to land in order to begin growing rice. Their argument was that, because so many men were away in the diamond fields during the beginning of the rainy season when fields have to be cleared (a man's job), the women were unable to grow sufficient rice for themselves and their families. Most of the work in the diamond fields takes place during the rainy season when the rains expose new gravel deposits for sifting. The Nimi Koro courts ruled, however, that women were, by definition, not farmers and, therefore, they had no rights to land (Rosen 1981:158).

In Soa Chiefdom there are no laws barring women's access to land, but it is difficult for a woman to get a piece of property from her lineage that is large enough to farm profitably or even allow her to grow enough rice to last a year. It would be unthinkable for a lineage to give a woman land to plant coffee, cocoa, or kola because once a farmer begins such a development the land is supposed to remain with him or his descendants until he is no longer using it. Usually hesitant to give women land for even a single rice crop, lineages are even more unwilling to allow them access to land for long periods of time. It is easier for a woman to get a smaller tract to grow cocoa yams or a small garden to raise produce to sell because these crops grow for only a year or two. It is also not unusual for a woman to garden on the land that she and her husband had used as a rice farm in the previous year. In these cases, the woman controls the money received from the sale of the crops, but she will use it to buy clothing and gifts for herself and her children and, perhaps, to buy rice should the family's supply diminish before the next year's harvest.

Most Kono rice production is based on shifting cultivation, a labor intensive process in which farms are moved to new areas each year. In the hilly and rocky terrain of the eastern Kono area, hillsides, valleys, and flatlands are farmed. Farmers rely on rainfall to irrigate most of their crops. Some farmers also plant wetland or swamp areas that are adjacent to their upland farms. Swamp cultivation will be discussed in more detail later in this chapter.

In shifting cultivation, crops can be planted on a new farm only after the trees and underbrush are cleared, dried, and burned, depositing a layer of ash fertilizer on the land. There is very little virgin forest left in the eastern Kono area. Most farms now occupy land that was farmed for three to seven years before. Between 1982 and 1984, farmers said that land should lie fallow for ten to fifteen years before replanting it, but that it is usually impossible to wait that long. The problem is not necessarily that there is a land shortage but, rather, that there is a shortage of land that lies close to any particular settlement. Individuals can sometimes establish settlements closer to their farmland, but this is often risky, and many would rather stay close to patrilineal kin rather than leave.

As a consequence, farmers must constantly make a trade-off between the intense labor required to clear land that has been fallow for a long period of time but is further from home and the lower yields available on land that has been farmed more recently but is closer to home. A common solution is to accept land relatively far from town but to alternate years of heavy and light labor, clearing a good piece of land one year and then farming it again during the next year. In the second year the boundaries of the farm may be expanded into uncultivated land nearby, somewhat offsetting the decline in production on the previously farmed portion. Another solution is to use a rotational system in which land is cultivated for rice in the first year and garden crops (groundnuts, cassava, or household gardens) in the second year, and then is allowed to fallow in the third year.

Most of the agricultural work is carried out by family units—a man, his wife or wives, their children, older relatives, and any others who may be living in the household during the season. In some cases a man whose wife is too old to work or who has few relatives in the area will work for another family unit in exchange for food during the growing season and a share of the crop at harvest time.

The size of a farm is determined by estimating the number of laborers who can be counted on to show up on a regular basis and the number of other workers who are available to help with tasks that require a larger labor force (e.g., brushing, hoeing, weeding, and harvesting). Overestimating these figures and clearing an area larger than can be farmed productively is an offense in the chiefdom and is subject to fines. People talk about farm size in terms of the number of bushels of rice that are actually planted rather than an estimate of acreage.[1] The quality of the soil and the type of seed rice available are also factors in the amount of seed planted in a given area.

Farm size also depends on how much land a farmer and his labor pool can clear before the rains begin. Burning before any rain has fallen increases the likelihood of causing large, uncontrollable and extremely dangerous brush fires that often dot the night horizon in March or April. Every year there are casualties from these fires, and it is not uncommon to hear that an entire village has been destroyed. In critically dry years the paramount chief may decree that no one can burn until he authorizes them to do so. In 1983 there were at least four large fires in Soa Chiefdom. One of them killed three men and destroyed four rice barns and several houses. Another destroyed an entire village. A third fire was set by a cigarette thrown from a passing truck and destroyed an entire coffee plantation. When one of these fires starts, there is no way to stop it, other than to let it burn itself out. If a farmer errs on the side of caution and waits for too many rains before burning, however, the brush will be too waterlogged for a good burn, the ash fertilizer will not be sufficient for a good crop, and much of the brush will have to be removed by hand before planting can take place.

Brushing (*fia chetia*) can begin as early as December or January. It is a task done almost entirely by men; women come to the work area only to bring the afternoon meal. About two weeks after the brushing is finished, workmen begin the laborious process of felling trees (*konteh-*

banda) on the property. Only one or two of the very largest trees may be left standing. On land that has been fallow for eleven years or more this means that farmers may have to cut trees that are 10 to 20 inches in diameter with locally produced metal cutlasses. If a piece of land has a number of large trees on it, the farmer may arrange for some of them to be cut into board for his own house or to sell. To ensure a good burn the weather must be dry for at least a week before the trees can be burned. Ideally, the cut undergrowth should have two to three weeks to dry.

Because predicting the onset of the rains is a very difficult proposition, Kono farmers coordinate their activities with a number of natural signs. Every year, just after the first two or three light rains, the termites (*bii*) leave their termite hills (*senda*) in massive swarms (the termites are escaping the rain soaked environment in the termite hills). The swarming lasts for one or two nights to the delight of children who run through town collecting thousands of them for roasting and eating. The termite swarms are a sign that steady rains are very close at hand. Farmers know they must stop brushing, if they have not already done so, and begin cutting trees so they are dry enough to burn before the heavy rains begin.

Only after the first burning (*minda*) of a piece of land do people begin referring to the work place as a farm (*seneo*) instead of a forest (*fiao*). After the first burn the farm also takes on an aura of relative safety. Farm space is both temporary and tenuous. By clearing and burning the forest, Kono men construct farm space, and dangerous forest regions are transformed into productive areas for human beings. The transformation of forest to farm can be seen as a triumph of order over disorder and of social order over individual interests (see Chapter 4). Forest space is alive with wild animals, as well as with devils, spirits, and other duplicitous antisocial beings whose intentions are rarely beneficial to humans. Not surprisingly when Kono talk about antisocial activities, they borrow images from the unbounded realm of nature. For example, those who engage in witchcraft transform themselves into forest creatures, such as snakes, before their heinous adventures. As unbounded space, the forest is unpredictable and uncontrollable. By contrast, towns are (ideally) predictable, and activities there are controlled by the social contracts that humans strike between obligations on the one hand and opportunities on the other.[2]

After the first burn women are freer to come and go as they please, and the coordinated agricultural labor for the year begins in earnest. Most farmers will actually do two burns. The first removes the smaller

TABLE 3

Calendar of Early Rainy Season Farming
Activities on One Farm

Date	Activity
February 5	Brushing begins
February 9	First drops of rain fall
March 22-23	Sporadic rain at night
March 23-24	Other farmers begin burning
March 26	First burn
March 30	Termites begin swarming
April 15	Second burn
April 22	First caterpillars spotted
April 24	Rice planting begins
April 27	First day of hard rain
May 9	Planting and plowing finished

material that has dried quickly. Several weeks later the second burn reduces the larger brush that failed to burn the first time. Anything that does not burn this time will be carried to the edge of the farm. If it is too big to be carried, it will be left where it lies and the farmers will plant around the obstruction.

Planting, the second stage of the agricultural cycle, is also governed by natural phenomena. It begins when caterpillars (*nyamusia*) are seen marching in long columns across paths and along the forest floor in order to escape their rain-soaked environment. At this point farmers begin planting their rice crop by sowing handfuls of the seed on the ground. In an area that relies on natural rainfall rather than irrigation, it is crucial to correctly gauge the amount of moisture in the ground. Rice will not sprout when the soil is too dry, and it will rot in the ground if there is too much moisture. The activities of one farmer during the beginning of the rains are charted in Table 3.

A variety of local types of upland rice are available, and most farmers will mix several kinds in order to get a successful crop under conditions that range from drought to flood. The mixture of rice seed will also be changed depending on the soil properties of different areas of a farm. Other seeds, such as cotton, tomato, and okra, are mixed in as well. After the rice seed has been scattered workers will hoe the soil lightly to cover the seed so that it will not blow or wash away but will still be able to sprout.

The organization of hoeing reflects the habitual emphasis on coordinated labor and on working in bounded spaces. The work throughout the day proceeds in sections. Pieces of land within each section (*gboo*) are marked off (*gbo te,* to cut or mark sections) and are given to an individual to work. These subsections are 6 or 7 feet on a side. As each worker finishes a subsection, an entire section is completed, and the group moves on to a new section, repeating the process. The emphasis is on group production, with no individual finishing more (or less) hoeing than any other.

The contrasts between bounded and unbounded space become more concrete in the next stages of rice production. Once the rice is planted, most farmers will fence their land in order to keep cutting grass (a rodent about the size of a house cat) and other animals from the rice. Traps (*gbai*), which are built into the fence every few yards, will yield much of the meat available to a farmer and his family during the production season. Fences (*fufu* or *fufu sansa*) protect crops from rodents and separate farm space from the relatively dangerous realm of the forest. In addition, the change from bounded to unbounded space is marked by rituals that are observed at entrances to and exits from farm space. Most Kono farmers rely on prescriptions designed by ritual specialists to guarantee good crops every year. The prescriptions or sacrifices (*sara*) used to mark the entrances to farm space can be as simple as removing one's shoes, dropping certain words from one's speech while at the farm, or stopping particular activities, such as whistling, when crossing into farm space. Essentially these changes in activity mark, in behavioral terms, the distinctions and contrasts between two kinds of space: the bounded and thus protected space of the farm, and the unbounded and thus dangerous and unpredictable forest space that surrounds it.

Another form of protection against the unpredictable aspects of nature can be seen in the placement of the *baffa,* or farm house. While fences encircle a farm, the *baffa* is usually placed in the center of contained farm space. Small children are often left to sleep under the baffa while their parents and siblings work in the fields. Women also cook the main meal of the day under the baffa. Baffas also serve as storage facilities for harvested rice, and ancestors are thought to come to the baffa at night to be close to their descendants. All of these activities make reference to protection in some way—children sleeping or women cooking are away from the protection of the rest of the work party; an entire year's crop can easily be devoured by an infestation of rodents, stolen by thieves, or otherwise tampered with by spirits; and the ambiguous attitude people have toward ancestors suggests they can be quite dangerous at times. Placing the *baffa* in the center of farm space allows the transformed forest (the farm) to insulate and protect people in the baffa from the uncertainties of the forest world.

As the rice sprouts to a height of 3 to 4 inches, the major agricultural tasks become weeding and scaring away birds. Women invite their relatives and friends to participate in work parties for the weeding. These become opportunities to gossip and instruct small children about the variety of crops that they must learn to cultivate. Often women trade weeding services, and a woman who weeds for her neighbor or relative can expect that woman to help her with her own weeding. Weeding is also organized as a coordinated activity. The workers are given a small section within a larger piece of land that has been marked off from the rest of the farm. Only when they have all finished their subsection will the group move on to a newly demarcated section.

Women and children are also responsible for scaring birds away from the crop. They take turns using sling shots to chase birds and spend long days (from sunup to sundown) on shaded platforms overlooking the rice fields and watching for flocks of birds as they settle in the waist-high crop. Women usually do other farm tasks, such as processing palm oil, while waiting for birds. Even in the midst of such activities, however, women keep a watchful eye on both their fields and their children. The afternoon air is filled with women on neighboring farms yelling at their children as they dose off in the drowsy afternoon sun while legions of birds settle in for a feast.

The yearly agricultural cycle ends at harvest time when large groups of men and women move through the fields to cut the ripened rice stalk by stalk. A stalk of rice is grasped about 8 inches below the kernels between the right thumb and a small metal knife or cane blade held in the right hand. In a quick motion the grip is tightened and the stalk is cut. The stalk is then transferred to the left hand with other previously cut stalks until the left hand is full. Then the whole bundle is tied and the process begins again.

The coordinated techniques of harvesting rice also make reference to bounded space and protection. The workers encircle a section of the rice farm and then cut inward. The Kono say that by providing a boundary for the rice they are able to control it and keep it from escaping into the forest. After it is cut, the rice is dried in the sun and beaten to remove the husks or stored for later use.

There is a distinct division of labor in agricultural production. Men are responsible for obtaining land from their lineage, brushing, obtaining rice seed, sowing the rice, and plowing it into the ground. Women are responsible for weeding (kobwe), helping with the harvest (kote), and processing the harvested rice for use throughout the year.

The division of labor in rice production is another example of the complementarity evident in other domains of Kono social life. Historically, no man would be given land by his lineage before he was married because it would be impossible for him to farm without the assistance and cooperation of a wife. Women have had a great deal of power in this system by virtue of their control of specific parts of the production process. A wife's ability to withdraw her labor at critical junctures ensured that her concerns in the marital relationship were, if not always met, at least aired. Although such withdrawal rarely occurs, men are ever aware of its potential threat.[3] With the introduction of a cash economy this relationship of complementarity is beginning to shift to one of dependence for women. The nature of this dependency is discussed more fully in Part II.

During times that require more labor than the family can provide, both husbands and wives are responsible for obtaining extra laborers. A man will invite male friends or relatives to assist in brushing, plowing, and harvesting. A woman will invite female friends or relatives to help with weeding and harvesting. Occasionally today laborers are hired, but they usually come for the day and are given a meal and palm wine for their services. A man who has invited such laborers may reciprocate by sending his sons or by going himself to assist them in their fields.

Occasionally, a wealthy individual will hire a group of bwikotemoe (medicine rice cutters) to harvest for him. Some towns have organized rice-cutting troupes who travel with their own musicians to cut rice for money. They are said to have magical powers that allow them to cut rice faster than normal people. While cutting, the workers sing to the accompaniment of drummers who set the pace for the day's work. As in family harvesting, they cut the rice with a small blade held in the right hand. The bwikotemoe wear metal rattles (waiya) tied to their right forearms, and they shake the rattle with each beat of music and cutting of a rice stalk. When the *bwikotemoe* are at a farm, people come to see them demonstrate their powers of rice cutting and magic, listen to their music, and assist with the harvest.

The hours of harvesting are interspersed with the magical performances for which *bwikotemoe* are famous, including such things as piercing their tongues with small metal skewers or driving metal knives into their calf muscles. The magician then disappears and, when he returns, the wounds have also disappeared. Some of them are also able to remove an eye from its socket and then replace it. To become a *bwikotemoe* one must die and be brought back to life; it is said this is the experience that makes the rice cutters powerful. The groups are primarily male, although I was told that women could also join. The troupe in the area where I worked consisted of about twenty-five people, all of them men. The troupe formed after some of its members saw a similar group from Guinea perform. In their own terms they became *bwikotemoe* in order to help their town organize successful harvests. They also spoke of the money they earned and the prestige they gained by being part of a troupe.[4]

Kono farmers are usually on the edge of survival in any single year. This is evident by comparing harvests and yields with the number of workers that need to be fed (Appendix A). It is clear that there are drought years, such as 1982, when families must buy or borrow rice in order to survive, or when lack of food may lead to illness and death among the elderly or young. In a survey of thirty-two households in 1982, only eight households produced enough rice to feed all of its household members. By contrast, a survey of forty-six households in 1983, a year of abundant rainfall, showed that all forty-six had rice surpluses, ranging from one to sixty-five bushels.

From this brief description of Kono agriculture it is possible to see parallels between agricultural production and social organization. The principles or structures that are most evident are complementarity and the reliance on others that complementarity implies. Agricultural production sets up dependant relationships between husbands and wives and between laborers and landholders. Power and success stem from the ability to accommodate others so that they will do their assigned jobs. Equally, power stems from the ability to withdraw labor when a patron or husband takes advantage of it.

Related to complementarity and balance in the relations of production is the principle of boundaries. Farm space is made safe by particular activities that include clearing brush, burning, and fencing. By containing farm space humans are protected from the uncertainties, unpredictabilities, and dangers of the forest, the same dangers that metaphorically symbolize witchcraft and uncontrolled individual intention. Such symbols reaffirm the coordinated nature of bounded activities, in this case agricultural production, as they simultaneously reify the dangers of the forest, individual intention, and witchcraft.

CLOTH PRODUCTION

Many Kono men and women, especially those of the older generation, are still active in the production of local, or country, cloth. Some of the patterns or structures seen in Kono social organization and agricultural production are also apparent in the division of labor in cloth production and in the cooperation and interdependence between social categories that this division fosters.

Cotton (*fande*) is grown by women who are also responsible for its transformation into thread (*yisi*). The cotton is planted with rice or with the vegetable crops that a woman considers her own (meaning she retains control of them and will use them for her family). She will be free to sell cotton if there is any surplus. Once the cotton is picked it is transported to town and stored until the woman has time to begin processing it. Because the production of thread is secondary to other household tasks, it is done during periods of free time—in the late afternoon or evening when most other household chores have been completed. The processing begins by drying the material in the sun, cleaning seeds and debris out of the cotton balls (*gbuo bo*), and working several cotton balls together into a unit. Once the cotton is cleaned, it is carded into loose coils, which are then ready to be spun (*fande fuane*) into thread. Today, spinning is usually done only by middle-aged or elderly women because younger women are not learning the skill (see Figure 14).

The spun thread is transferred from the bobbin (*endaka*) on which it is spun to a larger spool (*bonsoma*) and stored until a woman has enough to ask a weaver to work for her. If she wishes to dye the thread, she will take it to a dyer for processing before it is woven. Traditional Kono thread is a natural white (*agbe*) or very soft brown (*duu*), a natural coloration found in some strains of cotton. If the thread is dyed, it will be made light or dark indigo.

Complementarity enters the production process when a woman is ready to weave the thread into cloth. It is against town law for a woman to weave cloth. If she is caught, she will be fined ten leones ($.25 in 1984 dollars). There is also a prohibition against men spinning. Although this is not law, the penalty is extreme. It is said that a man who spins will become impotent. One old woman delighted in telling me of the clever way she went about getting her cloth woven. She had spun the thread and asked her husband to weave it for her. He set up the loom and started to weave but was constantly leaving the work to take care of his own business in other parts of the town. With all the interruptions it looked as if the weaving would never be finished, so the woman started to weave. Another man came by and told her that she had to stop weaving. The woman explained her plight, and the visitor said that he would weave it for her. Only then did the woman's cloth get woven. One implication of this story is that, just as a husband shows disrespect to his in-laws by not meeting his obligations to them, this woman's husband was being disrespectful by not attending to his wife's business after he had agreed to do so. A second implication is that the woman probably became the lover of the man who wove her cloth.

Kono country cloth is woven on a tripod loom. The cloth is actually woven in strips, which are then sewn together to make shirts, *lappas* (a length of cloth that a woman will wrap around her waist), or blankets. A man sits at the right side of his loom and the thread stretches out in front of him with the finished cloth rolled into a ball behind him. The two heddles of the loom are controlled by foot pedals. Once the weft thread is shot through the opening in the warp threads, the weaver switches the heddles with his feet, then tamps the new thread into the cloth with a beater, and proceeds with the next length of weft.

When asked why women are not allowed to weave, old men say that if a woman wove cloth she would have to sit with her legs apart to control the heddles, and young men would be able to look up her skirts. Several women told me that women used to weave, but I could find no reason for the switch from female to male weavers. According to one version of how the Kono came by their work specializations, it is said that God taught a man how to farm, he taught another man how to hunt, and another to be a blacksmith. He taught a woman how to fish and another woman to weave. These individuals then taught the skills to their children. The men taught their sons to farm, hunt, and work with metals. The woman who learned to fish passed the skill on to her daughter, but the woman who learned to weave passed the skill on to her son. Since that time weaving has been done by men (Willans 1909). Men say that weaving is the easy part of cloth production and that spinning fine thread is the difficult part. Men, however, blame the current decline in weaving on women, saying that they refuse to spin enough thread.

Women control the final cloth. Just as men control the rice harvest because they initiate the production process, women control cloth because they begin the production process. Weaving is something that women usually hire someone to do. The cloth itself will belong to the woman who spun the thread and arranged for the weaving to be done. A Kono woman will actually say that she wove a particular cloth, which means she hired a weaver who then wove it for her. While the name of the man who wove a particular cloth tends to be forgotten, it is much more likely that the spinner of the thread will be remembered because this is usually the person who has given away the cloth as a gift or still possesses it.

When a woman commissions a weaver, she provides the man's food for the days when he weaves, she sees that water for washing is provided, and she will try to get palm wine for him. She may also give the man six to eight leones, particularly if the man is not her husband. The weavers are not full-time specialists. Although most men can weave (*koa sa*), few can actually warp a loom (*koa don*), which is a much more specialized skill. In Kainkordu, with a population of about 1,200 in 1982, there were only nine men who knew how to warp a loom (see Figure 15).

Cloth production mirrors the division of labor by gender found in other production spheres and, thus, reinforces the idea that individuals are not capable of acting effectively alone. The word for cotton, *fande*, translates literally as father (*fa*) and (*n*) mother (*de*). I was told this word combination was used because cotton could not be used or processed without the cooperation of a man and woman. Whether or not this is the true derivation of the word is unclear (*fande* is also the word for cotton in Mende), but it is one explanation that people hold in their minds today.

For the Kono, as for other West African peoples, the production of cloth contains many references to the appropriate relationships between men and women. This is found in songs and stories about weaving, some of which are presented below. In the past, if a man was about to marry, he would often be sent to weave cloth for his new in-laws. In the first song a new husband remarks on the bad character of his mother-in-law.

He has woven thread for the woman, but she refuses to convince her daughter to spend the night with him. In fact, she has sent the daughter to sleep with another man. The chorus of this song is as follows:

> Gbak bai a ma,
> Koa e sa,
> Bienge ma,
> Aa dene e fu.
> The beater is bad,
> It won't weave cloth fine,
> The mother-in-law is bad,
> Her daughter is not going to marry.

In this song the mother-in-law is symbolized as a beater, the part of the loom that is used to beat the weft threads tightly into the warp and also used to keep the warp threads from getting tangled and unruly during the weaving process. The metaphorical equation of mothers-in-law and beaters refers to the tremendous influence women have on their daughters and the common complaint that mothers refuse to advise their daughters properly (meaning they refuse to take their sons-in law's sides in marital disputes).

The following story calls attention to the often sexual nature of relations of complementarity:

> In those days there was a woman. The woman liked men too much, but her occupation was to spin. When men came to greet her with cotton for her to spin, she was pleased. When women came to greet her with cotton to spin she was annoyed. She would ask the women if they didn't know how to spin, "You possess the same woman property as I between your legs. Go now and do your own spinning. Then when a man comes I will be able to do his job."
> While she was talking a man came to greet her.
> "Mother, good afternoon."
> "Who is it?" the spinner asked.
> "I am Sahr."
> She answered, "Come, I've just finished some thread. I have made it very fine. It was done with a new *endaka* (bobbin). Come, I will spin your thread for you. Come, I will spin your thread for you, then you can go."

The woman gave him a place to sit down outside. Then she took
her mat and spread it outside as well. The man brought out his cotton and the woman started singing.

Once she started spinning, the woman asked "Sahr, are you going
to pass the night here today?"

Sahr responded, "No, we are not going to sleep here this night,
but next time, alright?"

The woman was unhappy with this and finally convinced Sahr to
spend the night with her, and Sahr left in the morning with his thread.

A woman came to visit the spinner that morning, asking her to do
some work for her. The spinner said, "Don't bring your cotton here,
my *endaka* is broken. Every time you have cotton you bring it here for
me to spin, but you never come to bring me food when I am hungry.
You just come to have me spin for you. But, bring the thread, I will
do a small part of it for you. Then you can go and finish it yourself."
When the woman left, another man came to greet the spinner.

"I am Sahr."

"Ah, Sahr, is Tamba there? Is he well? And you have brought cotton.
Bring it and I will spin it for you. This *minga* (storage spindle), I have
just killed a fowl on it. It will do well. But are we going to sleep here?"

The man felt as if he wants to leave the same day, but to get his
cotton spun he answers her, "We are going to sleep here."

The spinner takes out her tools and starts to sing and work. After
she finished the work she convinces the man to stay and they sleep
together.

If a woman comes with cotton for spinning, the spinner will be
unhappy. That is the way it has been in the past. Women, in general,
don't like themselves. This is not new but has been so for a long
time. Men are the same way, they don't like themselves.

This story implies that spinning is a female task and that it is balanced
against, or complementary to, male tasks. A woman will do the work for
someone, but there are expectations in return, expectations that other
women usually cannot fulfill.

The following story and song also refer to the importance of balance in relations of production and what can happen when that balance
is disturbed:

The woman who does not spin for her husband is the one who is
liked [favored] by her husband. But when this wife comes to her

husband at night, she covers herself with the cloth spun by her co-
wives. The other women found this out, and an old woman in the
compound started to sing this song:

"A woman who does not spin for her husband is the woman who
is liked by the husband."

On hearing the song the husband came outside and started beating
the old woman. While he was beating her, the woman asked why he
was doing so. He answered it was because she was singing a bad song.
Finally, the town chief came and said they would have to settle the
case publicly. Both sides explained their side of the case, and the town
chief decided that the husband was in the wrong but, in the process
of hearing both sides, the woman was asked to sing the song again.

"A woman who does not spin for her husband is the woman who
is liked by her husband."

The man started yelling for the woman to stop singing or they
would enter into the quarrel all over again.

"A woman who does not spin for her husband is the woman who
is liked by her husband."

The wife then entered the discussion, saying she wanted to visit
her mother. "Always my husband says it is I who am spoiling the
house, but at the same time he condones my actions."

"A woman who does not spin for her husband is the woman who
is liked by her husband."

The wife then said that, if that was the case, she was going to take
her belongings and go to her people. Her husband asked her not to
go and asked the town chief to tell her not to go, but he refused. The
husband then said "We will go to the paramount chief and ask him
to settle the matter." "Alright," said the town chief, "but you were in
the wrong. You shouldn't have beaten the old woman for her song.
But when the paramount chief comes we will tell him."

"A woman who does not spin for her husband is the woman who
is liked by her husband."

The wife responded, saying "This is always the thing. We are going to settle the case, but we never settle it so I am leaving."

"A woman who does not spin for her husband is the woman who
is liked by her husband."

These stories, like the production process itself, speak of the appropriateness of relationships of complementarity between men and women
and the appropriate actions for each gender. In other words, all women
should spin, and men should require their wives to do so (meaning all
tasks women are supposed to perform). When an individual on either

side of the relationship of complementarity fails to do their part (e.g., a mother-in-law who does not uphold her obligation to a son-in-law, a woman who refuses to spin, or a husband who condones a wife's reticence to spin), the balance within the unit falls apart, usually to the detriment of all involved. As the first and third stories presented above show, the imbalance is not limited to the principal characters but extends into other social relationships as well.

What people describe as the traditional uses of cloth also reflects interdependence between categories of persons. Cloth was used as tribute to a chief. The chief wearing the finest cloth indicated the chief who had the greatest control over and support of his constituents. Even today, a chief's cloth is recognized as more complex in pattern and more colorful than other kinds of cloth (see Figure 16).

Cloth was also used in a variety of contexts and at a number of different stages in a person's life. At each stage, other people were involved in the construction or trajectory of the individual's life. Relatives provided cloth and, through their actions, sanctioned changes in an individual's status. For example, every girl who joined Sande was (and still is today) required to have an all-white country cloth, *lappa*. It was said that this cloth ensured that all the girls would appear as equals. The white cloth was also equated with purity. Wearing white *lappas* suggested that all the girls had passed successfully through a series of confessional and divination procedures that were designed to reveal any secrets they might be harboring and to guide them in the correct ways to free themselves of the dangers of secrecy. Both the mother and father or uncle of the girl cooperated in the production of the white *lappa* for the daughter.

In the past, country cloth was also a part of brideprice (see Chapter 3). A man gave his new mother-in-law cloth to replace the clothes spoiled when the bride was carried on her mother's back as an infant. The husband also gave his new brothers-in-law country cloth for shirts before his wife could co-habit with him. In the case of a first marriage, a man had to rely on his relatives to produce these cloths. In the case of marriage to a second wife, a female relative of the man or his first wife had to agree to the union and provide the thread to be woven. Today, trade cloth or money have become the norm in these exchanges.

About eighteen months after the birth of a child, a husband also had to give his wife enough country cloth to make a *lappa* and a shirt. The acceptance of this gift signalled a return to a sexual relationship after the post-partum taboo on sexual intercourse. Here, also, a man's female relatives or other wives had to recertify the marriage through their own labor. Today, trade cloth rather than country cloth is the norm.

Country cloth was also one of the items exchanged at funerals to sever the relationship between *fa den moe* and *bain den moe*. As in other contexts, trade cloth is substituted for country cloth today. Although all of these exchanges are still done with cloth, only the cloth for a girl about to join Sande must still be country cloth. In Chapter 8 I return to this point in considering the ways in which change affects Kono men and women differently.

Thus, in order to mark passage through most of the important stages of Kono life, one must have access to cloth. In the past this was only possible through production networks based primarily on kinship and marriage. The importance of cloth in Kono society and the division of labor found in cloth production implied that one must be attached to a network of producers that included both men and women. This, in turn, implied participation in a complex set of rights and obligations with other people. A young girl, for example, had to have family members willing to provide cotton for her, to spin thread for her, and to find someone to weave it before she could become an adult in the community. A man had to have relatives willing to help him marry, as well as to continue his marriage after the birth of a child. A proper burial also required an exchange of cloth. Individuals, then, were not responsible for the trajectory of their own lives or their own positions within the community. With the introduction of trade cloth these relationships of complementarity have changed in significant ways. These are discussed more fully in Chapter 8.

The expression of boundedness or containment in cloth production is less explicit and is related more to how cloth is used than how it is made. Briefly, the principle of containment in cloth production is found in the dual relationship between protection and control. Things that have to be protected must be contained, and things that must be controlled should be contained. Cloth, once it is made into a garment, does both. There are certain kinds of clothes, such as warrior's and hunter's shirts, that are particularly known for their abilities to contain and protect. For example, a shirt can strengthen an individual's defenses (a form of protection); historically, warriors used these shirts to ward off bullets or the spells of a challenger. Today, they might be worn by a politician for the same end. At the same time, warrior shirts might be used to publicly identify individuals as they strive for power. In a society in which individual aspirations are often thwarted by people's obligations to others, wearing such clothing identifies individual intention and, to some degree, makes it possible for others to control it. There is also a relationship here between containment and complementarity in that good cloth is made in a relationship of complementarity. Thus, coordinated labor provides protection to those wearing country cloth apparel.

DANCE PERFORMANCE

For some Kono, dance occasions are joyous entertainment; for others, they are dangerous arenas for playing out the tensions between individual goals and social obligations. Dance can also be a symbolic form of movement that validates action, speech, and social relationships. I first became aware of the non-entertainment dimensions of Kono dance when I participated in a series of speeches given to thank a departing Peace Corps volunteer. After the speeches the orators began to dance. Likewise, the new volunteer for the area was advised she should dance in order to show that what she had said in her remarks was true. In Kono terms, dancing showed that the speakers had really meant what they had said, another indication that actions are more real or truthful than words. I began to watch for other cases of validation. I noticed that town members were markedly disturbed when a high-ranking elder from a neighboring town refused to participate in a dance honoring a visiting dignitary. Because individuals can only dance if they harbor no bad feelings (*faa yone*), literally spoiled heart, it was assumed that the elder's refusal to dance showed a disagreement between the two men. In fact, from my interviews with the elder I knew that he simply did not like to dance and was embarrassed to do so in public.

The dangers of dance are rooted in the fact that skill in singing or dancing is often traced to the influence of dangerous and sometimes uncontrollable supernatural powers. Singers, dancers, and musicians are known to be involved with witchcraft and with other supernatural ways of enhancing their skills. Dance is used as one of the arenas both for the exhibition of these forces and for challenges between individuals exhibiting extraordinary powers.

The dance occasion I describe here comes from the public dances prior to Sande initiation ceremonies. This type of dance exhibits spatial features similar to those found in dances organized for funerals, visiting dignitaries, and the installations of paramount chiefs, section chiefs, and town chiefs. At such occasions dance serves primarily as entertainment and people look forward to these occasions. But these dances can also serve as validation of social allegiances and as a venue for dangerous challenges between supernatural powers.

The exact date for the Sande dances and the subsequent initiations is determined by phases of the moon. Once the date is set, arrangements begin in earnest. During the final month of preparation the initiate's father or the elder in her family takes on the responsibility of being the dance owner (*tombo ti*). He hires a singer, usually a woman, to represent his daughter in the celebrations. The singer in turn invites three or four women to knock *see* (a particular kind of gourd rattle) for her (see Figure 17). These individuals are called *see ko bo moe*, which translates roughly as "to pull them under the rattle," referring to the rattle's ability to control the dance group by pulling everyone within hearing distance into the rhythm and influence of a song. Although each girl should have someone to sing for her, often the families of several girls will pool resources to hire a singer between them. If there is not enough money to hire a singer, a family member with a good voice will be asked to sing instead; some of these individuals may eventually become professional singers. The dance owner also arranges for a *chiene* player (a *chiene* is a specific kind of slit drum), and for someone to act as controller of the dance (*tombo yo swe*). This individual will settle disputes arising at the dance, and he will control the actual dancing. Dancers come out of the audience itself. Most are male, especially in the later hours of the dance. Dance occasions are used as an opportunity to display family wealth and status, and they are planned, managed, and manipulated with the obvious intent of doing so.

Dancing begins sporadically several nights before the actual initiation ceremonies, but the most important night of the dance is on the eve of the initiation itself. During that night there may be four or five dance groups moving through town at any particular time. Although these are usually nighttime events, it is not uncommon for groups to form spontaneously and move through town during the day throughout the period of festivity. Before the dancing begins in the evening, each group gathers inside the house of the dance owner. While inside, the group is given advice (*da si*) by the dance owner. They are told to sing "fine," to remain "cool" throughout the night, and to stay in control. Small gifts may be given by the dance owner to the singers to further encourage the singers' endeavors. Palm wine is also passed around. It is generally known that the singers have their own supplies of alcohol, as well as magical agents to provide them with strength throughout the night. Finally, the music and singing begin. As it reaches a certain peak, the dance group moves outside to the veranda, led by the dance owner. The singing starts inside the house to allow singers, musicians, and participants to warm up out of the public eye. The songs are coordinated efforts, with the singer providing the main lyrics and the other participants singing out lines of the chorus in a kind of call-and-response pattern. When the group begins to sense a kind of cohesiveness among themselves, the singer begins moving into the street. The entourage of singers and musicians falls in around her, and other participants fall in behind her. Once in the street they begin a slow shuffling procession around the town, which will last most of the night.

As the procession moves through town in the early evening, it stops at the town chief's house, the paramount chief's house, and the house of the town's female elder. These visits notify the political leadership of a family's intent to initiate their daughter. The procession also visits ritual sites, such as the *tamba tina,* to notify the ancestors that their descendant is soon to become an adult. It also passes in front of the houses of family members and friends of the initiate, and people in these houses are expected to give small gifts of money to the singer and her group as encouragement to perform well. The initiate will stay in her family's house for the entire evening. She cannot dance for herself but must rely on others to show their support of her through their dancing. Periodically, the procession will return to the initiate's house, sometimes entering, sometimes singing on the veranda to offer the girl their encouragement. Figure 18 shows a diagram of the participants in the forward moving phase of one such procession.

The procession will stop periodically and the forward focus changes as a tight circle is formed around the performers (see Figure 19). This compact circle provides the arena (*tombo baama,* literally dance public, or dance outside) in which the dancers, facing the singers, exhibit their prowess and challenge the power of their rivals as well as the abilities of the singer. The point of these challenges is to be known as a good dancer, someone who is able to follow the rhythms of the singer and musicians. Not all of the people who dance are involved in these challenges, but those who are compete with both the singer and other dancers. The dancer tries to match and then surpass the talents of the singer by skillfully following the rhythms of song and accompaniment. There is an intricate balance between pushing the musicians into more difficult patterns and

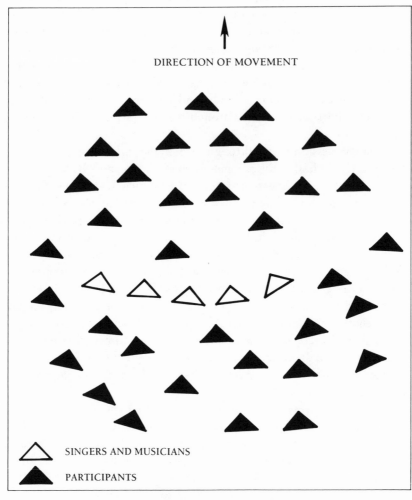

DIRECTION OF MOVEMENT

SINGERS AND MUSICIANS

PARTICIPANTS

FORWARD MOVEMENT OF DANCE PROCESSION

Fig. 18 Diagram of forward movement of a dance procession.

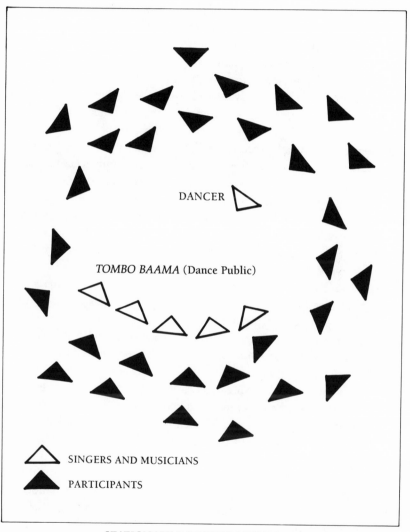

DANCER

TOMBO BAAMA (Dance Public)

SINGERS AND MUSICIANS

PARTICIPANTS

STATIONARY DANCE PROCESSION
(Participants facing dancer, singers, and musicians)

Fig. 19 Diagram of stationary phase of a dance procession.

exceeding their capabilities. There is also the implication in these performances that some participants might enlist the help of witches or other supernatural powers in order to assist them in their displays.

What follows is my description of one of these processions as it moved around town during a very successful dance occasion. At the height of the dancing the entire procession was moving slowly down the only street of town. This was several hours into the dance, and the mandatory sites had already been visited. There were fifty to seventy-five people packed tightly behind the singer, her assistants, and a drummer. Darkness and the dust of the dry season blurred both sight and smell. Individual movement was limited by the tightly packed crowd. With that limitation came the impossibility of movement in anything other than a kind of shuffling unison. Every few feet we would stop and someone, usually a man, would enter the central dance space. While he faced the singer, his movements changed from a shuffling movement to more individualized dance movement. At this point, the singer's rhythms became more intricate either in response to his movements or, sometimes, in order to push him further into dance. This often increased the rapidity of the dancer's steps or encouraged him to use more lateral space with arms and legs, generally adding to the intensity of the performance. While forward movement in the procession was relatively constrained, movement in the performance arena was much freer, with individuals being recognized for the peculiarities of their own performance styles.[5] This corresponds to the fact that individual reputations are built on the basis of performance within the arena; thus, stepping into the arena, to some degree, opens the door to individual expression as well as to the recognition of skill.

During the period when the dance arena was open, the onlookers maintained the beat of the previous shuffling movement but remained stationary, shifting their weight from one foot to the other. Everyone turned to face the inner circle. Women on the periphery of the dance space sometimes encouraged a particularly fine dancer by removing their headties and using them as fans for the performer. At a precise moment, the actions of both singer and dancer slowed in unison, were held for a tense instant, and in the next beat or two the dancer usually handed the singer and her assistants money in appreciation for their music. The dancer then turned, flowed back into the normal shuffling pace, and the entire group moved forward again. The time spent by dancers in the inner circle varied, but it was usually less than two minutes.

During the shuffling procession, as well as during the intervening periods of solo dancing, there was little sound except that of the drums, the sharp, almost painful, rattles, the voice of the singer, and the crowd echoing her lines. The participants in the center of this group were enveloped by sound and movement, and once inside it was difficult to get out of the group. The emphasis was on developing and maintaining the slow, controlled procession of the group. The formation of the central dance space slowed the forward pace even further. At one point it took us half an hour to go 200 yards. The focus of the dance group was markedly internal rather than external.

During the evening we encountered another dance group moving through town. As the groups drew near each other, each focused on maintaining its own song and rhythm, even when the temptation was to eliminate dissonance and slide into the resonating rhythm of the challenging group. After a few minutes of real effort, one singer and her group were unable to maintain their own rhythm, and someone yelled to the singer to move away. By putting more space between the groups the weaker singer and her smaller entourage were able to return to their own song, but the movement away was also an admission of weakness and defeat on the singer's part.

The singing continued until exhaustion began to set in around 3 or 4 o'clock in the morning. There had been no real climax in the evening, even during the challenges between dancing groups. There had only been a continual flow between moments that emphasized individual prowess and moments that emphasized the slow forward movement of the entire group. The element that united these moments was a gradual buildup of a sense of unity among participants.

As the group got smaller in the early hours of the morning, the atmosphere changed markedly. When the group was reduced to about eight stragglers, they seated themselves near the main road on some large boulders. By this time the singers had left and the dancing had stopped, but the stragglers carried on. One would begin singing, another would pick up the song, then there was silence for a while until someone else recalled another strain. Finally, this group also split up.

While this has been my description of a particularly successful dance event, Kono descriptions of the same event attributed its success to such things as the number of people involved in the dance; the quality of the singer's voice and songs, and her ability to entice so many to participate; the length of the night's dancing; and the absence of fights or other kinds of disturbances.

The principles of action, balance and complementarity, boundedness, and the pairing of clarity and obscurity can all be discussed from this description. The methods by which Kono physically manipulate and control individual intention or antisocial forces in domains other than dance can be used to understand how space is used as a mechanism to control individual intention in dance. As already discussed, Kono expressions of strong emotions are supposed to be internalized and contained within a strong bodily shell. Within a dance performance the secret, powerful, individualized, and antisocial forces that influence dancers, singers, and other participants are also spatially contained and thus controlled. Dancers and singers, as well as other individuals with extraordinary skills, must be contained because they have, by definition, moved away from social norms to some degree. Here again the tensions between individual goals and social roles or expectations become ambiguous and problematic. Singers and musicians are said to deal in "witch business" which is secret and, thus, individualized and antisocial. The taint of individuality exists even though the dances are considered a necessary part of an initiation ceremony and could not be accomplished without singers and musicians. In the challenges between dance groups the force of each group of musicians, singers, and dancers is contained within a circle of supporters. Just as wearing a warrior shirt identifies individual intention, the dance space also externalizes, or makes visible, the intentions of those individuals who would attempt to exceed normal social roles, perhaps even to the extent of delving intentionally in supernatural sources of power. This is further demonstrated by the fact that the dance arena is called *tombo baama,* or dance public/outside. The same term (*baama*) is used to describe the placement of other public actions. By making intention public, it is brought out in the open, channelled into acceptable forms, and thus its danger is reduced. The format for individual expression inherent in dance actually reiterates social control because the performer's ultimate goal—being recognized as a successful singer or dancer—can only be reached through the praises of other participants. Thus, once again, individual intention is subverted and brought under the control of others. Individuality is only *really* dangerous and destructive when it remains hidden, when someone decides to go through non-public channels to reach their goals.

It would be tempting to suggest that the dance event is an idealized and static model of an ideal Kono world, one in which antisocial forces can be tamed and controlled within a safe or make-believe environment. Having only a single description of a dance event might lend itself to this conclusion. However, what happens at dance events is usually much more problematic. The fluid and transitive nature of Kono space, in general, suggests that no space is free of manipulation and that all constructed spaces are subject to rapid disintegration. In problematic dance occasions the singer is unable to attract many participants, a boisterous individual upsets the delicate balance of the components that go into constructing a successful dance, or individual intention otherwise outweighs the constraints of the group. In these cases, as in patron-client relationships, clients and supporters simply disappear, removing the possibility of claiming success from any individual who fails to recognize the necessity of attracting and appeasing supporters.

I saw this kind of desertion happen on several occasions, one of which I describe here. At a large dance held to celebrate initiation into Bii, one family did not hire a professional singer but, instead, asked a male family member to sing (having a male singer is unusual, but it does not affect the point made in this description). The dance proceeded through the evening with the typical call-and-response pattern between singer and participants. After an hour or so, a man who had not been in town for other dances where I had recorded noticed my tape recorder and began singing louder than normal, at times even drowning out the main singer, presumably to impress the foreign researcher. The hired singer invited the man, who I later found out was visiting from Freetown, to lead a song, and at that point the event began to deteriorate. The song chosen by the new singer was more complicated than most I had heard at this kind of event. The participants were expected to remember a chorus that was several lines long (most of the choruses I had heard were single lines). After several attempts to learn the chorus line, the group still could only get half-way through before the line dribbled off into obscurity. Normally, a group picks up the line on the first hearing. The new singer proceeded with the song; after several more failed attempts to follow him, the majority of participants began wandering away, opting to attach themselves to a different singer, one where the experience of unison and balance was being more carefully maintained. In short, the new singer's claim to fame was denied by the simple fact that he could not hold a group of participants around him, and his personal goals were defeated. At that point I removed myself, feeling that my presence had, in some ways, contributed to the break up of the dance group. About a half hour later the group had reconstituted itself under the original singer and was continuing with the evening's festivities. When I asked people about the event the next day, there was a lot of laughter about the new singer, and I was told that he was not much of a singer but was just trying to show off. On the other hand, the singer, still trying to defend his actions, said that the people in the group really didn't know how to sing.

The principle of pairing clarity and obscurity, or leaving certain elements ambiguous, is also important in dance events. There are no formal criteria that define success. Rather, the emphasis is on constructing a certain sense of feeling (*gbuo dia,* or stomach sweetness) among participants. The qualitative nature of this kind of expectation allows individual agents to construct and shape dance events and the reputations of participants out of the contingencies of the moment. In this way the most pressing social concerns at that particular point in time can be used in evaluating action and defining expectations. To explain this more fully, I move to a comparison of the expression of principles across domains of experience.

REDUNDANCY AND PATTERN

In the early stages of my research I began looking at techniques of production in a variety of Kono activities—those that we would call "art" or "craft," such as spinning, dyeing, weaving, ceramics, music, and dance, as well as those that would be considered "non-art," such as funerals, household and agricultural labor, and child-rearing. In studying how people do things, I was looking for correspondences in the use of space, time, movement, language, conceptual framework, training, or other factors that could be discovered across various categories of production.

To borrow from computer terminology, this process of finding similarities is a kind of "sorting" by criteria that may change over time. As the criteria change, the end result—the interpretation or evaluation of action and thus the production of structural properties—changes as well. However, because the correspondences being discussed here are cognitive in nature, their descriptions can only be abstractions of reality. In a complicated process of building associations, one action or setting brings to mind another (or set of others) in complex ways that relate one domain to another, or one time (past, present, or future) to another, through metaphor and association. In short, redundancy suggests a perceptual problem that provides a kind of synergy across domains of production and across categories of time.

Following Bateson (1972a), I suggest that these correspondences, because they are repeated in a variety of domains and behavioral or objectives forms, serve as one part of the framework from which evaluations are made. Thus, redundancy makes something remarkable, noticeable, apparent, even meaningful. Redundancy also leads to appreciation and the sense of fitness or appropriateness associated with aesthetic judgment. But the notion of redundancy, as used here, is more complicated than this. It implies the recognition of similar idioms or forms in a variety of contexts (a perceptual problem), as well as the training of perceptual skills for the tendency to perceive particular kinds of similarities across domains. Finally, it implies the tendency to use such perceived similarities as the basis for solving new kinds of problems.

The correspondences described thus far relate to social organization and the organization of production in agriculture, cloth, and dance. They are, by necessity, abstractions of reality. As more is known about each domain of production, its metaphoric associations become more intricate and complex. The process of association described here is complex and multilayered. The associations become more personalized or idiosyncratic as the analysis moves closer to the individual psyche and individual experience. Only the most outward layers of associations are visible from a social scientist's vantage point.

It is also true that the emergence of various structural properties takes different idiomatic forms in particular contexts. For example, in its many transformations complementarity opens the way to definitions of categories of persons, as evidenced by the fact that only men are defined as farmers and only women can spin. Complementarity also opens the door to viewing the distribution of power and resources in ways that are both legally sanctioned and morally correct. This can be seen by the fact that in complementary relationships clients, laborers, and wives have the right to demand certain things from, respectively, patrons, landholders, and husbands. When such demands are not met, the protesting party has the right to withdraw its services. Everyone involved knows that at critical points in the production process such withdrawal can have disastrous effects, whether it is agricultural production or the production of a dance performance. Any individual who is not willing to withdraw under such circumstances is, at the least, considered foolish. Sentiment, then, as between husbands and wives, is infused with the obligations implied by complementarity, and the very nature of complementarity in its many forms reinforces the emphasis on coordinating action with others.

Containment and Boundaries

In general, all Kono production draws, in some way, from ideas of containment and the contrasts between bounded and unbounded space. Boundaries and containment have different expressions in various domains, however. As discussed in Chapter 3, spatial distance or being away from one's home is in some ways equated with being unbounded or out of control. Essentially, the identity providing aspects of space limit the range in which individuals can operate and still maintain those parts of their identity related to the rules of descent and the rights associated with their natal homes. As individuals move further from their homes, they are increasingly freed from the constraints of jural obligations. At the same time they become less able to utilize the advantages that patrilineal or matrifilial ties might provide. In essence, those away from their homes are in unbounded space, released from both the constraints and opportunities provided by the social connections established through birth and marriage. In other instances containment provides protection for the powerless or defenseless. At other times very dangerous things or people must be contained to control and utilize their power.

The contrasts between bounded and unbounded space are manifested in slightly different ways in agricultural production. Farm space is temporary and tenuous. It is constructed by transforming dangerous forest regions into productive areas for human beings. Forest space is alive with wild animals as well as with devils and spirits, duplicitous antisocial beings whose intentions are rarely beneficial to humans. Not surprisingly, when Kono talk about antisocial activities, they borrow images from the unbounded realm of nature to elaborate upon and explain antisocial activities. For example, those engaging in witchcraft transform themselves into forest creatures such as snakes before their heinous adventures. The forest, as unbounded space, is unpredictable, uncontrollable, not tied into the social contracts that humans strike between obligations on the one hand and opportunities on the other and must be protected against.

Town space is also separated from the dangers of the forest through actions that make reference to containment and bounded space. In the midst of a crisis (e.g., when a number of children have inexplicably died in a community or when crops of a particular town have repeatedly failed) a diviner or other specialist is consulted. The sacrifices that are commonly prescribed have to do with encircling the town to keep evil out or to keep witches who might already live in the town from eating children or otherwise wrecking havoc. Essentially, the act of encircling met-aphorically restores the boundaries of human decency and control to those in the town. In some cases, the encircling is done with homespun cotton thread that is literally stretched all the way around a small town. In other cases, I have seen only the paths leading to and from a town protected by planting witch traps in the form of old soft drink or beer bottles along the paths leading to the town. When witches try to cross over the bottles, their witch properties are entrapped, thereby contain-ing them and making them harmless. Sometimes small wicker baskets are woven into archways that people pass under as they enter a town. In all of these cases, those who would do harm to the town find that their witch properties or other tools of evil are trapped, rendering them powerless as they enter the town. The use of encircling or containment as strategies for defensive purposes goes back at least as far as the late nine-teenth century when the Kono planted bramble thickets around their towns for protection from warrior bands.

Similar to the placement of the *baffa* in the center of farm space, the most important ritual site for a town is also found in the center of town space. The *tamba tina* (described in Chapter 3), which symbolically links newborns to their natal home and ancestors, ideally is located in the cen-ter of a town. Of course, this central placement may change with the growth of a town or village.

As discussed previously, house space is also contained space. While farm space is humanly constructed and constantly reaffirmed through actions that differentiate it from the surrounding forest, the relationship between town space and house space is somewhat different. House space is contained because it is private and dangerous. What happens inside a house is unpredictable and uncontrollable. Witch traps similar to those sometimes found at the entrance to a town hang over doorways. There are also rituals of protection that can only be performed in doorways. Likewise, the first public appearance of a new child is associated with crossing over the threshold and moving from private space to public space. The dangers of being outside, on the other hand, are associated with overt challenges from others and failure to meet others' expecta-tions. Thus, there is a duality to bounded or contained space, and the same techniques are used to protect against outside forces as are used to protect against evil forces in the midst of social life.

At critical junctures certain categories of people become so dangerous that they must be physically contained in order to bound or control their actions. During post-burial ceremonies *bain den moe* and *fa den moe* participate in a ritual exchange in which the *bain den moe* are paid back for the efforts the deceased made on the part of the patrilineage of the *fa den moe*. During these exchanges the *bain den moe* remain inside a round house while the *fa den moe* remain outside. The goods to be exchanged are handed back and forth across the doorstep. In essence, this encircling controls the *bain den moe,* who may pose a threat to the offspring of the deceased if they are not satisfied by the post-burial exchanges. The potential danger of the *bain den moe* stems from the fact that a representative of the *bain den moe* maintains contact with the ancestors of the deceased's mother. If the *bain den moe* feel that their gift of a wife to the *fa den moe* has not been adequately repaid, they might convince the mother's ancestors to cause damage to the patriline of the *fa den moe*. Once such agreements are reached about the amount of goods to be given, the *bain den moe* leave their enclosure to bless the grandchildren of the deceased (the children who will continue the patriline of the *fa den moe*), thereby insuring the continuity of the lineage of the *fa den moe*.

In the use of cloth, boundedness is a technique that builds upon metaphors of the body as a container to strengthen actions and their effects. In warrior times some of the most powerful medicines used by warriors in battle were warrior shirts, an extra layer of cloth that could add further control to the body and thus focus the body's power for the advantage of an individual and his supporters. The shirts are said to have given warriors protection in battle by giving them physical strength, stopping bullets, and, in the most powerful examples, making their wearer invisible.

Complementarity

In many cases physically bounding or containing something sets apart the categories that are, in ideal situations, in relations of complementarity, as shown in Table 4. In other words, those activities and concepts that are potentially disruptive can be controlled and used for social reproduction when they exist in balanced or complementary relationships with the contrasting concept or action. Forests, then, are controlled through the construction of farms, and *bain den moe* are controlled through the correct actions of *fa den moe* (as in the encircling of *bain den moe* at post-burial ceremonies.

TABLE 4
Complementarities

forest	farm
bain den moe	*fa den moe*
matrifilial ties	patrilineal ties
obscurity	clarity
strangers/female	natives/male
private	public
unpredictable/chaotic/immoral	predictable/ordered/moral

When seen in this way, it is clear that what is on one side of the relation of complementarity actually helps structure the actions or conceptions of the corresponding side, and that much of social life is directed at maintaining the balance between complementarities. Individuals are constantly faced with balancing expressions of individual personality, sentiment, aspiration, and other idiosyncratic aspects of behavior against the obligations engendered by birth and descent rules. As described in Chapter 3, people must also balance the obligations inherent in rules of descent against the sentiments of matrifilial ties. In behavioral terms, the emphasis on complementarity is also evident in the division of labor found in most production processes. In cloth production, women are responsible for spinning cotton thread while men are responsible for weaving, and these lines are rarely crossed. In rice production, a man's successful crop depends on his ability to obtain land through his lineage and to convince his wife to do her share of the agricultural labor, including cooking for him every day on the farm, weeding at the proper time, helping with the harvest, and taking charge of processing the harvested rice. If a man fails to establish the proper relationships with either his lineage or his wife and her relatives, it is likely his crop will fail. Dance performance, as well, is a collective activity, and the degree of collective involvement within the town provides an indication of the talent of the singer and other performers. In the same way, a chief or elder rules only as long as he has supporters; consequently, much of his time, energy, and resources are spent ensuring that he meets their expectations.[6] In ideological terms, the efforts to balance the social world against the unpredictability of the forest serves as a framework for conceptualizing appropriate action. In fact, it is only possible to conceptualize order in Kono life by contrasting it with the images of disorder provided by the forest.

What I want to stress throughout this discussion of associations across domains is that in the very act of doing a particular task in one domain, reference is made to multiple domains. The actions of particular domains interpenetrate in changing and sometimes unpredictable ways. What I am suggesting is that, at one level, it is the process of association across domains and the formation of habits and redundancy or patterns of action that become important as models for action and being in the world and, in fact, form the basis of meaning and aesthetic judgment at any particular point in time.

It is not enough, however, for the outsider to note that such correspondences exist. What is essential is to couple this with an understanding that the correspondences only become real or effective if they are perceived or noted by individuals in their endeavors to match habit, pattern, or ideas of the way things are supposed to be against their interests and goals in particular situations.

This is basically a cognitive or conceptual problem, as it is based on actors' recognition of and action upon those configurations at any point in time. In Giddens's (1979) terms, these configurations can be called structural properties. I suggest that they guide the production of action as well as the evaluation of form and action. Not surprisingly, one of the other principles or structural properties in Kono life is an emphasis on action.

Action

Action is important in multiple ways. It is used to demonstrate power, social status, and knowledge. It is a means by which people gauge or make social affiliations public. Finally, it is used to demonstrate internal or emotional states. It is through their actions that people are known; in turn, the Kono are well versed in the demonstrative features of action.

One of the primary idioms (idioms being context-specific manifestations of particular structural properties) through which the importance of action is maintained is exchange. Exchanges are watched closely as indications of alignments within the community. When established patterns are violated, it is apparent to everyone that social relationships are out of balance and that someone in the relationship is not meeting a social obligation or is otherwise behaving inappropriately. It can also be said, in general, that exchanges demonstrate the entrance to or exit from social relationships. This is certainly true in marriage arrangements and burial ceremonies. While exchanges are often formalized, the idiom of exchange can also be found in informal relationships, such as the expectations that exchange engenders between friends.

Exchanges are negotiated in terms of actual goods or, more importantly, in terms of actions. The side that one takes in a dispute or in a dance event are only two of the ways of demonstrating social relationships and connections to others in ways that should guarantee future exchanges. Exchanges can be grouped into a series of categories, but the reader should keep in mind that these often overlap in actual practice.

First are exchanges that are used to validate or lend truth to stated intentions. When a stranger is introduced to a household, the head of the household will invariably vow his and his wife's assistance and hospitality. Along with the vow, it is common for a small gift to be given to the stranger (often the stranger will present small gifts to the head of the household as well). The usual gift in such instances is kola but if the stranger is male, the gift may be a cup of palm wine; if the stranger is a woman, the gift may be a small bundle of tomatoes, cassava leaf, or other foodstuffs from a household garden. It is also customary for a stranger to give small gifts to a town chief or paramount chief when first entering an area. Acceptance of the gift by the chief signals the chief's willingness to look after the visitor's interests during his or her stay. Likewise, gifts from the chief to the stranger imply a kind of tacit agreement to support the chief's leadership and, thus, serve as evidence of a particular kind of relationship. I was often struck by the lavishness of gifts given to non-Kono visitors. A missionary, for example, who had helped set up a clinic in a neighboring town was showered with country cloth robes and other examples of local crafts. Not long after he left Sierra Leone, however, I was asked to write a letter to him on behalf of the chiefdom asking if he could set up a similar clinic in Kainkordu. In another example of gift-giving as a way of instituting exchange, a government water engineer who was doing a feasibility study for a needed water project in Kainkordu was given country cloth, a goat, and several bushels of rice to encourage his efforts on behalf of the town.

Such gifts are, in part, a reflection of the interests of the community and an indication of the extent to which they will go to sway outsiders to assist in their efforts. On the other hand, they also reflect the kinds of actions that a wealthy chiefdom or town is supposed to take to demonstrate their wealth and good will toward official visitors. While such gifts cannot guarantee that requests will be met, failure to give gifts will certainly mean that visitors will not act on behalf of their hosts.

Learning, as well, implies exchange. Apprenticeships and the rights to skills that they validate are always preceded with the giving of small gifts and fees. In essence, paying such fees gives an individual the right to practice specific skills once they are learned. While individuals may have picked up certain skills through daily observation, actually practicing the skill without paying the fees usually dooms one's efforts. So embedded is the idea of payment for learning that what one is given freely is thought not really to be worth knowing.[7]

Marriage arrangements and subsequent relationships between husbands and wives are also validated and, thus, publicized by exchange. Sex, as well, is construed in terms of exchange, whether between husband and wife or between lovers. Although wives continually complain about their husband's girlfriends in terms of the drain on resources they cause, wives can also benefit from exchanges with their husbands. Women refrain from sexual relations with their husbands until a newborn is walking. At that point a man is supposed to present his wife with enough cloth to make a shirt and a *lappa*. By accepting the gift, a woman signifies she is ready to return to her husband's bed.

Patron-client relationships are also characterized by exchanges of resources, such as goods, support, and allegiance, between patron and client. The patron must meet the client's expectations or the client is likely to find more beneficial ways of investing his or her clientage (and vice versa).

The emphasis on action and exchange extends to the supernatural world as well, but in a way that marks the antisocial nature of witchcraft. Delving in witchcraft gives the individual powers that are superhuman. Part of the danger, however, is that witches always demand something in return. While demands from humans are predictable and logical, demands stemming from associations with witches can never be known in advance. They usually turn out to be what are considered in the Kono view to be heinous. One of the most feared is giving up one's own child or the child of a relative to be eaten (killed) by witches. Reaping the benefits of having a witch but then refusing to honor the exchange will usually end in death.

Maintaining good relations with the ancestors also requires action through exchange. Sacrifices must be made if one expects help from the ancestors. All interaction with ancestors, or with the deceased in general, is prefaced by leaving small items such as kola or a few coins on the deceased's grave. Ancestors are expected to provide something in return for their descendants' efforts. Ancestors who are perceived to have forgotten their descendants are themselves forgotten when it comes time to make sacrifices, and gradually the names of such recalcitrant ancestors will be lost.

Exchanges can also be used to conclude stages of a relationship and mark transitions to a new stage. Essentially, the exchanges of goods between *fa den moe* and *bain den moe* in post-burial ceremonies return to the *bain den moe* the value that his side of the family provided to the patrilineage of the deceased. At the same time, the exchanges provide the *bain den moe* with a public forum to settle any long standing disputes. Once the value of the exchange is agreed upon both the *fa den moe* and the *bain den moe*, and by extension the ancestors of the deceased's mother, relinquish any claims they may have on the descendants of the deceased. The giving of money by a son to his mother during his initiation into Poro is another example of how gifts can signal new phases of relationships.

The emphasis on exchange can also be interpreted as a way of aligning individuals with the expectations the Kono have of various categories of persons. Reputation and identity can only be established through action and connections to others. To establish connections (and thus social identity), one must participate in exchange. The individual who does not exchange with others is an anomaly, and thus suspect. Truck drivers, for example, are notorious for not participating in exchanges, in other words, for always demanding cash for transport, refusing to negotiate prices, and in other ways refusing to participate in flows of exchanges that can be negotiated. As a group they are considered to be hard-hearted; it is expected that at some point their hard-heartedness will come back to haunt them. The Kono attitude toward exchange mitigates against the accumulation of capital for investment. Individuals, particularly those with one foot in the cash economy, often find themselves in the position of choosing between maintaining a good reputation and advancing financially.

The failure to understand how the configurations or paradigms discussed here are arranged and formed through action and its interpretation or how such arrangements effect the production of meaning makes it impossible to know what action means, how structure is reproduced or changed over time, and how aesthetic evaluation effects the reproduction process. Idioms, then, are made meaningful or effective through their use in multiple domains. When actions comply with or correspond to patterns that are seen to crosscut domains of experience they are deemed appropriate, morally correct, or aesthetically pleasing. When they do not, they can be evaluated in negative terms and associated with the immorality of antisocial beings.

REDUNDANCY, CONTESTATION, AND CHANGE

While not identical to Giddens's explanation of paradigmatic forms, Bateson's (1972) discussion of the importance of redundancy suggests that with repetition, forms become more structure-like, more paradigmatic, and thus there is a quantitative aspect to the constitution of structural properties as Giddens defines them; the more particular forms are practiced or perceived, the more real and unquestionable or taken-for-granted they become. The cultural significance of the associations or paradigms set up by the perception of the repetition of these idioms in a variety of domains can only be explored through a demonstration of how the metaphors are contested, mixed, and reorganized in a variety of contexts. Aesthetic judgments, then, in the form of evaluations of the appropriate "sortings" of paradigmatic forms or resonances, are one of the primary mechanisms through which structure and action impinge upon each other.[8] This opens the door to viewing the repetition of forms or idioms, as well as the evaluation of forms, as acts that can be and often are contested enterprises. When interpretations of action are seen as constitutive of social or material forms, it is possible to consider the politics of interpretation and evaluation as well as the possibility of shifts in the very paradigmatic forms that constitute structure at any given point in time.

As the process of relating one domain to another occurs, so does a reshaping or retooling of the experiences at hand. Giddens (1976:128) writes that "[every] act which contributes to the reproduction of a structure is also an act of production, a novel enterprise, and as such may initiate change by altering that structure at the same time as it reproduces it—as the meanings of words change in and through their use." Such metaphoric retoolings are embedded in layers of personal experience that include habit, interests, and the idiosyncracies of personal experience.

While these are individualized perceptions and tempered by personality, they are also, to some degree, shared by those with similar life experiences, as will be seen in Chapter 6. They are part of what goes into the perception of shared identity and can, to some degree, be learned.

Finally, I would suggest that it is at the level of action and the perception of association or correspondences between actions that societies establish their uniqueness. While the major characteristics of Kono social life and production may appear similar to those found in societies that share similar subsistence patterns or an emphasis on coordinating the actions of individuals, it is the idiomatic forms of action, specifically how things are done and the associations or contrasts that emerge from that action, that form the patterns, habits of thought, and templates that suggest boundaries to the imagination and the conceptual possibilities for most members of particular societies.[9] In the next chapter we will move to this more general level of analysis to explore the ways in which the correspondences that emerge from domains of production select for or channel ideas about production and methods of criticism.

6

STRUCTURE INTO ACTION

Categories of Production
and Evaluation

This chapter looks at Kono categories of
production as an example of the ways in which structural properties
and individual perceptions of the behavioral idioms or resonances
that crosscut domains affect everyday life. In other words, I am interested in looking at how the perception of similarities across do-
ains form models for action and being in the world and constitute the
basis of meaning and aesthetic judgments. Through such judgments,
it is shown how structural properties are reproduced through action
over time.

My data for this exploration comes from informal discussions with
the Kono about categories of production and from subsequent formal interviews on the subject. By moving from the general to the specific in this
way, it is possible to consider the logic behind the divisions between
Kono categories of production and aesthetic evaluation in ways that
stress the constructive potential of human action. It is also possible to see
the circular relationship between structural properties and systems of
categorization or idioms, particularly the way idioms or systems of categorization reinforce and thus reproduce particular arrangements of
structural properties.

THE CATEGORIES OF PRODUCTION

From an outsider's perspective a description of Kono categories of production might begin by contrasting farm labor, household labor, craft
production, and art production, and then listing the activities within
each of these categories. Under farm labor, for example, one might list
brushing fields, sowing, weeding, scaring birds, setting traps, harvesting,
and a variety of other tasks; under household labor, cooking, carrying
water, sweeping, and child care, among other activities; under craft production, pottery making, spinning and weaving, mat-making, and blacksmithing; and under arts or performance, music, dance, story telling, and
possibly hair plaiting and scarification. Discussions of aesthetics would
center more than likely on those activities categorized as craft production
and arts and performance. Other activities might be considered, but only
in ways that would illuminate the activities already designated as craft,
art, or performance. For example, in examining a particular dance form,
one might note its similarity to movements used in some aspect of agricultural labor.

This arrangement of hypothetical categories, however, is based on an
idealized list of Euro-American categories. It bears little resemblance to
the ways in which rural Kono farmers actually categorize their productive world. Thus, instead of relying on the observers' categories, it is necessary to look at the categories that the Kono use themselves to see how
they fit together to both reproduce and structure Kono views of appropriate action. For the small group of farmers who provided information
on categories of production, Kono production is conceived of in terms of
a dichotomy between *wai chea*, which can be translated as productive
activity or work thing, *swin chea*, literally useless activity or useless
thing, or *sig bama*, literally sitting and doing nothing (Table 5). "Useless" in Kono terms includes spending too much time at palm wine bars
or on any other nonproductive activity (including anthropological research). *Swin chea* differs from the English category "relaxation" because of its negative connotations.

Nyane

Productive activities (*wai chea*) can be divided into at least three subcat-
egories: *nyane* (to make), *gbuo dia* (body sweetness), and *koo che*

TABLE 5
List of Kono Productive Activities (*Wai Chea*)

NYANE—to make	*GBUO DIA*—happiness stomach/body sweetness	*KOO CHE*—speaking
boda nyanda—making of clay pots	*kiene gbasi kwi*—drumming most often seen with dancing	*songo songwe*—noise
bai nyanda—cutlass making	*doune che*—eating	*bai sa*—settling of disputes
tumoe dea—net making	*si sa*—singing	*da si*—advice giving
waa dea—mat making	*si nyane*—song making (composing)	*si sa*—singing
sene sa—farming	*taai sa*—story telling	*si nyane*—song making (composing)
kaa da si—indigo dying	*tombwe don*—dancing	*taai sa*—story telling
kwa sa—weaving		
fande fuane—spinning		
tawa chea—cooking		

(speech thing or spoken form). There is a distinct line between making something (*nyane*) and the other two categories. The defining character-istic of activities considered to be *nyane* is that they end in the production of a tangible material form, whereas the activities of the other two cat-egories end in the production of intangible or ephemeral forms. Here, the divergences between the hypothetical model based on Euro-American categories and the Kono model of production and activity become more apparent. The category of making something tangible (*nyane*) includes farming, cooking, ceramic production, mat-making, blacksmithing, and other activities that produce a tangible form. As this list shows, what would be considered arts or crafts by Euro-American standards are clearly combined with nonartistic endeavors, such as farming, by the Kono. In other words, the Kono farmers I interviewed did not have a sep-arate category for activities that would be similar to the Euro-American category of art or craft.

Gbuo Dia

The line between activities that fall into stomach or body sweetness (*gbuo dia*) and speech activities (*koo che*) is less clearcut. Things that provide the quality of body sweetness or stomach sweetness provide a sense of overall satisfaction and contentment. Among these are dance oc-casions and the activities that are coordinated to produce a dance occa-sion, such as drumming, singing, dancing, and composition. Dances may be staged as part of a child's entry into Sande or Poro, the installation of a paramount chief or other political figure, post-burial ceremonies known alternatively as *di boenu,* or forty-day ceremonies, catching a thief, and numerous other important social events. Occasionally dance is unplanned and individuals dance through a town for sheer "gladdi-ness," but usually it occurs in association with one of the major occa-sions of life.

The fact that storytelling is also found under the heading of stomach or body sweetness would suggest that *gbuo dia* corresponds to a Euro-American category of performance arts, except for the fact that eating is also categorized as a kind of *gbuo dia*. The connection between these seemingly unrelated activities comes from the nature of the social rela-tionships that are constituted through and invigorated by these activities. The ideal forms of these activities generate a feeling of balance and har-mony among participants. For example, eating is a social occasion. Men and women usually eat separately, with children joining their mothers unless specifically invited by their father or another male relative to eat with them. When the food has been prepared, a woman sends a large steaming bowl of rice and a separate bowl of *plasas* (a vegetable stew, sometimes with dried fish, chicken, or meat) to her husband's rooms. The man will invite those present to eat with him, or if he is not home the rice will be saved for his return. It is common for a man to bring several male friends to join him in his meals. In the meantime, the women of the household and their children gather for their share of the meal. Co-wives usually cook separately and eat separately. The meal is eaten from a single communal platter or bowl, either with spoons or the right hand. Women send rice and *plasas* to neighboring houses as well. Often women in the same compound will send rice to each other as an indication of both friendship and cooperation.

Breaks in the patterns of these arrangements (sending rice to a husband late in the day or after dark, refusing to cook at all, or not sending rice to those in the same compound) signify problems in the various relationships. Food that is eaten under unpleasant circumstances, as when a dispute erupts during the actual meal, will not be perceived as tasting very good. Food is also one vehicle for poisoning and internalizing witchcraft, so consistently refusing to eat the rice someone has prepared is tantamount to accusing them of immoral practices. The idea of a fine meal, then, is one of the things people strive for in their everyday lives. The ideal is for eating to be a pleasant occasion in which social slights and suspicions are absent and the ideal compliment at the end of a meal is *N'gbuo dia* ("My stomach is sweet").

Similarly, the ideal dance is one that envelops numerous individuals— singers, musicians, and participants—in an atmosphere that balances the interests of individuals striving for recognition with an ideology that emphasizes cooperation. The unsuccessful dance, one that does not generate stomach sweetness, often erupts in fistfights, accusations of witchcraft, or other expressions of individual interests that have spun out of control.

Koo Che

The line between stomach sweetness (*gbuo dia*) and verbal things (*koo che*) is somewhat permeable. In *koo che* the emphasis is also on coordination and conciliation. Verbal things include activities that use speech to resolve differences between individuals or groups and to restore or maintain community balance. The Kono have formalized ways of airing grievances and settling disputes. When these methods are successful, social harmony is maintained or restored. Without discussion and mediation the grievances, suppressed angers, and frustrations of group living would destroy reciprocal ties within the group that ensure social, as well as physical, survival. The importance of resolving differences can not be overemphasized. This became clearer to me only as I participated in verbal mediations and discussed American methods for overcoming disagreements with some of my informants. After I had been in the Kono area for about a year, a group of young married women asked me how Americans resolved differences between relatives or friends. I explained that people would usually resolve problematic situations by ignoring the incident or trying to discuss it between themselves. I went on to say that if no resolution or satisfaction could be found from such talking and if the disagreement was serious enough, the individuals involved would probably begin to limit their contact or even end any future interaction entirely.

The women were astonished at my answer and explained their amazement by saying that only in extreme circumstances would a Kono resort to that kind of withdrawal. A Kono person who considers themselves wronged arranges for the dispute to be settled (bai sa) by a mediator agreed upon by both parties. By agreeing to a mediator both participants bind themselves to accept whatever decision is made and to follow any instructions or advice (da si) the mediator may give. During the airing of the case itself, each party has a chance to state their side and present witnesses. The mediator then decides who is in the right in the situation and, more importantly, gives advice (da si) to each side as to how best to get over the social breach and continue with the relationship. If damages are to be paid, the mediator determines these as well. Mediation emphasizes making social tensions explicit in a controlled setting and publicly defining or formalizing subsequent interactions between participants until the tension disappears. Such public discussions also externalize any grievances that might fester over time and cause bigger problems later. Mediation is sought in all non-civil disputes (disputes that are not referred to the paramount chief or courts for solution), including marital conflicts, theft, and disagreements between friends, no matter what the nature of the case. An example of how this process works can be seen in a marital dispute between a man named Thomas and his wife. The dispute eventually led to mediation between Thomas's wife and his girlfriend.

Thomas was a respected school teacher but had no relatives in the town where he was teaching. His wife, Sara, was also a stranger in the town, but they were both Kono and had made many friends in the community through their connections to the school and local churches. Sara was in her mid-twenties, Thomas was in his mid-thirties, and they had three children.

Sara was fond of explaining that her husband had been posted to an out-of-the-way town because of her. Before they married, she had been his student. Several older and wealthier men, including the headmaster of the school, had spoken to her family about marriage. Sara, however, was in love with Thomas even though her parents said he had nothing to offer her. Finally, she decided the only way she would be able to stay with Thomas was to become pregnant, which she did, and they were married. In order to escape the wrath of his employer, Thomas got a transfer to a very small town where the headmaster had no influence, a place where Thomas's real value was not recognized and, more importantly, where he was unable to meet people who could further his career. In Sara's mind she had traded marriage to an older, wealthier man for a love match. At times she was content with her lot, but sometimes she talked about how things might have been easier for her if she had decided on the older man.

Several years after coming to the town Thomas started to have an affair with one of his students. Sara knew what was happening, but there was relatively little she could do. Finally, she decided to visit her mother, taking her children and telling Thomas her mother needed help with her harvest. While she was gone, the girlfriend moved into Thomas's house and took over the cooking, washing, and other chores of a wife. Sara stayed away for several months, much longer than anyone expected, and only returned when Thomas went to bring her back. In the course of convincing Sara to return, he promised to end the affair.

The family was reunited, and the girlfriend moved out of the house. But the two women refused to speak to each other, and the bad feelings between them were evident. Finally, the girlfriend asked one of Sara's best friends to settle the dispute. When the case was discussed, each woman explained her side but said she wanted to end the bad feelings. Sara requested that the girlfriend's mother, who had become involved in the dispute, also agree to the mediator's terms. The student and mediator both agreed to speak to the mother to tell her to end the bad feelings. It was also agreed that the student would wash clothes for Sara one day a week and do other household chores as well. While this was a kind of penance, the prescribed tasks were also the kinds of things that a younger co-wife might do for her husband's senior wife. The affair itself was not open for discussion because wives have very little control over this area of their husband's lives. Instead, the situation was resolved by providing Sara with some of the services that a junior wife often provides a senior wife. The inclusion of the girlfriend's mother in the settlement guaranteed that the rift between Sara and the student would not be reopened through someone else's meddling.

The advice of mediators, then, returns disputing parties to balanced and harmonious relationships. Some individuals develop reputations as mediators par excellence and are sought out for their skills.

Similarly, noise (*songo songwe*) can be an important part of maintaining or restoring social harmony and balance in Kono communities. Noise is, in fact, a necessary part of some types of discussions and actually leads to a means of restoring social order and establishing reputations. Although noisy altercations between individuals or within groups are infrequent, they tend to occur at public events or when household disputes get out of control and one party wants to open the dispute to public scrutiny. At these times, the degree of outrage is reflected by the decibel level; the louder the protest and debate, the more people will become involved. The explosive anger expressed at these public events contrasts sharply to the measured tones and reasoning used in mediation or advice giving (*da si*). Individuals in this state, especially men, are usually characterized as out of control and not really responsible for their actions.

One particularly vivid outburst occurred at an all-night dance prior to a Sande initiation. The dances and the initiation itself are complex affairs that involve extended families and even whole communities in months of preparations. A disturbance at a dance can have ill effects on the initiates and usually results in people calling for a postponement or cancellation of the affair. There is a sense that bad feelings at the dance will spill over into the initiation itself and affect the ability of the initiates to recover from the cliterodectomy surgeries performed on the first day. Because of the degree of preparations for such large-scale events, postponing a pre-initiation dance is a difficult, if not impossible, task. The threat of such disturbances generates a great deal of anger, as can be seen from the following description of a relatively small dance, which drew about 150 participants to a village that normally housed about thirty people.

Shortly after the dance began, shouting and then a fistfight erupted between two men. Some of those present attributed the disturbance to political differences between the two men; others attributed it to an affair that one of the men was having with the other man's girlfriend, but the rapidly escalating verbiage made it difficult to hear exactly what the men said to each other. The other men present stopped the fight, and one of the protagonists ran off. The men then started to debate whether to notify the paramount chief of the dispute's possible political nature or just to fine the men themselves.

When the dispute broke out, Sande elders circulated through the crowd calling all Sande women to a meeting. When the meeting broke up about an hour later, the women announced that they were deeply offended by the fight and asked that compensation be paid to the Sande elders. Essentially, the women argued that the men, by being unable to control their ranks, had disrupted the Sande celebration and, potentially, the initiation. The women demanded compensation for the insult, and the men refused. The verbal matches that ensued went on for about an hour and a half with all of the women and a few men, mostly male relatives of the initiate and their friends, aligned against the rest of the men. At one point the women withdrew again to try to reach a consensus among themselves. When they returned to the center of town and again demanded compensation, however, the shouting erupted all over again.

Gradually, almost imperceptibly, the next hour and a half resulted in a decision as to what should happen to the offending men and how much compensation the men as a group should pay. What became obvious throughout this process was that the noisy shouting bouts eventually led to the emergence of certain individuals as spokespersons. Their advice and performance styles gained the respect and attention of the rest of the group. As this happened, fewer and fewer people took part in the debate, and what had been a cacophony gave way to a consensus. The individual whose voice finally prevailed was a younger man (about thirty-five), who was well-respected for his knowledge of "country ways" in the chiefdom headquarters where he lived; he was also a relative of the initiate and well-known in the town where the dance was being held. The men finally paid the fine (four leones in total, about $.36 in 1982 dollars), and their spokesperson apologized for any problems they had caused. The women accepted the apology through their leaders and, after another hour of regrouping, speeches, and cooling off, the dance continued.

The process that I have described here is similar to that followed whenever noisy disputes got out of control. Reaching a consensus in this way is very much a participatory process. Here, as in advice-giving, verbal behavior plays a part in the search for a balance between individual intentions and the maintenance of community harmony. Individuals, such as the man who resolved the tension at the dance, advance themselves by promoting harmony rather than disrupting it. The words that finally sway the crowd, as well as the individuals whose persistence and verbal skills are recognized, will be remembered, cited, and perhaps even sought after in the settling of future disputes.

Singing (*si sa*) also belongs to *koo che*, both because it is a verbal act and because it is a means of expressing dissatisfaction in Kono life. As in many West African groups, singers (usually women among the Kono) are given license to express criticism in performance contexts that far exceeds the boundaries allowed them in everyday life. This is evident in two verses of a song that I recorded during the dance performances prior to initiation into Bii in 1983.

Musu yama yama e fon nyandon.
A yama yama e fon nyandon.
A yama yama du chandon che a yima yon fondye.
O mai ye wo kwo fo chenen ne e du chandon, moi e chenon.
O mai ye wo tu musu mbe chenjana, moi e chenon.

One woman in this compound is bad.
There is a bad thing in this compound.
There is a bad thing in this town but especially in this compound.
O there is a big man in this town who likes to provoke, let us not go there.
There is a jealous woman in this house, let us not go there.

Although not all songs express such criticism, those that do often publicize community problems as dance groups move through a town. By doing so, community members give notice to wrongdoers that their actions are being watched and that community sentiments may be turning against them. To be popular, Kono singers must be tapped into the gossip networks of the communities where they perform. They must understand the tensions that exist, and they must master the subtlety that allows them to refer to those tensions in ways that push people toward, rather than away from, community values. Singing, then, also plays a role in maintaining social harmony and is most appreciated when it helps to do so.

The more ephemeral categories of production (*gbuo dia*) and *koo che*) contribute to the production of social cohesion by holding up the ideals of balance and harmony and, at the same time, by demonstrating appropriate ways of expressing disharmony and of restoring social relationships. These ideals provide the background against which actual experiences are judged and evaluated. All dances remain problematic sites of contestation (as demonstrated by the description of the Bii initiation dance in Chapter 5), and few social relationships remain trouble-free indefinitely.

Rights and Obligations in Productive Activities

One of the critical things about Kono conceptions of productive activity is the fact that making something (*nyane*), body sweetness (*gbuo dia*), and speech things (*koo che*) all fall into the category of productive activities. This suggests an important kind of equivalence among the three that I would like to explore here. Rural Kono, as well as other subsistence agriculturalists, live in a social world, one in which behavior ensuring agricultural production, or survival in general, is not limited solely to techniques related to subsistence. The uncertainties of the Kono agricultural system are offset, in most instances, by rules concerning the rights and obligations that individuals have vis-a-vis others. Some of these are customary, as in the trading of rice and *plasas* between women in the same compound or women who share the same cooking fire. The Kono also feel obligated to invite anyone entering a house where people are eating to join in the meal. Complying with these mores enhances an individual's reputation as a person of training or manners.

More formal arrangements exist among family members. A husband is required, as part of marital obligations, to provide food for visitors from his wife's family, no matter how long they stay. One of the most common complaints men have about their wives is that a wife's relatives, especially her younger brothers, can visit her indefinitely and expect to be fed without contributing to the household labor pool. It is not unusual to see adolescent males travelling from relative to relative in order to escape the hunger in their mother's household in the period of time just before the yearly harvests or to avoid work on their father's farm during the brushing or harvesting periods. Refusing food to these visitors or other in-laws can eventually lead to a summons before the paramount chief or, in extreme cases, to dissolution of the marriage. Joking relationships between a man and his sister's children are another example of formal relationships that can potentially offset short periods of hunger through the petty thefts that such relationships allow.

Essentially, such formal obligations provide most individuals with alternate strategies for obtaining food should their own crops fail. Providing rice to relatives or neighbors at a time of need actualizes a potential network of relationships that one can call upon at other times. These are not directly reciprocal relationships but, instead, are relationships marking possibilities in which each side keeps loose track of what is expected of themselves and what they can expect from others.

While the kinds of reciprocal relationships described here are seen most readily in dealing with foodstuffs and agricultural production, capital, for the Kono, comes in a variety of forms. It can include cash, control over crops and laborers, and participants in a dance occasion. It can also include political influence. Expectations within these partnerships range from contributions of rice or labor when a child is joining society, gifts of money to help defray funeral expenses, assistance in finding seed rice for next year's crop, and support during a dance sponsored by a "lending" family. Those who meet their obligations are praised for their good behavior (*a sone nyi,* "his/her behavior is good"). Those failing to meet obligations are less likely to have people to turn to when they are in need.

While it might be tempting to place agriculture at a causal or determining level in this model, that is not my intention nor is it the Kono view. Instead, the kinds of reciprocal relationships I am describing are not seen as ways of guaranteeing survival but as ways of living a good and satisfying life. Necessity and good social form are entwined in ways that, even when the individual is no longer tied to an agricultural lifestyle, the social forms that accompany that lifestyle remain valued and worth continuing because that is what, in Kono terms, good behavior or good character (*a sone nyi*) dictate.

When exercised, these sets of rights and obligations tie individuals to continually changing social networks. The more reciprocal obligations are performed the more likely future obligations are to be called into play. Repeated demands and obligations strengthen an individual's position in particular networks, increase the size and strength of their safety net, and extend individual control over others. Because of this aspect of control, the dimension of not indebting oneself to too many people also exists.

Movement out of the network or circle of rights and obligations implies a lessening of one's possibilities within that particular circle; to be able to make demands on others implies placing oneself in a position to have to acquiesce to other's demands. In what might be compared to a kind of high stakes poker, those not interested in advancing their reputations beyond being recognized as a good person try to position themselves in ways that will allow them the highest benefits with the fewest costs. Those who are in chiefly lineages or who otherwise are interested in increasing their status are more ready to accrue debt from others as a way of advancing themselves and demonstrating their influence. Often such plays bring a degree of turmoil because they force the individual to choose between conflicting loyalties, ideas of what a good person should be doing, and knowing that personal advancement sometimes depends on alternative strategies. As a result of such choices, those individuals who overextend themselves or who align themselves in new and innovative ways can sometimes find themselves defeated, with the alternatives they had counted on and invested in crumbling beneath them.

This is what happened to Peter, a well-respected teacher in his community. In general, teachers are in a very precarious position in Sierra Leone because they have a guaranteed salary, which tends to be a magnet for those in their families whose crops have failed or are otherwise in need. Placed in the difficult position of never being able to satisfy their family's needs, many teachers ask for posts away from their families and their demands. Peter, however, was teaching in a town where many of his relatives lived. He was respected in the town because he was not perceived as a stranger as many of the other teachers were. He was also married.

In addition to teaching, Peter and his wife cultivated a farm every year. Sometimes students from his classes provided farm labor; at other times family members would help and Peter's wife would, in turn, assist on their farms. Although Peter was doing all right financially, he could see no way of saving money from his salary and getting away from farming. His wife began to complain, saying that she had nothing although she worked twice as hard as other women. In fact, she probably did work harder than most women to make up for Peter's absence from the farm while he was teaching.

Gradually, Peter became involved with one of the local churches and the charismatic European priest in charge of the region. He was baptized and occasionally worked as a translator for the priest or assisted in parish work in other ways. It was clear that he was attaching himself as a client to the priest in the same way another Kono man might attach himself to a lineage elder or paramount chief. As in other kinds of reciprocal relationships, the obligations on either side are not spelled out, but each side has an idea when they are being taken advantage of. Together, Peter and the priest planned to work on improving the schools and health care in the region, and Peter had the idea that eventually the priest would be in a position to help him with further schooling or to offer him a position that paid more than a teacher's salary. Given the economic position of priests in this part of Sierra Leone, both of these expectations were probably unrealistic, but Peter's judgment was clouded by the belief that all foreigners have unlimited resources from which to draw.

As Peter was cultivating his relationship with the priest and spending more and more of his time on church affairs, he had less time for either farming or family business. He and his wife stopped cultivating a farm every year and started using more of their cash to buy rice. This left even less money to distribute to needy family members. His wife also decided to go into small-scale marketing, buying local produce and taking it to sell in the markets of Koidu and then returning with goods to sell in their home town.

Things had reached a kind of waiting state when I first met Peter and his wife in 1982. Within about a year and a half, however, two things happened that destroyed Peter's plans. First, the priest became ill and left Sierra Leone, never to return. When he was finally replaced, it was clear the new priest had his own plans for projects in the region, and they did not include Peter. Then, about six months later the government found itself unable to pay teachers' salaries on a regular basis. When this first began to happen, paychecks were skipped a month at a time but were usually made up in the next month's pay. It was impossible, however, to predict when a check would be withheld.

The situation deteriorated further. By 1984 teachers were not paid for six months at a time, and by 1988 they had not been paid for a year and very little teaching was going on.

Needless to say, these unpredicted changes left Peter in a very serious position. When I saw him shortly after the priest left the country, his hair was dirty and uncombed and his general appearance was unkept, both signs, in Kono terms, that he was near a psychological crisis. Having been shut off somewhat from his family, he had to spend the next year reestablishing his rights to land and other resources controlled by his lineage and otherwise realigning himself with his lineage. This process was complicated by the fact that he had very few assets to trade in a patron-client relationship. When I saw Peter again in 1988, he had reestablished ties with his family, but it was clear that he had not escaped from the situation unscathed. His wife left him, after having been convinced by her family that he had lost everything and that, if she stayed with him, she would remain a farmer for the rest of her life. Her family arranged another marriage for her with an older, more prosperous man whose economic future was secure.

The point of this story is that in Kono society people's actions can, to a large degree, engender obligations and expectations and their activities can serve to align them in continually changing social networks that go beyond family or marital alliances. These obligations are not givens but are part of the chaos and uncertainty of everyday life. The mechanisms through which connections between people are actualized are directly related to *gbuo dia* and *koo che*. Dance, as one kind of useful endeavor, ties people together in networks of reciprocal obligations. For example, a boy's father's brother is obligated to participate in the dances surrounding his nephew's entry into Poro; his failure to participate would be interpreted as a sign of problems within the family. Slighting someone in this way may have implications for the older man's ability to make a farm the next year as the young man in question, or perhaps his entire immediate family, may withhold labor because of the uncle's breach of etiquette. Thus, dance is called a kind of *wai chea,* a kind of productive activity or work. By engendering expectations of reciprocity, such activities as dancing, settling disputes, and exchanging food operationalize exchange networks that are tenuous, calculated, and controlled. These networks also provide a safety net in a sometimes hostile agricultural environment where the unpredictability of weather or illness can have disastrous effects on a family's capacity to produce enough food to survive through the next harvest.

The reciprocal relationships described here also have an effect on the sides people take and the settlements they perceive as appropriate when they are asked to help settle a dispute. It is not uncommon for personal histories or perceived obligations to enter into how people side in settling marriage disputes. An anecdote from my fieldnotes illustrates how prior relationships with disputants might color decisions of right and wrong. A married couple I had spent considerable time with had exchanged accusations of neglect and adultery. At one point the wife, who had been unable to muster much community support for her grievances, confronted her husband in the center of town and loudly accused him of having an affair with another woman. As a result of this embarrassing public disturbance, gossip against the wife, who was from an important family, reached an all-time high. A friend of hers, who had not actually witnessed the event, however, told me she did not believe the things people had told her about her friend. It was obvious she could not bring herself to blame the wife. Instead, she said that she really did not know what was happening or who was in the right. What she did know was that, when she first came to the town as a stranger there, the woman involved in the dispute and her mother had been very kind to her. These kindnesses made her unable to define the woman as guilty now. Loyalty, then, is tied into the set of rights and obligations that people have in relationships to others. In this case, loyalties were as important as what happened in the social rupture and actually influenced the way the dispute was perceived. The mediators who were asked to settle this case advised the husband to be more concerned with the feelings of his wife and told the wife that she could not confront her husband in public. If feeling for the wife and her family had not been as strong as it was in the community, the mediators could have suggested a much harsher penalty.

To return to the relationship between the three categories of useful activity (*nyane, gbuo dia,* and *koo che*), it is important to note that all of them contain activities in which individuals must be engaged in order to be seen as useful members of a community. By participating in these activities, people actualize the ties that bind them to particular networks and publicly demonstrate those ties, associations, and obligations to others. These activities become gauges of individuals on two levels. First, they serve as a means by which individuals are able to measure their own position in the community—who can he or she ask for something, and who has the right to make demands on them. Second, they provide the community as a whole with a means of gauging the character of individuals—who meets the obligations they accrue, and who does not. In this way, such activities as dance or dispute settlement become obligations individuals must participate in to ensure the continuation of subsistence activities. Because many of these nonagricultural activities take place in the dry season, it becomes increasingly clear why dry season activities are as important to the yearly cycle as are the agricultural tasks of the rainy season. Thus, a balancing or complementarity of the two seasons becomes conceptually important.

Individuals who feel themselves becoming detached from the networks they have established sometimes go to great lengths to ensure their continued participation. As suggested by the discussion of space and identity in Chapter 4, managing these networks is particularly difficult for those whose activities take them away from their natal homes. I once saw a young man jeopardize his year's enrollment in secondary school by delaying a trip back to school for several days because he had been called upon to help settle a family dispute. The student explained his late departure by saying that he felt he had to stay at home to resolve the dispute in order to maintain his place in the family. It would have been easy enough to find a substitute, if he had wanted to, but this was out of the question. Because his position within the family was already tenuous by virtue of his leaving the community for school, it would have further weakened if he had left before the case could be settled.

The points I want to emphasize from this discussion are, first, that *gbuo dia* and *koo che* are embedded in the same network of rights and obligations that actualize subsistence activities and, second, that they are conceptually at the same level of importance as the category *nyane*. Thus, farming is work, but so are dancing, singing, storytelling, and the other activities that are defined as *wai chea*. While the activities of *gbuo dia* and *koo che* may be physically gruelling or emotionally trying at times, the degree of difficulty is not what defines these activities as work. Rather, it is through *gbuo dia* and *koo che* that individuals are able to cement and make visible the ties and associations that are a necessary part of material production. Likewise, individuals are able to engage in the production of material forms only through the production of the immaterial or ephemeral forms that constitute *gbuo dia* and *koo che*.

FORMS OF AESTHETIC CRITICISM

The division between *nyane* and the more ephemeral forms, *gbuo dia* and *koo che,* can also be seen in the forms of aesthetic evaluation that are applied to each category of production (see Table 6). The most frequently used Kono term of appreciation is *a nyi*, which translates "it is good." The words *a nyi* will be used to describe a new pot, whether it is metalware (*da*) or terra cotta (*boda*), providing it is an object to be admired.

If the object is flawed in some way, the description will be *a ma nyi* ("it is not good"). If an older vessel is worn to the point where it can no longer be used, it will be thrown out with the explanation *a ma nyi* ("it is not good") or *a yonda* ("it is spoiled or ruined"). The quality of goodness can be used to describe any material form. For example, men use *a nyi* to talk about feminine beauty. A physically attractive woman will be described with the phrase *a gbo nyi* ("her body is fine"), which implies appreciation as well as sexual interest on the part of the man. The praise used for a woman in whom one is not interested is *a sone nyi,* which means "her character is fine," but character can also include physical attributes. Both forms can theoretically be used by women to describe men, but it would be very unusual for a woman to use *a gbo nyi* to say "his body is fine."

Further clarification of Kono aesthetic judgment comes from examining the limitations in their application. They are applied only to human action or to places or things that have some value to the Kono themselves. Thus, a hillside might be praised, but only because it has been left fallow for years and is now suitable for rice farming, or a waterside might be commented upon, but only in connection with the cool or sweet water one could get from it. Scenery, per se, is not commented on.

Goodness can also be used to describe specific actions or the activities that fall under body sweetness (*gbuo dia*) and spoken things (*koo che*). When used in this way, the commentary is not about movement in formal terms but rather about evaluations of the reasons for the action. If a young married woman says she is going to the weekly market in a neighboring town, a likely response is *a nyi* (good) or *a nyi kaka* (very good). The judgment, however, relates to the evaluator's perception of the needs of the market-goer, or alternatively, to the interests of the evaluator. If the woman says she is going in order to buy fish or a new pot or to consult a diviner, the response will be positive, as long as the stated needs meet the evaluator's perceptions of the young woman's situation or if the market-goer had promised to return with something for the commentator. If the market-goer makes the three-mile walk to the market every week without having any particular reason for going and ignores her household to do so, however, the response may not be so positive. It will be assumed she is going to meet a lover or for some other less than honorable reason. It is also important to point out that individuals do not have the right to make such comments about those senior to them. A woman, for example, would not question an older man's motivations while she might question those of a young boy. She could certainly make negative comments about a woman her own age but probably not about an older woman. In the same way when a dance occasion is praised with the quality of goodness (*a nyi*), it is because the reason for the dance, rather than the dance itself, was a good one.

Praise of skill or understanding is another form of appreciation that cuts across all forms of productive activity. *A kosan fa* ("she understands it") refers to the perceived skill with which someone carries out a task, as in *a kosan fa sene sa* ("he knows how to make a farm"), or *a kosan fa tawa chea* ("she knows how to cook"). Commentary on skill is an important way of commenting on terra cotta production, mat-making, blacksmithing, dancing, story-telling, singing, and all other forms of production.

A kosan fa can also refer to a person's right to carry out a particular task. For example, *a kosan fa kaa da si* means "she knows how to use indigo (*kaa*) to dye cotton thread," but it also implies that the woman has paid the appropriate fees and maintained the laws which allow her to practice the craft successfully. To some degree, having formalized training and the rights to particular knowledge can also mean one has skill. In trying to elicit which weavers were perceived as skillful in producing the patterns typical of Kono strip weaving, for example, I was told that, if someone knows how to warp a loom, they are skillful and the patterns they produce are fine.

Appraisals of someone as skillful can also extend beyond the task at hand. Weavers will be praised if the cloth they produce is tightly woven, but this appraisal is related metaphorically to the complementarity embedded in relationships between women who spin and men who weave. The focus here is not as much on the end product as it is on the process of production and labor coordination and, by extension, on the complementarity of gender roles that successful production implies.

The distinctions between making tangible forms and producing ephemeral forms are reflected in forms of criticism used specifically for ephemeral forms. *A di* ("it is sweet" or "it is good") is applied to singing, drumming, cooking food, dancing, and apparently all other activities that are ephemeral or impermanent. *N gbuo dia* ("my stomach is sweet" or "my body is sweet") expresses satisfaction at the successful coordination of elements that result in a sense of pleasure or satisfaction. This phrase is used to express satisfaction with such things as a delicious meal, participation at a dance, the way a case or dispute is settled, or a

TABLE 6
Categories of Criticism

Nyane	Gbuo dia	Koo che
a nyi	a nyi[1]	a nyi[1]
a kosan fa	a kosan fa	a kosan fa
	n'gbuo dia	n'gbuo dia
	a di	a di

[1]In these cases, a nyi is used to refer only to the reasons behind such actions, not to the forms themselves.

gift. The important factor in using this phrase is the successful manipulation of elements leading up to or surrounding an event. If stomach sweetness is used to praise a meal, it refers not only to the quality of the cooking but also to the social experience of eating. N gbuo dia will not be used to describe a rushed or socially unpleasant meal no matter how delicious the food is. In the same way, the phrase will be used only when certain qualities of a dance are realized or when the manner in which a case is settled or a gift is given is praiseworthy. In legal matters and advice-giving this implies the use of tactics "to save face" for those involved and to smooth over public disturbances rather than to pinpoint and punish wrongdoers in the name of justice.

Of the four forms of criticism discussed here, a nyi (goodness), a kosan fa (understanding or skill), a di (sweetness), and gbuo dia (body or stomach sweetness), the first two can be used in all forms of production and the latter two are used only to describe ephemeral forms. These distinctions, as seen in Table 6, suggest that different kinds of things are praised in nonmaterial forms than in material forms. While skill and goodness are qualities that can be used to describe all forms of production, the qualities of sweetness or body sweetness are used only to describe short-lived and ephemeral activities.

It is no coincidence that Kono praise for the ephemeral is often conceptualized and personalized as sensory experience. As I have already discussed, people position themselves in the production of social forms, such as dispute settlement, eating with a particular group of people, or dancing at an occasion sponsored by a particular family, for a variety of reasons. These reasons include, but are not limited to, gauging one's own obligations towards others, evaluating what one can expect from others in return, and estimating community expectations. As social affiliations change, so do the allegiances, possibilities, and expectations that open for the individual actor. The physical body is an important seat for managing individuality and serves as one arena in which the choices between intention or individual interests and obligations to others are often fought. It is not a difficult leap, therefore, to suggest that as relationships within a Kono community change over time, particular kinds of social events will no longer "taste sweet" or produce sweetness for particular individuals. As interests and relationships in events change, so do the sensual experiences that, to some degree, guide appreciation or evaluation in ways that mingle the sensory with the emotional experience of events. In this way individual perceptions and interests play an ongoing role in evaluation and the production of structural properties. I will return to this point in the second half of this volume.

It is possible to apply these arguments to material production by returning to my earlier statement that the production of material forms is only possible through the production of the ephemeral forms of Kono life. The social networks that simultaneously activate and constitute the rights and responsibilities that are such a major part of the production of ephemeral forms, such as dance and dispute settlement, also contribute a portion of the resources, such as labor, that is necessary for the production of material form.

CONCLUSIONS

The conclusions that can be drawn from this analysis of categories of production and criticism suggest a number of principles that the Kono use to evaluate action and form. Complementarity and the emphasis on action are both reproduced here in varying degrees. First, the analysis provides an insight into how various categories of production are viewed and used. It suggests that most rural Kono do not distinguish between "art" and "non-art" as the Euro-American elite art world does. Instead, they make a distinction between the production of tangible things and the production of intangible social forms. They praise tangible things if they have been skillfully produced or if they are useful to their owner. The Kono make judgments on the basis of what people do with things, rather than on how many things they accumulate. Thus, Kono interpretations of people's actions become important components of criticism. Likewise, there is little evidence that the Kono criticize material form for its own sake. Objects that have no relevance to their needs fall outside the class of things or forms that they evaluate.

Second, the analysis shows how social forms are perceived and used. The Kono evaluate such forms on the basis of the degree of harmony that they establish between individuals. They know and judge people and their connections to each other through public acts, such as participation in a dance event or assistance on a farm. Carrying this further, it is not surprising to find that the Kono perceive private acts, which exclude public associations, in negative terms. This, in turn, suggests that the Kono have a predisposition for attention to the actions of others, as well as one's own actions, and a corresponding emphasis on the evaluation of action by others. The ambiguous relationship between clarity and obscurity is important here. What is obscure is clarified only through publicly stated judgments of action and the acceptance of such judgments.

Third, this analysis has suggested that categories of production and aesthetic criteria are culture specific. While there is a degree of variation in both, depending on life experiences, social role or position, age and gender, and other such factors, the logic and rationale behind the categories of production and appreciation relate to a series of principles or structural properties that are produced or reproduced, although in changing forms, by actions over time and in multiple domains in Kono society itself. While there are similarities between rural Kono and their neighbors, on the whole the perception of analogies across domains is more alike among those sharing Kono ancestry than it is for those who do not. This line, however, is not fixed. Those leaving rural areas for Koidu or other cities may, in some instances, find themselves having more in common with their non-Kono neighbors than they do with their relatives or friends in their natal homes.

This chapter ends our focus on the ways in which structure shapes action, emotion, and aesthetic criticism in Kono life. The analysis, however, would remain incomplete without turning to a consideration of the ways in which action shapes structure. Judgments as to the correctness or appropriateness of form begin with individuals and their interests. The would-be singer described in Chapter 5 acted as he did because of his interests in that particular situation. The mechanism that allows changes in the constituting capacity of structures or principles at any point in time are tied to the perceptions and interests of the individuals involved and their capacity to get others to see things in the same way. Because paradigmatic forms are the product of individual perceptions, variation among individuals must be explored, both in terms of the specific paradigmatic forms that are foregrounded at any given point in time and in terms of whose arrangement of paradigmatic forms is accepted as correct and uncontestable. These relate to questions of power, contestation, and the other ways in which action affects structure, the topics of Part II of this volume.

2

ACTION INTO STRUCTURE

7

POWER, AUTHORITY, AND THE IMPORTANCE OF ACTION

Thus far, I have described Kono social organization and techniques of production in relatively static terms. In the previous chapters, I have examined the structures and principles of Kono life in order to see how they shape the goals and ideals that people strive towards and thus tend to reproduce as patterns of action over time. Relatively little has been said, however, about how those patterns and habitual actions change. This question provides the focus of the remainder of this volume. My framework for addressing this problem is to focus on the consequences, both intended and unintended, of action over time.

From this perspective, structure can be seen as virtual, rather than actual, and as ever mutable and changing. Giddens (1979) writes that structure consists of sets of paradigmatic associations at specific points in time, that it has no concrete reality. Structure is visible only through action and the negotiations and manipulations associated with action as actors attempt to fulfill the expectations of others as well as to make the world meaningful for themselves. While structure itself is never produced or reproduced, what is produced in action are stocks of knowledge, sets of acceptable and unacceptable paradigmatic associations, and the framework for contesting particular sets of associations. Such associations are comparable to the patterns (e.g., complementarity, boundedness, and a modulation between clarity and obscurity) discussed in

190   Kris L. Hardin

Chapters 3 through 6. I have argued that such patterns can be seen as the mechanisms that link domains of production or experience, that evaluation plays a major role in the ways that connections are made between domains, and that structural properties are produced through this linking of domains.

Only in the repetition, through action, of these sets of associations and stocks of knowledge are the habits and patterns that manifest structural properties established. What is produced in structuring (the product of action), then, are the traditions, rules and resources, sentiments, habits, and expectations that shape, but do not determine, action. Looking at action in this way leads to a view of structure as a flexible and ever-altering entity that is capable of responding to the contingencies of everyday life.

The relationship between action and structural properties, then, is circular. Action affects the configuration of structural properties (and thus the interpretation of action) and, at the same time, the habits, rules, and resources embedded within structural properties guide action (Giddens 1979). Within this dialectic, change is inevitable. Recognizing the dialectic allows consideration of the role of aesthetics in the production of structural properties, the production of action, and the process of change. This is similar to Karp and Maynard's description of Evans-Pritchard's use of agency in *The Nuer*. They write that "through evaluation . . . agents reproduce their structure in action. As value terms are invoked they are altered, 'manipulated,' to form an unintended system that exhibits constancy of form over time" (Karp and Maynard 1983:487). In other words, it is through evaluation, and especially through the changing factors that play into the evaluation of a specific act or setting, that it is possible to see the ways in which social and cultural norms shift over time as norms produce action and as action, in turn, produces norms.

While aesthetic judgments often reflect the habits embedded within accepted, dominant, or even hegemonic arrangements of structural properties, they can also provide a window into alternative arrangements of paradigmatic forms in unique and important ways. See, for example, Hebdige (1979) on resistance and styles of dress and Willis (1977) on the perceptions and values of working class adolescents in Britain. It is often in the contest between differing aesthetic judgments (or different perceptions of paradigmatic associations) that regimes of interpretation change or, alternatively, are further solidified. To understand such changes, three dimensions of social life must be explored. First are the Kono concepts of power and authority and how they are attained. Especially important here are the ways in which individuals ensure that their interpretations of action will count, in other words, that their interpretations will be reproduced over time.[1] Second are the variations in the perception of paradigmatic forms and the changing interests of individuals in perception. Third are the specific ways in which various domains change in relation to each other. Various domains of life will change at different rates, and the ways in which one domain penetrates and acts as a metaphor for others shifts over time, meaning that the very paradigmatic associations that produce structural properties will shift as well.[2]

In this chapter, I begin by considering what power and authority are and how people learn to use them. This raises questions about the reproduction of sets of knowledge or paradigmatic forms; it also demonstrates how changes in relations of power or authority might lead to the rearrangement of interpretive paradigms and, in turn, to changes in structural properties.

As I noted in Chapter 3, one of the Kono words for power is *gbaseia*. This refers to an individual's ability to gain access to and control resources, as well as to shape future action. Someone who has *gbaseia* can control the actions of others through an astute use of resources. Those with *gbaseia* tend to serve as patrons, using rice, women, jobs, land, and other resources to tie clients to their political, social, and economic agendas. Patrons are respected but also closely watched by their clients, who are ever wary that they will not receive a fair return for their allegiance. Force tends not to be a feature of patron-client relationships because clients will move to other patrons if force is used to ensure compliance. For most situations, force is the preserve of certain chiefdom officials (e.g., paramount chiefs and court officials) who have the legal authority to back up their threats with the use of police personnel.

Physical strength is also recognized as a kind of power. While it is something to be admired, however, it does not carry with it the possibilities of control or influence over others that *gbaseia* implies.

Power is attained in two related ways. First, individuals can inherit positions of power from male or female relatives. These include, for example, positions of leadership within a family or lineage or being an elder in Sande or Poro. As wage employment becomes more important, positions of power can also be attained through hiring. Teachers and medical personnel hold positions of power within the community because of the resources they control. Holding positions of power, however, is not enough. Individuals must also demonstrate that they have the right and authority to exercise the powers inherent in the social positions they hold. To do this, they must demonstrate the ability to harness knowledge, medicines, witchcraft, and other supernatural means in socially appropriate ways. A chief who is unable to fulfill this second avenue to power will still be chief but he will have very little authority over those under him.

The requirement that power be demonstrated in credible ways ensures that, while inheritance is important, it is not enough to guarantee social position. Status and power relations, then, are dependent upon the judgments of others. Essentially, then, all relations of power are to some degree relations of patronage, and all patrons are required to meet the demands of their clients to maintain their status. In this system, part of a client's allegiance to a patron includes agreeing with and repeating a patron's interpretations of actions and events. Without such support, the patron or leader becomes relatively ineffective. In this way charisma, personal style, the ability to demonstrate certain kinds of knowledge, and other aspects of individual identity are as important as inherited traits in the pursuit of status, power, and the authority that power implies.

It is this aspect of evaluation that is critical for understanding the dialogic relationship between patrons and clients as well as between structure and action. While the dialectic between structure and action is posited as a universal, in fact, how the dialectic operates and the ways in which action may affect structure in particular places depends on the ways people attach meanings to action, what action can mean, and how variations in meanings or actions are reconciled in particular places. Because the possibility of multiple meanings or interpretations of action exists, insights into action and its meaning are integrally related to questions of power and authority, specifically, the ways in which power relationships are used in contexts of evaluation.

Mauss (1979:105) described action as a "system of symbolic assemblages." It is within this "system" that movement becomes infused with the physical, psychological, sociological, and affective associations that become habitual "in the life of the individual and the history of the society" and allow for action to be meaningful (Mauss 1979:120). From this perspective, it is clear that ways of meaning or providing movement with content are as important as the specific movements themselves, that the application of meaning to movement transforms movement into action, and that the way such transformations occur varies between cultures. Here, I am making a distinction between movement or behavior and action. I consider movement to be the full repertoire of movement that is humanly possible, while I take action to be those units of movement that are interpreted as meaningful.

For the Kono specifically, the relationships between action and meaning and between power and the interpretation of action become clearer by understanding how people learn to control action and knowledge of its meanings. As Williams (1982:177) suggests, explanations of movement that fail to take account of a system of associations describe behavior only in an "ethological" sense; they ignore the human capacity of reflexivity and the human potential to categorize and use action. At issue here is not only *what* action means but also the broader question of *how* it means. It is only in this sense that affect and aesthetics can enter into a consideration of action and the capacity for interpretation.[3]

What is necessary, then, is a consideration of action in Kono terms. The degree to which action is emphasized in Kono life has already been discussed in this volume. Proverbs provide further insight into a taxonomy of actions. A *fo kwi na che a che kwi*, which translates "it is not speech, but action" and *Yo fo bwiendo, ni a ma kan, a nyi*, "If what you say comes to pass (if you really do it), it is good" are only two of the many sayings that emphasize actual doing over saying one will do something. While speech is one kind of action, it is less important than actually doing something. This contrasts with other Mande groups, such as the Bamana, who say that an individual is known by his or her speech and go to great lengths to cultivate the art of speech. It is probably worth noting here that the Kono do not have the category of *griot*, specialists in the recitation of genealogies and history, which is found in most other Mande areas. Instead, Kono pay particular attention to what people do and accomplish, and words mean very little unless actions reinforce them. This is partially related to the fact that action is capable of revealing internal or emotional states. As I mentioned in Chapter 4, the Kono body (*gbuo*) is conceived of as a shell that is filled from infancy by learning and experience, and emotions are internalized, actually experienced, through various parts of the body. For example, dancing at an initiation or a government dignitary's visit not only signifies support in ways that words cannot, but it also demonstrates *faa chima* (a cool heart) and the absence of malice. Considering the importance of bodily experience in Kono action, it is not surprising to see the metaphorical use of sensation to refer to understanding and knowledge. Kono will say *E ya min?*, which translates "Have you heard it?" But the same verb, *min*, also refers to knowing, understanding, and drinking. Thus, both information and knowledge are physically encapsulated within the individual's body in much the same way as water, food, witch properties, or emotions are. Knowledge must be taken inside to be known, to be acted upon, or to be useful.

Because knowledge is, in some sense, experiential and embodied in action, it is possible to have widely varying individual perceptions and interpretations of action, in much the same way that different individuals adopt unique or idiosyncratic styles of movement. Such variation has implications for an individual's ability to define or impose meanings on situations or actions or to interpret action in ways that count. In this way, interpretation can, in fact, be seen as one of the resources that powerful Kono individuals control. In order to understand the level at which Kono power and authority, action, and evaluation intersect, it is necessary to examine how appropriate actions are learned.

LEARNING ABOUT ACTION AND AUTHORITY

Learning imbues individuals with culture-specific ways of attaching meaning and affect to movement. Some of the outlines of a Kono framework for interpreting action have already been sketched in previous chapters. Briefly, there is a link between action and knowledge. Personal experience is central to Kono claims to knowledge, as can be seen in the way people talk about events and their knowledge of them. In this way, Kono are reticent to speculate publicly on the distant past since "we were not there, so how could we know what happened." Most Kono are equally reluctant to discuss or describe contemporary events that they did not witness or that they claim not to have experienced themselves, especially if their own version of events differs from accepted interpretations. This applies to knowledge of everyday events (e.g., marital disputes, fights, etc.), as well as to knowledge of witchcraft and the secret phases of both Poro and Sande initiations. Although individuals clearly have a great deal of personal knowledge about both, demonstrating that knowledge in public or in inappropriate ways signals a kind of participation that, in the case of witchcraft, marks one as a witch and, in the case of initiation societies, marks one as an individual who is dangerous and cannot be trusted. Clearly, then, there is a boundary between what an individual knows and what that individual has the authority to say they know in a public context.

Discrepancies between public and private speech relate largely to questions of authority or an individual's claims to have the status to influence thought, opinion, or action. As exemplified in the case of a woman's refusal to comment on a married couple's dispute (see Chapter 6), the authority to speak is something that is weighed very carefully. In this case, the woman began by saying that she did not really know what had happened but that her support for the wife was based on the fact that the wife and her mother had shown her repeated kindnesses. Even though the woman had undoubtedly been told by others exactly what had transpired between the married couple, as a non-native of the town, she had no authority to speak about the events, especially since she was unwilling to condemn the wife's actions as others were doing. Speaking in public, then, has two dimensions—authority and interests—and truth often lies somewhere in between. Only those recognized with the authority to speak in particular situations will be deemed credible and will, in turn, have the power to describe events for others.

Gossip between friends, however, is very different from public pronouncements. Witchcraft, for example, is something that is not normally discussed in public. In private, however, among people of relatively the same age and status, it is discussed, as can be seen in the following case. During my fieldwork in the summer of 1988, I witnessed what can only be described as a tragedy. A woman from Kainkordu purchased what she was told was a chemical for delousing when, in fact, it was a defoliant known as Tricula or Tricinol.[4] When it enters the skin, it attacks the central nervous system. The woman brought the chemical back to town on a Thursday night and on Friday morning she rubbed it into her hair and put on a head tie to allow the chemical to work. She did the same to her daughter's hair and to the hair of five other women and girls in the compound. Then she left for her farm. On the way she felt a burning sensation and stopped at a stream to wash out her hair. That night the woman's daughter went into convulsions and died. By Saturday morning another young girl had died, and the woman's mother was very sick. By Saturday afternoon the mother, too, was dead. The woman and the three others who had used the chemical were terrified that they, too, would die.

On Friday night, after the death of the first girl and before anyone outside the family knew the death was related to the chemical, I spent the evening with a woman my age whom I knew quite well and a young male relative of hers. There were also several others in the room and, of course, our conversation turned to the dead girl and the others who were sick. My friend Mani related the story of a woman in Kainkordu whom she thought to be a witch. She described how the woman was always trying to give food or other things to young children. Mani's theory was that the woman had probably gotten close to the dead girl's family and that they were suffering for it now. The young man then related a dream in which he had been told not to accept favors from this woman or eat food that she had prepared (both indications that the woman was probably a witch). Thus, within the confines of private conversations among relative equals, talk of witchcraft is possible. While rumors of witchcraft are something that can be discussed privately, public talk is akin to accusation, which is rare and which only certain people have the authority to make. In this case, once it became generally known that the deaths were related to the use of the chemical, the talk of witchcraft subsided.

As suggested above, there are times when witchcraft is discussed publicly. In these cases, however, the actors are limited to people with certain kinds of authority. In one of the few public pronouncements of witchcraft that I witnessed, the town chief of Kainkordu and several chiefdom elders asked the town crier, an elderly man who paraded through the town every evening proclaiming the news and upcoming events, to warn the people of Kainkordu that a witch had come into town. As the town crier moved through town, he repeatedly advised parents to keep their children inside that night. He then described the witch as a trader from another region of Sierra Leone, a light-skinned stranger who had entered Kainkordu that day and who was reputed to have eaten children in a nearby town. At the end of the message, the town crier addressed the woman directly, telling her that the town knew of her presence and that it was in her best interests to leave before the following day. Exposed in this way, the woman found she was unable to work in the town, and everyone was relieved to find that she had left by the next morning.

In this case, the town chief and chiefdom elders had the authority to comment publicly on witchcraft because of their status and because failing to do so could have brought real danger to the town. Furthermore, they are already assumed to be delving into witchcraft, further underlining the experiential dimension of knowledge that I have described. Thus, those without the ability to demonstrate such claims to knowledge (such as my friend Mani), also lack the authority to publicly accuse someone of witchcraft.

The connection among knowledge, power, and authority are also apparent in the control that Sande elders maintain over knowledge of childbirth. Most men, unmarried women, and childless women will claim to know nothing about childbirth, saying they cannot understand it when they have not experienced it. Bledsoe (1980; see also Hardin n.d.), in discussing Sande among the Mende, suggests that one way Sande elders maintain power and authority over women in their communities is through their monopoly of knowledge related to reproduction. As women age in areas of West Africa that have Sande, they accumulate more and more knowledge related to illness and reproduction, especially those women who become Sande leaders. This provides them with a degree of power and authority in Kono life that at times rivals that held by all but the most senior men.

The degree of variation in the interpretation of action is somewhat lessened by the process of enculturation as individuals begin to embody culture-specific ranges of movement possibilities in childhood and, at the same time, begin to learn about the capacity for action in demonstrating knowledge and power. In early infancy (and possibly prenatally) perceptions of the movements of others begin to shape a movement template that simultaneously enables and limits the enculturated body's capacities for action. Mauss (1979:102) describes this process as "prestigious imitation":

> The child . . . imitates actions which have succeeded and which he has seen successfully performed by people in whom he has confidence and who have authority over him. The action is imposed from without, from above, even if it is an exclusively biological action, involving his body. The individual borrows the series of movements which constitute it from the action executed in front of him or with him by others.

For the Kono, the possibility of "prestigious imitation" becomes important after a child reaches the age of about eighteen months and is able to walk relatively well. Before this point, there are relatively few expectations for the child. In fact, the child is catered to by both its mother and other family members. If it cries, attempts are made to determine why, to distract it, and to stop the crying. Even slight indications of sickness cause the mother great concern, especially if she has lost other children in infancy. The Kono believe that young children make the choice of staying in this world (*dunuya*) and that they are particularly vulnerable to enticements to leave during the first eighteen months. In fact, the infant mortality rate in this area in the early 1980s was quite high. My estimates were that 50 to 55 percent of children born between 1975 and 1984 died in their first year. An infant's decision to stay in this world is related to the quality of care they are given. It is especially up to a mother, but also to other family members, to persuade the child to stay.

At about eighteen months, when the child's mother is freed from postpartum sexual taboos and pregnancy becomes a possibility again, the child is propelled into a new stage of life. In this stage, the child is expected to begin to learn appropriate behavior, that actions have consequences, and that life is oriented around obligations to others rather than to the pursuit of individual goals. In Chapter 4, I suggested that the system of birth-order naming tempers the expression of Kono individuality and emphasizes allegiance to Kono ideals of appropriate behavior, including compliance to the expectations of others and social obligations in general. Emotional habits instilled in the process of weaning, which begins at about eighteen months, further reinforce this orientation.

Although previously breast-fed on demand, once weaning starts the child is allowed to cry for his or her mother's breast. The infant might be picked up, but the child will be prevented, at least initially, from actually nursing. Other food might be substituted, but only if it is readily available. Cries often turn into screams of frustration and rage, to the amusement of onlookers, but the child is repeatedly thwarted in its attempts to reach its mother's breast. The child is denied the breast anywhere from several minutes to half an hour before finally being allowed to nurse or, in some cases, falling asleep from exhaustion. It was apparent from watching individual mothers that there was no pattern to the length of time they would hold out before allowing the child to nurse (although those just starting the process seemed to allow nursing sooner than those further along).

The length of time it takes to wean a child also varies among women. When a woman realizes she is pregnant, the process is sped up. If pregnancy is not a factor, the child may be allowed to nurse intermittently for another year and a half. Kono women seem to like having a nursing child and are in no real hurry to have the child weaned unless they become pregnant.

The unpredictability of access to the breast limits the child's ability to intuit the patterns that would allow either prediction or control of the situation. In this way the child begins to learn, through denial and unpredictability, that he or she responds to, rather than determines, the actions of others and, by extension, the world-at-large. Essentially, this is the first point at which children are introduced to the fact that, as they mature, they will move through a series of socially constructed categories of personhood, each with its own set of capacities, emotions, and conceptions of self. At this initial threshold, the child learns a lesson that will surface in a variety of contexts and transformations for the remainder of his or her life—that the demonstration of rage (as in crying incessantly) will have little effect on the actions of others and that the child or individual has little ability to control the situations that surround him or her.

Once weaned, young girls and boys begin a period in which they gradually become more involved with household duties and obligations. In what can only be called prestigious imitation, small girls will mimic the actions of their mothers or other female relatives in a make-believe world of household labor—discarded tomato paste tins are appropriated for cooking pots, three small stones become supports for the pot, twigs become firewood, and weeds become potato leaf *plasas* (sauce). As a girl becomes skilled at imitation, she is gradually brought into the adult arena and allowed to help with the real cooking process. Girls receive little verbal instruction, only inclusion or acceptance in the adult arena once the task has been internalized. Young boys are likely to be given household tasks, such as fetching water and splitting wood, and the amount of labor is gradually increased as they mature physically. They spend their free time with male playmates constructing and playing with toys, sometimes fighting, and sometimes trying to follow their fathers on their daily tasks.

At about five or six, though, young boys are expected to begin learning the skills they will use as adult men, and their attachment to their fathers becomes more a part of daily experience. They will be expected to go to the farm to help with the work in any way they can and in any other way to begin imitating male roles.

Along with the embodiment of actual skills through imitation and approximate duplication of movement in the child (or adult) come complexes that include attitudes, psychological predispositions, and emotional responses. These serve as blueprints for both thinking about the world and being in it. Bateson (1972b:159–76), in a discussion of deutero-learning refers to the "habits of mind" or apperceptive habits that are learned along with the mastering of particular skills. In other words, as a skill is learned, the student also incorporates a range of other cultural information that can shape world view, personality, and other factors that channel action. But the physiological process by which specific repertoires of movement either structure personality or become imbued with meaning and affect remain unclear. Bateson and Mead's (1942) groundbreaking research suggested that how children or adults are taught to move or complete specific tasks (in other words, how specific patterns of movement are internalized) is as important as the specific movements or techniques themselves. For example, the lack of emotional climax that Bateson and Mead found typical of Balinese personalities was related to patterns in the treatment of infant's bodies during periods of interaction with others. Action, from its inception, then, begins channeling habits, perception, and psychological predispositions at an unconscious level.

Through prestigious imitation, the body picks up the actions of others as these are encountered on a daily basis. Such imitation and, in fact, most forms of Kono learning are accompanied by almost no verbal instruction. Young girls, for example, are taught to wash clothes in a stream by being badgered or excluded from working until they pick up the task properly. My field notes reveal many instances of this kind of learning, as seen in the following excerpt:

> I went to wash clothes with Finda, the younger wife of a town elder, and two small girls from her compound, Sia who was eight or nine years old and Yai who was thirteen years old. At one point Finda started yelling at Sia to be more careful with the clothes. Sia started crying and Finda told her to leave. I asked what was wrong and Finda said Sia did not know how to knock clothes.[5] She repeatedly told Sia to go back to town, but Sia continued to cry and work, refusing to leave. Yai just continued working through all this, not saying anything. Eventually, Finda stopped telling Sia to go, and Sia stayed in the stream knocking clothes.

At no point in the morning's work was Sia told what she was doing wrong or how she might improve her technique. Instead, she was expected to imitate the actions of those whose techniques were correct. In this case Finda, as the only adult present (besides myself), had the authority to reprimand the two younger girls. At the same time, however, she was learning authority herself. She pushed Sia only far enough to upset her but not far enough to drive her away from the work party, which would have meant more work for Yai and herself.

A corollary of this is that an individual with authority, by not explicitly defining the criteria that make up good or bad action, is able to maintain authority more readily. Again, this brings up the question of obscurity in relationship to evaluation and judgment and suggests that evaluation is to some degree subjective and related to the interests of the person making the judgment.

For Kono adults, learning new skills also occurs through action and the conscious approximation of body movements, with very little verbal instruction. During my fieldwork I "studied" cloth production, pottery production, dance, agricultural production, and household labor by finding people willing to teach them to me. In order to learn to spin, I approached a woman with the appropriate small gifts and asked if she would help me learn. She agreed, and we spent many afternoons sitting on her veranda spinning, much to the amusement of her neighbors. My teacher would spin for a while and then hand me the spindle, thread, and other tools. As I fumbled with them, the woman would laugh and then grab the spindle back saying "No, no, like this." She then proceeded with the task, handing everything back to me periodically. Although I felt my skills were improving, she continued to grab the tools from me, and I became more and more frustrated. I was unable to see any real difference between what she was doing and what I was doing. What I really wanted from her was a verbal explanation of what I was doing wrong in specific terms. For example, I expected her to tell me that, if I held the spindle lower, the thread would be a finer texture, or that the thread was breaking because I was not pulling on the bobbin evenly. These are the kinds of statements I would have been able to translate into action. No matter how I tried, however, I could not elicit this kind of instruction. My attempts to do so merely increased the level of mirth and intensified her determination that I just was not serious about learning.

This kind of instruction can be related to discussions of identity and authority. By becoming an apprentice I gave my teacher the right to criticize me publicly. Apprentices tend to remain under their teacher's authority for as long as the teacher lives. This is especially the case for students who live in the same community as their instructors. I witnessed this extended relationship between a very elderly potter and her student. Even though the student had been working with the older woman for ten years or more (and was almost as old as her teacher), people still came to the older woman to arrange for their pots. The younger woman did not take commissions on her own and, instead, still acted as the older woman's assistant, even though she was a competent craftsperson in her own right. It was not until the older woman died that she emerged as an independent producer.

Although I never became an expert spinner, I did begin to recognize the same emphasis on action (or the experiential) and nonverbal instruction in a wide range of Kono teaching practices. Afraid that as an outsider I might be taught in a different way than a Kono individual, I made it a point to observe other adults being taught and found the same reliance on nonverbal, experiential techniques. Patterns of teaching in agricultural work, spinning, household labor, and most other skills rely on the body's ability to incorporate the actions of others over time. Although I was not involved with the instruction periods of Poro or Sande, it is my impression that the experiential mode is important in these organizations as well. While stories, proverbs, and songs are important tools in teaching adult roles, so is action. For example, when the new initiates are taken from the Sande bush to the waterside to wash or to work on a Sande elder's farm, each girl walks through town holding a raffia mat around her. Modesty is not only talked about but it is also enforced in action.[6] Likewise, there is a period of time after initiation but before their final release from the bush that Kono Sande initiates are allowed to move through town during the day without their raffia covers. If they are greeted by a man or woman who is not a member of Sande, however, they are not allowed to shake hands (the normal greeting) with them nor have any bodily contact. This exemplifies the way in which the distinctions between members and nonmembers are instilled, but such distinctions are carried out in experiential, not verbal, terms. In fact, the strength of Sande may stem from such embodied experiences. It is not enough to define members as a group, but it is similarity of experience that binds members together in the lifelong associations that Sande provides. While it is impossible for me to compare the extent to which verbal or experiential techniques are employed in Poro or Sande instruction, these examples make it clear that the experiential is an important dimension of Sande instruction.[7] It is only through doing, then, that one learns. Verbal instruction can not be substituted for this process of imitation.

By the time children learn how to learn they also begin learning how to manage their emotions and to take responsibility for their emotional outbursts, as can be seen from another example drawn from observations of the girls Sia and Yai. Neither of these girls had been initiated into Sande yet. The mother of Yai, the older of the two girls, who lived in Koidu, had sent her daughter to the countryside to recuperate from a long illness. She was very thin, and when I first met her I assumed she was only eight or nine, rather than thirteen years old. The second girl was also being fostered in the household. One day when a group of women from the household went to find firewood, the girls came with us. Before leaving town they began arguing about something, and Yai cursed the other girl's mother. When the eldest wife in the household overheard the curse, she stopped the entire work party. She called to the two girls and told her younger co-wife to take them to the path alongside her house to let them fight. Both girls were about the same height, but Yai was thinner and weaker. Within a few seconds the younger girl had knocked Yai down a small slope where she skinned her knee. She got up and started crying. The co-wife pulled her up the slope and put her face to face with the other girl and the fighting started over. Although this time the struggle continued for a longer time, it was obvious the younger girl was the stronger of the two. After thirty seconds, the elder wife separated them and the fight was over. The rest of the work party stood around the two girls laughing, mostly at Yai for her foolishness. The laughter contrasted markedly with the rage, frustration, and seriousness apparent on the faces of the two girls. When the elder wife separated the girls, she was also laughing. Once the disagreement was settled, obviously in the younger girl's favor, the argument was over, and any other bickering between the girls that day was quickly stopped by the adults.

The older girl had been taught, in a public forum, that her emotional outbursts were not only inappropriate but, more importantly, that they were also hollow because she lacked the strength to back up her threats. As a result, her actions had been ridiculed. Individuals without the ability to translate speech into action are ridiculed. Speech itself, then, is not a causative; it requires individual action to make it meaningful. It is not what you say you can do but what you actually do that matters.[8]

Even among Kono children of this age, then, emotions such as anger are to be controlled and internalized, and actions (in this case a fight) are the final arbitrators in many kinds of decisions. A basic part of growing up is learning to control emotions, learning the importance of action, and learning what actions one can credibly make.

While young girls learn about capacity and control from older women, young boys learn similar lessons from their relatives and peers. During the full moons of the dry season in Kainkordu most young men in town can be found in the streets practicing fighting, imagining what their lives would have been like in warrior times, and matching themselves against their cohorts. The hierarchies that encircle Kono males for most of their lives are begun in the actions surrounding these battles and deeds.

The few children who are unable to demonstrate such capacities as emotional control and the correct relationship between speech and action tend to become the targets of directed abuse designed to channel their actions along appropriate lines as they near the age of initiation. These children are often placed in situations where they must act out the patterns that they have failed to learn through "prestigious imitation." In the case of the girls' fight, this meant placing the misbehaving girl in a situation that she could control only by adopting appropriate adult behavior (essentially ignoring a situation she did not have the power to change). With practice, the girl hopefully will no longer have to be controlled by adults but will adopt appropriate behavior on her own. A similar lesson can be seen in the following case.

Tamba was a nine-year-old boy, somewhat small for his age, and obviously unable to control his emotions. The slightest reprimand would bring tears to his eyes and sometimes his whimpering would continue for some time. As the time approached for him to be initiated into Poro and this behavior continued, his parents became more concerned. Criticism of the boy's emotional outbursts intensified, beginning with verbal commands to stop crying: *A to!* "Stop it!" and *I da a ton!* "Shut your mouth!" If he did not stop, his mother would begin slapping his legs. She would continue to do this until Tamba was no longer crying audibly (even though the tears might still be running down his face). When the punishment continued for too long or became too harsh, another relative, usually the boy's grandmother or the mother's sister, would step in to stop it. By the time I left the field in 1984, the boy had still not succeeded in controlling his behavior to his parent's satisfaction.

At the time, I found this sequence of events inexplicable. With distance, it has become apparent that the mother's actions were directed at getting her son to internalize his emotions. The slaps and verbal jibes always stopped when the boy was no longer making noise. The increasing intensity with which Tamba was punished was directly related to his nearing the age of initiation. In his parent's eyes, he had yet to demonstrate the maturity expected of a boy about to be initiated. While Poro marks a stage in maturation for all boys, initiation before a boy is able to control his body and emotions will open him to the jibes of Poro elders as well as other initiates in the struggles to establish a hierarchy among initiates that usually lasts for life. Because they did not want their son to become a victim of such pressures, Tamba's parents were working very hard to change his behavior before he entered the bush.

Along with what might be called a prohibition on the expression of emotions, young children learn to express or make public anger, discontent, and other social imbalances in authoritative ways. One way of addressing perceived abuse, and thus resisting it, is inaction or, as I began calling it in my field notes, "awayness."[9]

"Awayness" implies temporary withdrawal from the social sphere or from normal activities, and it usually results in a renegotiation of the allocation of power within a particular situation. Let me give an example. I was sitting with a group of five or six women and girls who were taking turns at pounding rice. While two pounded, four or five others talked and watched. Mafoo, a wife of the compound headman, approached and yelled across the area for Yai (the same girl who lost the fight) to go out to her garden to cut potato leaf. This meant that Yai would have to leave what had turned into a pleasant and relatively relaxing social occasion to walk through the forest to the woman's garden alone, a distance of about half a mile. As an older woman from Yai's compound, Mafoo had every right to ask Yai to do errands for her. However, she rarely gave Yai food when she cooked and she constantly berated her. For these reasons, Yai did not really like her.

Yai did not move for several minutes and Mafoo yelled again. At that point Yai turned on the stone she was sitting on, showing only her profile, and she appeared to be gazing off into the distance. Mafoo yelled several times, still with no apparent response from Yai. Eventually Yai got up, went into the house, and returned with a pan. At that point, she seated herself on our side of the pounding area, about three feet from Mafoo. Yai still refused to look at her or acknowledge that she had been asked to do something, and Mafoo continued to yell at her to go to the garden, calling her lazy.

Finally, Mafoo realized that Yai was not going to comply with her demand. She renegotiated the terms of her request and told Yai that the two of them would go to the garden together. Still, there was no response from Yai, and Mafoo's yelling and verbal abuse continued. About twenty-five minutes later, Yai got up, looked at Mafoo, and, without saying anything, set off towards the garden, and Mafoo followed.

"Awayness," then, constitutes one form of resistance in Kono life. People call it into play not only to avoid following rules but also to notify others that, perhaps, they too are no longer playing according to the rules. A child who feels taken advantage of, a wife whose husband is not meeting his obligations to her family, a client whose patron is no longer meeting obligations or expectations are all likely to use "awayness" or withdrawal to extricate themselves from a situation or to give notice that they feel they are being abused.

Part of socialization for the Kono, then, implies learning how to act appropriately in specific situations and how to accurately gauge one's authority and social position relative to others. Learning also implies how to physically incorporate categories of emotion that underlie social interaction, how to use action to demonstrate particular capacities and knowledge, and how to resist the demands of those more powerful in acceptable ways.

MANAGING AUTHORITY, POWER, AND ACTION

Understanding what people have to learn about action also implies developing the ability to interpret the capacities of others through their actions. In the Kono world, this translates into, for example, designating specific individuals as knowledgeable or powerful because of their actions, the possibility of manipulating action to demonstrate knowledge, and using action to demonstrate changes in social status and capacity. Much of Kono social life, in fact, could be described as a kind of theater. Individuals are constantly negotiating or playing with relative authority and status. In a status system that is systematically unequal but in which the inequality is not based solely on heredity and, thus, is not fixed, there is the continual possibility of bettering one's position vis-a-vis others. As individuals learn new skills or about new medicines or notice that their neighbor's abilities seem to be fading slightly, there is someone always ready to better their own position by challenging anyone who is perceived to be weaker. This adds much of the joy and excitement to situations of chaos or disruption, such as that described in Chapter 6 as *songo songwe*. It also adds much of the interest to other social events, as individuals watch the actions of others for signs of new weaknesses or strengths and adjust their actions accordingly.

The direct relationship between action and knowledge allows particular actions to be interpreted to mean knowledge about particular things. Thus, individuals may have rights to specific actions, such as buying particular medicines or skills. Performing such actions without having the right to do so condemns the individual to certain failure. During part of my apprenticeship to an indigo dyer, I employed an interpreter. I paid the traditional fee for the knowledge of dyeing for myself but was not required to do so for my male interpreter (dyers are always women). While translating for me, my assistant also learned much of the herbal knowledge and methods surrounding the dye process. One day in jest I said that, if he found no job after I left the field, he would be able to work dyeing thread. He responded immediately, saying that would be impossible. When I asked why, he did not say that dyeing was a woman's task, as I had expected him to. Instead, he replied that, because he had not paid the fees to learn the skill, he had no right to practice it, and if he did, the thread would never hold color properly. While individuals can use action to demonstrate particular capacities, the rampant use of demonstration is held in check by a belief that they will fail if they do not have the specific rights to do so or the powers to fulfill the demonstrations.

While fear of failure is a powerful check on illegitimate claims to knowledge, the use of action as an indicator of knowledge and capacity suggests the kinds of persons who are likely to advance in Kono social life. These are the individuals who are willing to take chances, to question authority publicly, and to use the constraints that hamper most individuals to make themselves even more powerful. One such case, as described in Chapter 4, is the chiefdom elder who adopted the name "Temne" to counter what was intended to be a slur. By daring to publicly challenge the slur, he ensured the continuation of his control over others.

These actions call to mind a second implication of the relationship between action and knowledge. This is the manipulation of action in order to demonstrate or make claims to particular kinds of knowledge. Thus, particular actions can be interpreted as indicative of specific internal states, powers, or rights. As was discussed in Chapter 4, Kono individuals (and other Mande peoples) acquire legitimate status only through action and by placing themselves in the public eye (Arnoldi 1986). The control on overt claims to power is that such claims open the individual to an onslaught of tests ranging from public commentary to dangerous encounters with supernatural powers. Singers, politicians, Poro and Sande elders, and other public figures attain their positions through the intricate manipulation of such factors as personal inheritance and identity, resources they are able to distribute to clients, control of supernatural powers, and the ability to withstand challenges. The venue for these activities is always public. This is in direct contrast to illegitimate claims to power, which are established through actions, such as witchcraft, that are orchestrated outside of the public eye.

Before filling an important social role, individuals must publicly demonstrate their power, and thus their right, to do so. Demonstrations of power rely on the control of a variety of resources, both material and supernatural. The ability to perform in this way implies turning to or being influenced by supernatural forces, which provide the abilities needed for positions of leadership. Just as warriors of the past were known to have achieved their positions through the use of supernatural power, it is assumed that today's big men use supernatural means as well. Knowledge of the supernatural, power, and individual intention, then, are linked. In short, the patron must distinguish himself or herself as an individual. This is often a dangerous undertaking that requires the ability to meet tests from both human and supernatural forces and, thus, demonstrates one's control of and superiority over them.

The dividing point between legitimate and illegitimate power, however, is ambiguous. Legitimate power is public and thus kept in check by the actions of others, while illegitimate power is secret, dangerous, and out-of-public control. The extent to which public individuals also delve into the secret aspects of power, however, is clouded. Such ambiguity makes it possible for a public figure to fall from grace in a relatively short time if accused of witchcraft and if the accusation is deemed creditable.

The claims, challenges, and tests of power and knowledge can be seen in the actions of a government official who visited the eastern Kono area in order to gain support for a political campaign. While he was not Kono, he had been born in the Kono area, was fluent in Kono, prided himself on his knowledge of Kono culture, and had several Kono advisers. However, he had spent much of his young adult life outside Sierra Leone and had been educated primarily in European schools. Upon his return to Sierra Leone, he had become involved in government work and was interested both in preserving traditions and in using those traditions to identify and meet the needs of the eastern Kono area. He was very aware that, because he was relatively young and had spent years away from the area, he was not trusted by conservative forces within the community. People assumed he had little knowledge of what they call "country ways," the traditions that are defined as the guiding force of much of Kono action. Anyone without this knowledge is presumed to have little power since, for most rural Kono, power is attained through heredity and control over medicines and other supernatural forces that have been handed down at least since warrior times. People also suspected that the man would bring radical ideas and upsetting changes because of his foreign schooling. In a rural community such changes are perceived as a threat to the existing power base. Aware of these problems, the official put a great deal of effort into managing locally recognizable idioms to demonstrate his knowledge of local customs, his right to manipulate the knowledge people associate with power, and, consequently, his ability to command power and authority. Although he did this in a number of arenas, the analysis presented here focuses on dress.

Usually when officials visited, they dressed in trousers and European shirts or polyester "safari suits" (trousers and matching short-sleeved shirts modelled originally after colonial "safari" shirts). This particular official arrived in town for a market-day political rally dressed in trousers and a kola-dyed brown country cloth shirt. When I commented on this clothing, several people told me with satisfaction that this was a warrior shirt and that the visitor must, indeed, be a powerful man.[10] It is important to point out here that these speakers were also supporters of the man.

Later I discovered that warrior shirts themselves are imbued with power and are said to be able to protect the wearer from bullets, witch spells, or other kinds of harm. Often the shirts have protective amulets hidden in them, or the fabric itself may provide a protective skin that makes the wearer impervious to bullets, poisons, or other dangerous elements. Essentially, the shirts demonstrate power in visual terms. It is extremely dangerous for someone to wear them if they lack the ability to activate the powers of the shirt.

Among the Kono, the demonstration of power implies challenges. This is the case whether the context is one in which a little girl curses another one or one in which a politician attempts to challenge the power base of a community. Antisocial forces within the community, either human or supernatural, interpret or quantify the power displayed by the shirt, and then they challenge the wearer to display his powers by counteracting their spells.

Obviously, individuals become easy prey if they are caught in one of these shirts without having the degree of power it attributes to them. In a sense, men who wear these shirts take part in a game of visual dares. To declare oneself to be powerful is to open oneself up to challenges. The uncertainty of knowing who is in the audience, in human or supernatural terms, increases the stakes. For the Kono, knowledge and claims to power can only be demonstrated through action, sometimes in deadly contests with the supernatural.[11]

Claims to power and the authority power implies are validated only if performances are deemed authentic by an audience. Authenticity is, to a large degree, a question of behavioral style and the ability to demonstrate one's right to behave in a certain way. As in other kinds of decisions, such evaluations are always filtered through the viewer's allegiance and interests, and, together, style and allegiance identify the winners of what are sometimes very subtle contestations. The importance of behavioral style brings us back to the pairing of clarity versus obscurity. It is clear that what is ambiguous is often interpreted through an individual's interests. Thus, if an individual who has been challenged should sicken or die or if someone in his family should die, those in disagreement with the challenged individual will attribute the illness or death to weakness. Those without such interests will assume the connection to be coincidence. Although I will discuss allegiance and interests and their effect on evaluation in the next chapter, the important point here is that power or the authority to act is derived from the support of others.

A third implication of the relationship between knowledge, action, and power in the Kono world is related to the use of changes in bodily practice to demonstrate changes in status and capacity. In such demonstrations, the emphasis is once again on the experiential by linking knowing and doing in physical terms. For example, treating the bodily shell in certain ways can signify entry into new social categories, as can be seen in the ceremonies preceding a boy's initiation into Poro. The initial stages provide public demonstrations of changes in status. They also provide models for future behavior and legitimate the newly adopted behavior patterns.

Before Poro initiates (usually between the ages of seven and twelve) are actually taken into seclusion, they are "danced" in procession to the town controlling the Poro bush. At one point during the hours of dancing and feasting, the boys' mothers are led a short way from the town and are seated in a line along the path leading to the Poro bush. Once the women have arranged themselves across the path in the typical straight-legged, straight-backed sitting position of women, their sons are brought down the path—a few at a time—by a Poro elder. As the boys pass by, each woman grabs her own son. To the boy's surprise (he knows nothing of what will happen to him once he leaves the town) and the amusement of the other women, the mother pulls the son onto her lap and offers him her breast, as if he were still nursing. For a few seconds, the body positions of mother and son are once again identical to those of mother and nursing infant. Then, a Poro member grabs the boy, raises him to his feet, and tells him to drop the coins he has been holding in his hands into his mother's lap. The boys are then pulled by their Poro brothers further into the bush, away from their mothers, the town, and their childhood. They will not return until they have been reborn as young men.

This performance is the beginning of a boy's recognition of the reciprocity inherent in adult relationships, as discussed in Chapter 3. It is also an indication that he now has the right, or obligation, to behave towards his mother in this way.

It is significant that such changes in status, which are essentially changes in capacity and in the kinds of knowledge and authority the individual is allowed access to, are played out in experiential terms. The boys physically experience the change in status from infant to young adult. This example strengthens the point I am making about the importance of the relationship between action and knowledge and the power or authority that particular kinds of knowledge bestow. The fact that such status changes are carried out in physical terms suggests that action and its interpretation defines Kono categories of persons, as well as the right to "perform" adult status. That sons and mothers are involved in this part of the ritual makes each a witness to and, thus, accomplice in the reorienting of their relationship; a son can no longer demand freely, and a mother is no longer expected to give without return.

This ritual also marks changes in power relations between mother and son. A son can no longer expect the unconditional support of his mother. Instead, he will be required to demonstrate his affiliation to her in new ways, much as a client uses goods and deeds to demonstrate his affiliation to a patron. The son's change in status, then, is also a change for his mother, and the ritual provides the models for both partners in the new relationship.

CONCLUSIONS

In the Kono world, individuals attain power or authority through the demonstration of power and knowledge, which often entails both control of supernatural forces and effective demonstration of that control. As small children, Kono individuals begin to learn that authority is socially sanctioned. Children also learn about the importance of action as a way of demonstrating authority and the ways to resist what they perceive to be unjustly applied authority. As they mature, Kono children learn how to use action to demonstrate capacity and knowledge and how to compare their own capacity for socially sanctioned authority with the capacities of those around them.

As adults, those capable of demonstrating power, authority, knowledge, and control of the supernatural forces this implies are likely to be able to attract followers and clients, people who are willing to trade allegiance for the prestige and resources likely to drift their way as a result of being attached to a powerful person. While the most powerful men are usually lineage heads and the most powerful women are Sande elders, powerful individuals may also establish themselves outside lineage hierarchies as traders or as other individuals who have access to alternative resources. A good example is the trader described in Chapter 4 who was able to rise in the political hierarchy because of the resources he acquired in trading. Critical here is the demonstration of power. When a powerful individual's actions are no longer deemed credible, clients and supporters disappear. As a result, a singer, a chief, a husband, or a lineage elder, for example, find themselves not only without followers but also without the capacity to have their actions count in ways that construct social and cultural frameworks. The singer returns to the normal life of a wife, but with a future often marred by alcoholism, sickness, and a degree of anomie. She no longer has the power or authority to criticize, and thereby alter the actions of others. When a chief loses power, he finds himself unable to influence the elders who were once under his control. When a husband loses his power, he finds himself unable to control his wives, who disappear into the houses of other men or engage in thievery to support themselves, and often he finds himself rumored to be impotent. A lineage elder finds himself labelled as old, unable to guide the lineage wisely, and possibly a witch. Often he will see his son or younger brother take over the role of lineage advisor and patron (see Chapter 3).

Such falls from power are often accompanied by rumors of witchcraft. While everyone expects powerful individuals to delve into supernatural powers, it is only when those powers begin fading that rumors of witchcraft emerge. Here, again, action and power and, more importantly, people's judgments of the actions of others define categories of persons and an individual's place within those categories. In short, it is judgment that provides a degree of clarity in the relatively obscure relations of power and authority that are continually in flux and open for interpretation. Part of this flux stems from the fact that heredity alone is not enough to ensure attaining power and authority but that these aspects of social life also rely on questions of charisma, personal style, and the ability to demonstrate power, authority, and knowledge in credible ways. Power and authority, then, are social achievements that are inherently the result of the judgments of others. This raises questions of interests, aesthetics, and how people evaluate—issues that will be discussed in the next chapter.

This also raises questions about change. As new individuals rise to positions of power and authority, new interpretive frameworks emerge in ways that have the potential to reshape perceptions of the relationships among domains of production and experience. These changes also have the potential to reshape the emergence of structural properties and, as a result, the ways in which structural properties will affect action in the future.

8

AESTHETICS AND CONTESTATION

Reproducing and Resorting Paradigms

In the previous chapter, I explored the issues of power and authority and the ways in which people learn to use them. The emphasis was on examining the constructive aspects of power and authority or the ways in which individuals work to have their interpretation of events accepted by others. In this chapter, I carry this discussion a step further and consider how variations in the perception of paradigmatic forms and the changing interests of individuals affect their interpretation of events, aesthetic judgments, and, in turn, the instantiation of structural properties.

As discussed in previous chapters, social structure exists in varying forms, configurations, or arrangements of structural properties at particular points in time (Giddens 1979:64). The particular arrangements at any point in time affect the interpretation of events and actions. Sahlins (1981) has described these configurations as relations of conjunction between structure and action that change from one historical moment to the next. These conjunctions include action itself, as well as the habitual montage of associations that forms the stocks of knowledge or conceptual frameworks that provide action with meaning in both the actor's and interpreter's mind. For the Kono, these patterns include, but are in no way limited to, the idioms of containment and the marking of boundaries, exchange, and contrasts between the rules of descent and the sentiments attached to matrifilial ties. When perceived across domains of experience, such idioms work to produce such structural properties as complementarity, particular ways of pairing clarity and obscurity, and the importance of action. Thus, idioms are both the behavioral manifestations of organizing principles or structural properties and the means by which particular arrangements of structural properties emerge.[1] It is impossible to divorce the idiomatic forms from the associations underlying them, as action only becomes visible for interpretation through such associations. As noted in Chapter 7, in the process of identifying and interpreting action, particular configurations of idioms and their underlying principles gain strength as they are repeated. Essentially such patterns become increasingly valid with practice and eventually they become models for shaping future actions and interpretations in the form of structural properties.

The search for redundancy, analogy, and resonance that stimulates the emergence of idiomatic forms is primarily a problem of perception; thus, it is a process rooted in individual perceptions and agency. While shared identity or culture goes a long way towards schooling similar perceptions, inevitable differences in perception do emerge, most noticeably along the boundaries of persons that share similar experiences and interests, for example, class, gender, and age.

All societies have ways of drawing agents into cultural norms, essentially rounding off the corners of individual or subcultural identity and interests and making it possible for both individuals and various groups to work and live together. As is apparent from the Kono material, notions of personhood and individual capacity, early infant learning, and the tightly interwoven connections between actions, knowledge, and judgment are only some of the means by which individual perceptions are channelled along lines of similitude. Even so, not all individuals who share aspects of identity or culture perceive in identical ways, thus providing the possibility of a range of different interpretations of action. While social science has tended to talk about the shared aspects of perception in terms of norms that enable communication, shared knowledge, and coordination of activities among individuals, in fact what are discussed as norms are merely approximations rather than identically held truths.

D'Azevedo (1958:708) implied that differences in perception are important in aesthetic evaluation when he wrote that aesthetic effect emerges from "the correspondences perceived between the qualities of an aesthetic object and their affinities in the subjective experience of the individual." In other words, aesthetic judgment is an individualized pursuit, tied more to past history or subjective experience than to formal qualities. What he suggests, then, is that the very perception of formal qualities is tied to personal experience, and such differences in perceptions are the basis of contradictory aesthetic judgments. In another example of differences in perception, Schneider (1971) notes that Pakot men and women appreciate in different ways, and that these dissimilarities have to do with differences in life experiences.

There are several ways in which variations in perception can lead to variations in the interpretation of action. First, actors abstract relevant or noticeable phenomena from the range of possibilities surrounding them. Thus, particular movements are interpreted as meaningful—a smile, a frown, a hand gesture, a style of walking—while other movements remain entirely unnoticed. Second, once movement sequences are perceived and thus abstracted for interpretation, the actor also has choices as to how he or she will interpret what is seen, felt, or heard.

At each level (abstraction or interpretation), differences between individuals can arise from several sources. First and chief among these is the way individual experiences channel perception and interpretation in unique ways. For example, such qualities as genius or madness channel lived experiences in ways that can lead to radically differing perceptions. Training for particular kinds of skills also schools perceptions in specific ways. Photographers, psychiatrists, biologists, and musicians, for example, are likely to notice different aspects of the same interchange and, thus, interpret it in different ways. The differences related to training or occupation often extend into multiple domains of life. Baxandall (1972) demonstrates this particularly well in a discussion of changes in Renaissance painting styles as merchants became major patrons of the arts. The merchant class brought new skills and expectations, such as the ability to gauge volume, to the interpretation of Renaissance painting. These new interests dramatically altered previously favored styles.

Second, physiological (including biochemical) variations have been shown to effect personality, perception, and other ways of interpreting the world. Schizophrenia is an extreme example of how physiological conditions can affect the perception of events. Less extreme conditions such as failing eyesight and fluctuations in blood sugar levels have all been shown to affect sensory perception.

A third way has to do with the ways in which an individual's goals and predispositions can be inextricably entwined with the perception and interpretation of events. What this means for the interpretation of events in general is that, if an individual has an interest in perceiving events in a particular way, he or she will tend to do so, regardless of the validity of alternative explanations.

All three sources of difference produce contradictions in the interpretation or evaluation of events. Settling contradictions, essentially deciding whose interpretation is correct, has implications both for questions of power and status and for the very reproduction of social forms. As individuals relate one domain to another and evaluate which paradigmatic configurations are better or more appropriate, both the experiences at hand and the models for conceptualizing future action are reshaped.

To examine the changing shape of structural properties, then, it is important to arrive at a way of looking at the integration and coordination of multiple subjectivities in ways that produce paradigms or hegemonies of interpretation at particular points in time. It is also important to find a way of looking at how interpretations are contested and managed and how shifts occur in paradigmatic formations when alternate paradigms come to the fore. Essentially, this implies what Giddens (1979) would call a "theory of action." He (1979:49) suggests this must include ". . . a theory of the human agent, or of the subject; an account of the conditions and consequences of action; and an interpretation of 'structure' as somehow embroiled in both those conditions and consequences."

In the following section, I discuss each element in turn in order to get at the ways in which Kono action, in the form of aesthetic judgment, mediates between action and structure and, thus, facilitates structural change.

THE POLITICS OF SUBJECTIVE EXPERIENCE

Bourdieu discusses the problem of variation in terms of the habitus. Borrowing from Mauss (1979) and others (Bourdieu 1990), Bourdieu (1977:86) defines habitus as:

> . . . a subjective but not individual system of internalized structures, schemes of perception, conception, and action common to all members of the same group or class and constituting the precondition for all objectification and apperception; and the objective coordination of practices and the sharing of a world view could be founded on the perfect impersonality and interchangeability of singular practices and views.

Bourdieu (1977) goes on to write that individual systems of dispositions or personal style should be seen as structural variants of the same habitus, providing that the actors fall within the same class or social group. He sees the habitus as the mechanism that allows for mutual understanding by those within the same social group and for similar interpretations of the actions of those outside the group. In Bourdieu's terms, habitus is constituted by a pool of resources, even interpretive skills, which all individuals of the same class or group share, resources that are separate from, and in addition to, the peculiar or idiosyncratic experiences of individual lives.

In practical terms, however, applying the concept of habitus, as it is construed by Bourdieu, is problematic. From my own work it is apparent that interpretations of action do tend to vary along the lines of age, sex, occupation, personal history, perceptual skills, and individual interests. Essentially, however, Bourdieu's perspective locks people into social positions in ways that, while generally may be the case, cannot explain variation or the power and constructive potential that variation may provide. There are, for example, points at which affiliations to perspectives or perceptions based on age or gender may collide. In such cases, individuals are forced to choose between what are usually conflicting actions. A case in point are the Kono men whose ties to their lineage and its interests outweighed their ties to other men in the dispute between women and men during the Sande initiation dance described in Chapter 6. Other cases of such conflicts are provided in Willis's (1977) description of working class adolescents who manage to escape both the obstructions to upward mobility embedded within working class values and the upper class capacities for exclusion as they rise in Britain's social hierarchy.

I would argue that Bourdieu's view of the solidity and essential solidarity provided by the habitus neglects the conflicts and variations that occur in everyday life. While his use of habitus assumes that the variations in individuals' interpretations of action are insignificant, I suggest that, in fact, they are potentially very powerful and must be taken into account.[2] In other words, reactions to events are not constant across all members of the same class or social group at all times. In fact, it is quite possible that such alignments are constantly being negotiated, a possibility that Bourdieu's position makes it impossible to explore.

A review of the contested forms already described in this ethnography further highlights the deficiencies of Bourdieu's approach. In the case of the singer whose following disappeared, a particular social formation that feeds on consensus and concerted action won over several other possibilities (see Chapter 5). One alternative might have been an alignment of men as opposed to women, in which case the male participants would have continued to follow the singer while the female participants might have drifted away. Similarly, in the discussion of an argument during the dances prior to Sande initiation, it was clear that the individual who finally settled the disagreement chose to side with his family rather than his own Poro mates (see Chapter 6). Both of these cases suggest that affiliations rarely hold under all circumstances and that individuals have a great deal of leeway as to which allegiances, schemes of perception and conception, and consequent actions they choose to uphold at any particular point in time. My point here is that individual opinion is not constrained by single-stranded sets of affiliations but, instead, results from the manipulation and coordination of affiliations and interests in varying and complex ways.

A more accurate depiction of habitus, then, is that individuals incorporate, to varying degrees, the conceptual and behavioral habits of those with whom they share a common background or affiliations; it must be accepted that variations in individual experience and in personal interests can affect schemes of perception and action. While Bourdieu sees everyone of the same group or class sharing in the same set of possibilities, habitus is more accurately depicted as a universe filled with people whose interpretations of experience can be represented as partially overlapping. When situations change, so do the configurations of the overlap, depending on the facet of experience being selected for or foregrounded at any particular time. Individuals of the same sex, age, occupation, etc. are likely to share similar perspectives and views because they are likely to have common histories, habits, and experiences. But such coherence cannot always be expected, and more individualized patterns must be taken account of. When the analysis becomes more fine-tuned, the elements of contrast become more idiosyncratic and individualized to the point of being related to characteristics of personal psychologies, specific social relationships, or biological states. In short, I suggest that the common denominators that Bourdieu assumes to exist cannot, in practice, be isolated in real life and, if they could be, they would be so general as to be useless. While class, age, or gender may constrain and confine, they do not determine. It is in the possibilities of indeterminancy that fluctuations in interpretation, power, and structure are possible.

Furthermore, the notion of habitus is far more useful to social science if it is considered in more flexible terms, capable of dealing with the changing interests of individual participants, variations in perceptual skills, and other factors. A more flexible definition would make it possible to take into account what Needham (1983) has discussed as changes of aspect or point of view, aspect being defined as the varying connotations and uses of an object of thought. In considering the arrangement of aphorisms, maxims, paradigms, and metaphors and the "flashes of comprehension" that result from these arrangements, he suggests that logical processes, such as particular ways of structuring cause and effect relations, occur within particular arrangements of aspects. In other words, as the arrangement of aspects changes, so, too, will seemingly logical and essential or taken-for-granted understandings of the world. Needham's work implies that the configuration or weighting of interests is constantly in flux and that these configurations at specific points in time affect both the production and interpretation of action, depending on the perception of contexts in time and space.

Forge (1970), likewise, has considered variations in perception and related these variations to the context of events. In one context, particular actions or forms are meaningful. In others, they may have no meaning or have entirely different meanings. Following this orientation, I would suggest that the production and interpretation of action are subject to changes of aspect based on changing individual interests and perceptions of the exigencies of particular situations.

Change of aspect can be shown in a relatively simple example, which becomes more complex as more specific levels of interests and connotations are broached. In asking others about the state of a particular marriage dispute, I was often asked a question in return: "Did the wife go to the farm today?" If my answer was yes, my informants responded that the dispute was over, at least for the time being. At this level of generality, interpretations of the wife's actions are made based on the actions of most other women in the town who are not involved in marriage disputes and personal experience of an economic system that places most husbands and wives in relationships of complementarity. However, there are other levels that can be examined.

One of these is the potential for actors to manipulate the demonstrative features of action. An unhappy wife will use her daily walk to the farm as a public opportunity to display the state of her marriage (she has few public opportunities to make such demonstrations). By walking slowly and disinterestedly, by leaving town later and later each day, or by refusing to go to the farm altogether, she can signal that all is not well in her particular household. Just as the particular ways that perception and knowledge are configured by the wife allows her to express her internal state, similar personal configurations inform the interpreter's definition of the situation. The identification of "disinterest" or reticence in a wife's gait can only be discerned by relating this particular action to a number of contrastive situations. For example, this can be done by contrasting this particular journey to the entire corpus of the woman's past and potential trips to her husband's farm: How does she walk when she is tired? Is she late because there was a household emergency that kept her up late the night before? Is she ill, and how does she walk when she is ill?

Equally important is the relationship of interpreter to actor. It is essential to realize that interpreters of action are also agents and that they have interests in interpreting the meaning of another's actions in specific ways. A jealous co-wife, a sympathetic sister, a mother-in-law, or a potential lover will likely have different interpretations of the same action. Furthermore, whether or not an interpreter's definition of action will be accepted by others depends on his or her position within the community. Thus, definitions can serve as both an indication of, or a means for, solidifying power and authority.

These multiple variables underscore the individual nature of interpretation and suggest that, while the sharing of interpretations across classes of people does occur, the sharings are not identical. In addition to differences in individual interpretations and their effects on perceptions and interpretations of action, there is also a kinesthetic dimension to subjectivity that involves comparisons of how the interpreter of action might behave in certain situations or would behave if he or she filled the social position of, for example, the wife in the discussion above. Until recently, questions of socialization ignored somatic modes of attention or embodiment as potent forces in incorporating individuals within social bodies. Relatively little is known about the role of kinesthesia, for example, in the often subconscious interpretations of movement. Kinesthesia has been defined as a sensory activity that is mediated by the end organs of muscles, tendons, and joints and stimulated by body movement and tension. The result of this sensory activity is mimesis, a copying of action— seeing and then feeling the action performed by others and incorporating it into one's own body.[3]

Jackson (1983) discusses this awareness of others in mimetic rituals in which individuals "play the other" and thus know, or incorporate, the constituent features of the behaviors of categories of others within their own bodies. In his Kuranko examples he suggests that disruptive situations, such as periods surrounding rituals that mark changes in social status, and thus changes in patterns of social interaction, set the stage for recombinations of movement patterns that "allow each person to discover in his or her own personality, a way of producing, out of momentary chaos, something which will contribute to a renewal of the social order" and that allows individuals to "periodically recognize the other in themselves and see themselves in the other" (Jackson 1983:336).

In the mimetic performances during Kuranko initiation rituals, men impersonate women and vice versa. Similar kinds of sex reversals can be found during Kono initiation rituals and funerary rites, when particular characteristics of a deceased man may be mimed by female *nimoti* (the younger sisters of the deceased's spouse). Jackson (1983) discusses the restructuring power of these mimetic performances in conjunction with male/female relationships—men "knowing" women and women "knowing" men and in so doing allowing a degree of prediction and coordination of interests and activities. In terms of aesthetics, this process of mimicking allows a kind of comparison of one's own patterns of action to those of others in such a way that one's own patterns of action are also reaffirmed or, in some cases, reconstituted.

Based on the Kono data, which also includes examples across occupational, age, and status differences, I would suggest this process of mimicking, at varying degrees of consciousness, is much more widespread and, in fact, provides one of the factors that allows understanding among categories of persons and definitions of categories of otherness. Perhaps a few examples of this kind of "knowing" will help here. Young girls perform dances that mimic the actions of Maraka women (another Mande group). The mimicry, however, presents the Maraka as lewd and shameless women who touch their breasts and genitals when they dance. These performances both define otherness and construct appropriate patterns of action for Kono women. In another example, the Kono often recognize or point out strangers by their body movements. "He dances like a Mende" is a phrase that can be used to identify a stranger attending a dance or, conversely, to critique the quality of a Kono man's performance in ways that highlight what Kono behavior is. At the same time, these patterns emphasize experiential knowing rather than verbal description of otherness. One day a group of women and I greeted an elderly woman in her house. We were invited into her room, and at one point the conversation turned to my presence in the community and how difficult it must be to be far from home. The talk then shifted to a series of praises for my being in the community and my behavior. The elderly woman said that I was a good person because I always took time to greet people, and I was willing to spend time with people. She then began comparing me with a European woman who had married into her family and had visited the town a few times. Much to the amusement and approval of the others present the old woman got up from her stool and mimicked the movements of the European woman as she moved through town. She rushed across the room in jerky movements, bounding with each step. She held her head down without turning to either side as she passed. The mime then turned her talents towards me and proceeded to show the group how I moved through the town, using slow movements with head held high and turning from side to side acknowledging the people I passed. All agreed that this, indeed, was the way I moved and that it was appropriate, *a nyi*, as well as surprising for a foreigner.[4]

In other cases of knowing, young boys mimic the singers who perform for initiations into Sande. Male adolescents also mimic the actions of warriors in fights, which helps to establish a kind of pecking order between males, just as wars once established a hierarchy among warriors. Mimesis, then, can tie individuals into a social whole through experience of the other. This playing of the other allows for some degree of prediction and interpretation and, as in the case of the warriors, a reinterpretation of the actions of others, or switching of aspect.

As the Kono examples show, this "trying on" often takes place at ritual occasions, but it also occurs at other times. It is one dimension through which individuals "know" and, thus, evaluate others. At times, it is merely a physiological process within an individual's own body, either consciously or unconsciously. At other times, it is overtly public for all to see and judge. Much of the time, it lies somewhere in between. In some respects, then, even within the multiplicity of a given population there are mechanisms for arriving at the likely meanings of the actions of others and for constructing a universe filled with people whose interpretations of experience can be represented as different but partially overlapping.

The fact that much of this "trying on" is done through body movement again reflects the importance attached to action and its interpretation in the Kono world. Otherness, in the form of madness, is also most apparent through varying styles of movement. Quick or jerky movements, lack of movement, disinterest, and lack of attention to the flow of life are interpreted as signs of madness. Supernatural otherness also is indicated by various transformations of normal human movement. Masked figures associated with Yombo (the masked figure described briefly in Chapter 4) and Poro consistently confuse directionality by disguising front from back with both movement and costume. Komokunde, one of the most frequently described devils of the area, is characterized as having a face and feet which are going in opposite directions. These transformations of ordinary body movements are used to show differences from normal patterns of human movement and to associate these differences with the realm of the supernatural.

The meaning of movement in all these cases comes through juxtaposing normal movement (i.e., "Kono" or one's own style) against other forms of movement and then fitting deviations from the norm into various categories of others. Sarles (1975:32) suggests this process of contrasting is at least partially physiological:

> ... [O]ur bodies are highly attuned to others' bodies ... especially to deviations from "normal" (our own?) states. But perhaps this is the sense in which we know what "abnormal" is, i.e. our own bodies find themselves forced to change or alter their images in ways that we label "uncomfortable" [parentheses in original].

The strings of associations on which abnormal and normal movements are based, however, must be continually reconstituted or reproduced in order for them to remain effective, in order for movement to remain meaningful.

Recognition of the changing nature of habitus, depending on circumstances, also allows an individual's own goals and interests in particular situations to be taken into account. Again, this is clear in the case of the dance event that fell apart (see Chapter 5). As a result of the crowd's decision to abandon the would-be singer, a certain set of paradigmatic forms or structural resources were reproduced. These had to do with complementarity and balance. These principles were reinforced when the crowd refused to adopt the alternative set of idioms proposed by the would-be singer.

A broad interpretation of habitus also allows for consideration of individuals who just can not get behavior quite right, those whose personal histories or quirks keep them from succeeding in a particular society.

These are the individuals who are perceived as slightly out-of-step or out-of-time. Examples of these kinds of individuals can be found in any community. One such man in the eastern Kono area was Sahr. During World War II he had served with the British Army in Burma and other places.[5] Like many of the other Kono men who served, he was given some job training in the army. After he returned to Sierra Leone he had two choices—to look for work outside his hometown or to return home, become a farmer, and perhaps to occasionally practice the engineering skills he had learned in the army. Sahr opted to return home. His readjustment to rural life, however, proved to be difficult. In the army he had risen to a certain level of power and authority over others because of his training as an engineer. Back home, where he was a relatively junior member of a founding patrilineage, he had little status and few resources to trade for a position of power. While in the army, he had learned to define himself through an alternate authority system, one in which status was achieved by virtue of his knowledge and skills, and one that allowed him to escape the relatively low status he was assigned in his home. His perception of the world and of his place in the world had been altered, and he found it very difficult to deny those perceptions once he returned home.

On the other hand, men who had also served with the British but who had more senior positions in the patrilineage (e.g., as senior sons of a lineage elder) had little trouble adjusting to life when they returned home. They moved back into already-established networks and familiar sets of behavioral idioms. They also had at their disposal lineage resources (land, marriage alliances, inheritance, wives and their offspring), which their positions allowed. To some extent, they were able to capitalize on their foreign experience by using it to validate their claims for increased social position and status within their lineages. (This was the case even if they had received no special training or skills while in the army.)

Individuals like Sahr were caught making claims to authority by virtue of their special training, a kind of capital that in the late 1940s was relatively unrecognized. Sahr's training did not provide him with the same respect that formal education would have (as discussed in Chapter 3). At this period in time employment by the government as a clerk or other functionary was the expected outcome of a secondary education. Because Sahr chose not to follow this path and did not have the certificates associated with completing an educational program, many of those around him discounted his accomplishments. Unwilling to define himself as an ordinary person again and unable to convince others of the value of his training, Sahr was trapped. Because his claims to power were framed in idioms that did not recognize the complementary relationship between the powerful and their supporters, his claims were unacceptable. Gradually he became the laughing stock of the community. As the years wore on he became an alcoholic, living more and more on the fringes of society. As his perception of himself became more and more estranged from the way others saw him, there were rumors that his behavior was being caused by witches. Eventually, the attitudes towards him were also carried over to his son.

In this rather extreme example, it is apparent that life experiences affect what Bourdieu (1977:86) called the "internalized structures, schemes of perception, conception and action" of the habitus and that individual intent and personal experiences play a part in the perception and interpretation of meanings and action. Special training was not enough to guarantee Sahr a position in his hometown during the late 1940s, even in something as fundamentally important to development as engineering. His special training was not linked to the patron-client or lineage relationships that normally establish rights and creditable claims to power. The hierarchies established by lineage affiliation, however, are not monolithic and static, as can be seen in the case of a Kono trader described in Chapter 4. He, too, was a junior son of an important lineage and, thus, likely to be passed over in questions of inheritance. By amassing a small fortune as a trader, however, he became a powerful patron and was recognized as such by the community at about the same time Sahr returned from military service. In the trader's case, wealth (as opposed Sahr's special training) was perceived as a creditable way to demonstrate the right to power and authority. Through wealth and, most importantly, through acceptable idioms of exchange, the trader was linked to the notions of complementarity and balance that are part of the accepted ways of demonstrating and achieving status.

By 1983, the framework for incorporating individuals with special skills into new status positions had shifted somewhat, as was demonstrated by the European-trained official who was able to lay claim to valuable agricultural land even after farm work had begun that year (see Chapter 3). He received the contested piece of land not only because he was an important man in his lineage but also because it was hoped that his special training and his connections to officials in the capital city would somehow benefit the community in the future. This demonstrates a shift in what are conceived of as manipulable resources and the idioms for manifesting power and rights. Those, like Sahr, with resources that do not fit into the patronage system or whose internal schemes of perception do not coincide with objective criteria for advancement, must either change their schemes of perception or they are subtly marginalized. A second point demonstrated by these three cases is that schemes of perception change over time. Here, it is clear that such changes occurred as new forms of complementarity emerged and as new idioms for controlling individual intention were worked out.

The fact that differences in what are accepted as legitimate claims to power or resources exist is significant in that it reveals part of the cultural configuration of power in the Kono world. For the Kono, the legitimation of individual interpretations of action and experience is external to the individual. When individual claims fail to be validated by others, the individual is perceived as somehow being different or behaving inappropriately. Power and authority, in the Kono world view, then, are realized through the actions of others. This is reminiscent of Foucault's (1980:93) discussion of the circularity of mechanisms of power as they are affected by truth and right. The rules of right set limits to the use of power, while power produces truth and validates the rules of right. Those with power or group support define what is right or appropriate, and, in turn, what is right or appropriate signals those with power. Not only is this a question of determining right or power at particular points in time, but such judgments also form the basis of models for future action.

In applying questions of power and right to the discussion of habitus and a theory of human agents, it is clear that Kono individuals only attain power or authority through others. Such support establishes rights, allows individual expression, and signals comprehension. It also signals the acceptance of particular relationships between meaning and form, specific paradigmatic associations, and specific weightings of the principles of complementarity, containment, and action, and, finally, specific relations between clarity and obscurity. A lack of support and comprehension is expressed through ridicule, exclusion, or other acts that devalue the impact of individual expression. This process distinguishes truth from non-truth as it designates those claims that are valid from those that are not. In the process of this designation, the standards for the production of power, truth, and rights in future situations are established.

From this discussion it is apparent that once the importance of subjective experience in aesthetic evaluation is recognized, it cannot be ignored. While it is tempting to see this process as one that continually reproduces structure or brings to the fore the same structural properties, in fact, the paradigms do shift. Each contest—between singers, between insiders and outsiders, and between those with resources and those without—holds within it the possibility of shifts in the paradigmatic framework and associative links across domains of experience. As particular kinds of contests are repeated, in other words as "old" paradigmatic frameworks are repeatedly questioned, the alternatives themselves become more patterned, more capable of producing their own truths, and new paradigms emerge. How new paradigmatic forms take shape brings us to Giddens's (1979:49) next criteria for an adequate theory of action—"an account of the conditions and consequences of action."

THE CONDITIONS AND CONSEQUENCES OF ACTION

In a partial sense, the conditions of action are the material upon which changes of aspect or alternative paradigmatic associations rest. They relate to the structural properties that channel action at any particular point in time. Conditions may be both acknowledged and unacknowledged. Acknowledged conditions are an actor's reasons for an action, the rationalizations that allude to factors affecting an actor's choice of actions at a specific time. These can be related to environmental pressures, social pressures and interests, context, and other elements from the setting of the interaction. The rationalizations or explanations for action that are given in particular circumstances foreground or make visible the contingent features of a situation that are perceived as most important at that time. They can also provide insights into how an actor goes about resolving competing allegiances.

Unacknowledged conditions are much more difficult to apprehend but, nonetheless, need to be explored. They are related, at least partially, to the psychological and kinesthetic factors discussed in the section on habitus, particularly how it actually feels to be in one kind of situation as opposed to another. It is important to keep in mind that, in many cases, the emotions and judgments being discussed are not disembodied but are often, at least partially, based on how particular situations feel to participants.

Discussing the consequences of action brings us back to a discussion of power and authority. Are individuals' definitions of situations (or

ways of associating paradigmatic features) precluded or negated by the
definitions given by more powerful individuals? In the case of the engineer presented earlier in this chapter, the answer is yes. Power here is defined as control over resources and the ability to construct models for
future action. Upon returning to Kainkordu after World War II, individuals with access to resources were able to supplant or redefine the social
position of the trained engineer. At the same time, they reaffirmed a particular behavioral idiom about access to power and status, specifically a
reliance on the rules of descent and complementarity.

Another set of examples of the consequences of action and the ways in
which paradigmatic frames are reproduced can be found in my field ma-
terials from the mid-1980s. The following example shows how the resolution of conflicts between divergent paradigmatic frames or competing
idioms are worked out in action.

Thanksgiving Dance

A general description of Kono dance occasions for initiations, funerals,
and other celebrations has already been presented (Chapter 5). The configurations of structural properties that usually emerge in these performances are related to two idioms: the bounding of individual intention,
and complementarity, as expressed in the use of space and in particular
styles of social interaction and movement. Similar idioms are also found
in other domains of Kono life, including the descent system, agricultural
production, cloth production, and the organization of various rituals.
Taken as a set, these idioms give shape to the structural properties that
organize experience over time and are often used in both the appraisal
and production of action. To participate in one of these domains is to
implicitly make reference to and reinforce these idioms and to reproduce
particular arrangements of structural properties.

The dance forms presented during local thanksgiving celebrations and
agricultural shows (both province-wide and chiefdom-wide) are noticeably different from initiation dances. My descriptions of this difference
will come from the competitive dances performed during the relatively
small, annual chiefdom-wide thanksgiving celebrations organized by foreign missionaries in the Kainkordu area. The dance form itself was probably introduced during the colonial period at province-wide agricultural
shows in which dance troupes from neighboring areas competed for recognition and prizes.[6] The form, however, remains an important part of

post-colonial agricultural fairs and also serves as an integral part of entertainment for visiting dignitaries. For example, I witnessed the same kind of dance performance when Siaka Stevens, then President of Sierra Leone, visited Koidu for an All People's Congress (APC) party convention in 1983.

For these occasions dance groups, musicians, and singers from neighboring towns are invited to exhibit their skills in front of an audience that includes visiting dignitaries or other authority figures. The dignitaries then decide who the best performers are. In the case that I describe here, the dignitaries were foreign missionaries. While the dances themselves are similar to those held for initiations or funerals, the framework of the performance is considerably altered. The competitions I witnessed were held during the day in a large field in which an area 50 to 70 feet wide was fenced off for the performers. Guards were posted around the perimeter of the area to keep onlookers away from the central performance space. Visiting dignitaries were seated on one side of the performance space.

Most of the professionals participating in the thanksgiving celebrations had performed in similar situations before. Less experienced dance groups, however, had trouble making the transition to the new open space. In one case, a group of young girls associated with Sande froze shortly after they entered the arena. They were from a relatively large town in the chiefdom and had many supporters in the crowd that day. However, they were not accustomed to performing in an open space and were unable to build the intense sensory overload that they associated with dance and successful performance. As a result, their performance "fell apart." Although they never actually stopped dancing, there was a quality of self consciousness and slowness in their movements. This was apparent to the onlookers who commented that something was wrong or that something was keeping the dancers from being fully engaged in the dance.

At this point, the crowd that had been pushing against the short fence throughout the competition finally pushed it over. The guards gave up their efforts to try to control the crowd, and the crowd took what they perceived as their "rightful" place around the performers. As soon as the audience was relatively close, the dance group began performing with most of their usual enthusiasm.

It will be useful here to compare the varying references and associations of the thanksgiving dance to the other dance events that I have described in previous chapters. In the dances for Sande initiations, singers and performance groups are successful if they are able to establish an atmosphere of harmony and unity among participants. This is done by constituting space in ways that make reference to containment and controlling the expression of individuality. In this process, individual intention is recognized but then subverted by the group. These dance occasions are recognized as successful when the performance of containment and control of the individual are successful.

The thanksgiving dance described here is of a completely different order than the initiation dances. The initial stages of the event were characterized by unbounded space, with primacy given to individual performers, with a separation of performers and audience, and with loss of the larger group's control over the performers. Furthermore, the success of the performance was to be determined by individuals who were not actually participating in the performance. Presumably, these designations could not be connected to the appraisal of the relationships generated among actual participants within the performance event. All of these factors run counter to the idioms or habits of action that were so praised in other dance occasions.

The fact that the crowd broke through the barrier separating them from the performance also suggests that the initial arrangement was perceived as somewhat unsuccessful. As the crowd broke through, the set of references, associations, and idioms present during other successful dance occasions were reinstated. The result was that containment and group control were once again primary for the participants. In interpretations of the event, the latter part of the program, when the crowd was actually participating in the dance, was considered to have been more successful than the initial stages.

In the initial stages of the thanksgiving dance, commonly held aesthetic principles were violated by the contingencies of a relatively new situation. Those with experience in similar performance situations were able to make the adjustment more successfully than those without that experience. Again, this demonstrates that ideas of appropriateness are related to subjective experience. It implies that successful participation in the new type of dance occasion depended on some degree of incorporation, even embodiment, of actions and idioms different from those normally used. Specifically, the new idioms included a freeing of individual performers from the control of the group. A successful participation in

AESTHETICS AND CONTESTATION   233

these dance occasions came through alterations in practice, as well as realignment, of the paradigmatic associations behind action. With realignment came a new set of associations and sense of being in the world. In
other words, new structural properties emerged that emphasize individuality at the expense of complementarity. Similar realignments seem to
be occurring in other domains as individuals begin thinking about the
possibilities of accumulating cash and other resources in new ways and,
consequently, begin thinking about themselves and their capacities in
new ways as well.

What I am suggesting here is that within the initial organization of the
thanksgiving dance, when the audience and performers were separated,
are the seeds of the kinds of realignments that could significantly change
the relations of conjunction between action and idioms and between idioms and the emergence of structural properties. These realignments are
not limited to dance performances alone but also potentially affect a
wide range of associations in other contexts as well. As situations are
repeated or essentially practiced, even situations such as the unsuccessful
thanksgiving dance, new associations, relationships, or paradigmatic
forms come into being or enter the realm of possibility. In essence, as
habits of one domain become apparent to participants, they simultaneously open the way for the recognition of similar kinds of experiences
in other domains. These new associations are constituted and derived
from specific moments of action. With repetition of those moments and
associations comes familiarity, acceptance, and eventually appreciation.
It is important to note, however, that the shape of these new associations
or paradigms is unpredictable.

In the case of the thanksgiving dance, the formation of new behavioral
idioms is more than just a question of repetition. Here, it is also a question of power. Within the confines of the thanksgiving dance occasion,
new arrangements of space and new kinds of social relationships are authorized and given credibility. Specifically, the new relationships include
a separation of performer from audience, judgment by those not actually
involved in the performance, and deemphasis on the construction of
bounded space within the performance event. Relationships that were
judged unsatisfactory by participants in other situations become satisfactory when authorized by an elite. In the thanksgiving example, it was
recognition by a foreign elite, but this is not always the case. In the
dance competitions for agricultural shows and the visit of Sierra Leone's

President to Koidu, it was a Sierra Leonean elite making the choices. While it may once have been a foreign pattern, it is clear that it has now been adopted by many Sierra Leoneans as well.

Regardless of whether the impetus for the introduction of the new form is foreign or local, it is apparent that local performers are incorporating the new patterns of behavior. For these performers, the goal is to be successful within the confines of the particular event at hand. Efforts toward that end necessarily mean efforts to adopt the criteria of success determined by those making the judgments. As Foucault (1980:59) suggests, "if power is strong, this is because it produces effects at the level of desire . . . and also at the level of knowledge. Far from preventing knowledge, power produces it." Knowledge, here, in its widest sense, refers to alternate interpretations of being in the world and the ranking of these varying interpretations.

The Town Meeting

A second vignette that demonstrates a specific case of contestation and the reproduction of a paradigmatic framework concerns the use of space in a town meeting. The meeting was organized by the school headmaster and his teachers to discuss how to get townspeople to contribute labor for making mudbrick blocks for the walls of a new school building. I happened to arrive at the school compound as the junior teachers were directing the children in arranging benches for the outdoor meeting. They were placing them in straight rows, in much the same configuration as benches inside the classrooms. When the headmaster came outside, he changed the arrangement to a circle. Although he gave no explanation for the change, it became apparent to me from later observations that almost all meetings of any importance were conducted in enclosed, circular spaces. Dance performances, dispute settlements, and agricultural labor are a few of the activities that also use the circular idiom, and all of these settings make some reference to boundaries and containment. Significantly, the only real exceptions to the rule on circularity can be found in two relatively recent contexts—the local court and the schoolhouse.

By arranging the school benches in rows, the teachers reproduced the spatial arrangement of the classroom, a setting over which they have control and within which they routinely operate as powerful individuals. Most community members (200 to 250 showed up for the meeting that day), on the other hand, find the school setting foreign and uncomfortable since they have had little personal experience of it. One result of maintaining the school arrangement during a public meeting would be to extend the teachers' control to decision-making within the community, an arena in which they normally have very little effect. The teachers' lack of control within the community itself comes from the fact that most are thought of as "strangers," people without family ties in the community. While the teachers felt their education should provide them with a measure of prestige within the community, the community saw them as young men and, thus, unsettled and relatively unknowledgeable. Moreover, it perceived those who were unmarried as irresponsible. On the other hand, the community viewed the headmaster, who was slightly older than his teachers and whose family lived in the community, as a mediator between new and traditional lifeways. This provided him with a certain amount of importance and respect within the community.

Embedded within the spatial arrangement of benches is the fact that those who are most comfortable within a particular environment will tend to participate in, if not control, that environment. Those who are not used to a particular environment and, thus, are uncomfortable in it, will tend to remain in secondary positions, unaware of the rules and unable to make creditable statements or put themselves forward in the situation. The headmaster was well aware that in Kono thinking, nonparticipants, or those locked out of relations of complementarity, are not necessarily bound to carry out decisions they have not contributed to and that the withdrawal of labor or other forms of noncompliance is a primary way of showing dissatisfaction, which meany that the bricks for the school would not get made.

By rearranging the bench pattern, the headmaster encouraged more community participation in the discussions and, in fact, allowed community members to control the situation. By returning the arena to a bounded format, he returned the situation to normal social discourse in which community rules and norms of behavior, including complementarity, could emerge. His action also effectively blocked the degree to which the teachers could contribute to the discussions. As a result, during the course of the meeting each household present agreed to produce a certain number of blocks within a certain amount of time, which meant that the new school building could be built.

At the same time, the decision to change the seating arrangements to correspond more closely to the ideas of appropriate space held by the larger community did not damage the headmaster's position relative to the community; in fact, it reestablished, in a public setting, his superior rank vis-a-vis his teachers. The headmaster said he rearranged the benches "so everyone would be able to talk." Essentially, the rearrangement linked a relatively foreign context (the school) to a familiar situation (community decision-making) in a way that left the community in control. The political consequences here are obvious—the work was completed, the headmaster's position was reinforced, and the community's input in school affairs continued. By opting to support community interests in a setting that promoted complementarity and boundedness, he reaffirmed community interests at the expense of the interests of his teachers.

This example of contestation, as in the thanksgiving dance, reproduces, rather than realigns, particular sets of structural properties. In the Kono social contract that balances obligations with opportunities, the idiom of encircling space also refers to the construction of power and power relations in multiple domains. In the agricultural domain, it is the power of human beings over the dangerous and unpredictable forces inhabiting forest space. In dance, it is the power of social groups to publicize and thus control the actions and intentions of individuals. In the case of the community meeting, power was constructed at several levels—the headmaster's ability to impose his will on others and the community's ability to enforce its aesthetic criteria on individuals not from the community. In what can be considered two competing paradigmatic forms, one spatial idiom, which is centered around using bounded circular forms, took precedence over a very different spatial idiom, which is centered on linear and hierarchical forms and which is found predominantly in the classroom and the court system. In both of these relatively new forms, the power hierarchies are rigidly structured, and consensus or complementarity is downplayed. The circular form of the town meeting brought participants back to the familiarity of consensual participation and the control manifested in the delicate balance between bounded and unbounded space that plays into aesthetic judgments of moral and immoral or appropriate and inappropriate in so many other domains of Kono life. As suggested in the dance example, however, just below the surface of the contest between the headmaster and teachers lay new potentialities—new arrangements of space and power, new meanings, essentially alternative paradigmatic frameworks that may, at some point, emerge as more powerful or appropriate.

Agricultural Production

The last example of contestation and reproduction I want to discuss has to do with changes in agricultural production. Eastern Kono are currently working through the impact of two innovations designed to alleviate the uncertainties of agricultural production. The first is swamp rice cultivation and the second is mechanization.

In contrast to upland rice, which was domesticated sometime between 3000 B.C. and A.D. 700 (Porteres 1976, cited in Atherton 1979), swamp rice was introduced in the eastern Kono area sometime in the 1940s. The introduction of swamp rice was part of a government program between 1935 and 1947 to introduce improved seed varieties for swamp cultivation. In 1988, several elderly Kono told me that rice had been introduced from Kamiendo or Koardu, Kono/Kissy areas to the east of Soa Chiefdom, by a British government official. There is no question that the push toward swamp cultivation occurred not only to alleviate food shortages but also because the Europeans disapproved of shifting cultivation. Their disapproval was based on three factors. The first was impatience with a reliance on natural forces, such as rainfall. The second was an unwillingness to invest the time and energy necessary to fully understand the specificity of techniques of shifting cultivation. Enhancing such techniques can occur only with expert knowledge of the microenvironments in which they are utilized. Without such specific knowledge large-scale agricultural programs prescribing fertilizer and other changes in techniques tend to fail because of their inability to tailor programs to specific environments (Richards 1985:79). A third factor was the fear that valuable export crops, such as timber, groundnuts, and palm oil kernels, would be damaged by brush fires associated with shifting cultivation (Richards 1985:21).

The emphasis on swamp cultivation in Sierra Leone continues today, as evidenced by the fact that, as of 1988, Peace Corps agricultural volunteers were still trained primarily to work in swamp development. In the Kono area, however, swamp cultivation has not been as successful as upland cultivation. This is due to both environmental factors and labor and land tenure practices. First, in contrast to the more easterly areas of Kamiendo and Koardu or more southerly and westerly areas inhabited by Mende farmers, Soa Chiefdom has relatively few swamps. Those that do exist are either too large for a single family to farm or too small for a family to produce enough rice to last a full year. A family that farms a small swamp must usually also make an upland farm, which is in a different area and requires coordinating labor in two locales. In the case of larger swamps, appropriate modes of community-wide labor coordination have not been devised. Attempts by Peace Corps volunteers, missionaries, and health workers to organize the cultivation of large swamps have, to date, failed. These failures are attributed to the fact that a community-controlled swamp farm would involve new patterns of cooperation among men and their families. As I noted in Chapter 3, long-term cooperation among Kono men, even those in the same patrilineage, is rare.

Second, swamp work tends to be regarded with less enthusiasm than upland farming for economic reasons as well. In order to get two crops a year, which is possible in some areas of Sierra Leone, Kainkordu farmers must use fertilizers, which are both costly and difficult to obtain because of poor local transportation. In 1983, one bag of fertilizer cost approximately 16 leones (the monthly salary of a school teacher was 20 to 25 leones at that time), and it took three or four bags to cover a medium-sized swamp. The expense of 48 to 64 leones (about $1.44 to $1.92 in 1983 U.S. dollars) was out of the reach of all but the wealthiest farmers in town. In addition to the cost, there are problems with its effectiveness. As noted by Richards (1985:61), soil conditions vary widely from area to area, and agricultural agents are rarely acquainted with the specific conditions in the areas where they prescribe soil amendments. As a result, massive amounts of money have been spent for what are sometimes limited improvements. When such development attempts fail, farmers become less and less interested in the suggestions of the government, the United Nations Development Project, the Peace Corps, and other development workers. Instead, they prefer their old and trusted methods as well as their own, locally engendered formulas for innovation.

A third reason for the lack of interest in swamp rice is the amount of time its cultivation requires. Practically speaking, the Kono year is divided into two seasons. People work very hard on their farms in the rainy season. During the dry season they devote their attention to all of the details of life that agricultural work precludes, especially funerary rituals, initiations, and other family-based activities. Producing two rice crops a year from a swamp necessarily means doing agricultural labor for at least part of the dry season. As I discussed in Chapter 2, the emphasis on two parts of the year is essential for the construction of a good life among the Kono. The activities of the dry season are, in many ways, as integral to agricultural production as is the sowing or harvesting of rice. As one agricultural technician explained to me, once he finished harvesting his swamp rice he felt that his work for the year was done. He could not understand why the development agent he was working for expected him to continue working, despite the fact that he was being paid a twelve-month salary. For many of the Kono, the idea of working during the dry season has yet to be integrated into their calendar.

A fourth reason for the failure of swamp rice cultivation to take precedence over upland rice farming has to do with the land tenure system. In addition to fertilizers, swamp rice cultivation requires the development of the swamp, a process in which walls are constructed within the swamp to channel and control the amount of water present at any point in time. Initially, this is a labor intensive process, although once the swamp is developed it requires relatively little maintenance. Farmers are reluctant to develop swamps because their long-term access to the swamp is left to the discretion of lineage elders. The case (see Chapter 3) in which an individual's coffee plantation was taken from him and given to an elder brother is not unusual. All but the most powerful people are wary of investing large amounts of labor in any particular piece of land for fear it will be reallocated once it proves to be profitable. It seems as if the relatively recent introduction of swamp cultivation has collided with the land tenure system guiding upland rice production. Families have tended to hold the rights to upland tracts of land for generations. Such histories of family rights do not exist for swampland. As a result, rights to swampland are in constant negotiation. Those most physically able to develop swampland—young men and women—are precisely the individuals who are most likely to lose it if someone more senior challenges their claim to the land. Thus, young people are often reluctant to invest a great deal of energy in swamp development.

The final, and perhaps the most important, reason for the lack of enthusiasm for swamp cultivation is the connotation of the swamp. Most Kono talk about swamps as cold, damp, and sickly places in which to work. The Kono word for cold (meaning cold weather) and malaria (chima) is the same word used to describe the swamps. In addition, the swamps are home to a variety of poisonous snakes, which increases the danger of swamp work. Most Kono also say they just prefer the taste of upland rice varieties to that of swamp rice. Consequently, upland rice varieties often bring higher prices in the markets.

As this discussion indicates, structural properties such as complementarity, as they are manifested in such idioms as the division of labor in rice production and the division of the Kono year into two distinct seasons, have worked against full-scale swamp rice cultivation in Soa Chiefdom. While it is obvious that these are not the only reasons, they do seem to be powerful factors in the lack of interest in swamp work.

The second innovation that is part of the discourse of ways to improve agricultural production centers around mechanization, a departure from current techniques that is more dream than reality. During my initial fieldwork in 1982–1984, when I asked what changes farmers would like to see in the Soa area, their overwhelming response was mechanization. As with swamp cultivation, this technique is a holdover from the colonial view of shifting cultivation as primitive and ineffective. In what Richards (1985:13) describes as a "new 'frontal attack' on agricultural development" after World War II, "machines rather than the skills of the small-holder were to be the cutting edge of agricultural change" in Britain's colonies. Although the government and development policy (because there is so much foreign aid, these are sometimes two separate things) were beginning to shift back to an emphasis on agricultural techniques and knowledge already in place, most Kono farmers were still envisioning a day when tractors would free them from the toils of shifting cultivation.

The few instances in which mechanization has been introduced in the Soa area, however, have failed dismally. In one case a government representative, who had access to a tractor, plowed a hugh expanse of flat land, but disputes and endless discussions about who actually had access to the land stalled planting that year. By the next planting season elephant grass, which is nearly impossible to eradicate once it takes hold, had sprouted throughout the farm, and to this day the entire area remains covered in the grass. Other failures have been due to the fact that tractors, when they have been available, were incorporated into patron-client relationships. Farmers willing to become clients got their fields plowed; those not so willing were unable to take advantage of the new technology. Eventually, the lack of fuel and spare parts, as well as inadequate maintenance, silenced the few tractors that made their way into the area. The relics of this dream of mechanization can be seen rusting along the roadsides or in backyards. In addition to the social and economic barriers to mechanization, it is clear that many, if not most, farms in the hilly region are inaccessible to mechanized equipment.

Although mechanization was readily accepted as a goal in the Kono area, in actual fact the behavioral idioms associated with land tenure practices and modes of labor organization worked against the successful adoption of tractors in places where they were available. Coupled with the lack of foreign exchange (for replacement parts) in Sierra Leone as a whole, these problems have made mechanization more of a nightmare than a dream. As a result, by 1988 people's attitudes toward mechanization had become much more tentative than they had been in the early 1980s, and adequate transportation for crops had replaced mechanization as the change most farmers mentioned when asked what would help them become better farmers.

In the cases discussed thus far, the consequences of action have, to some degree, facilitated the reproduction of particular sets of structural properties. Those in power or those whose decisions are given weight (e.g., community members responsible for establishing reputation and status, the audience reclaiming the thanksgiving dance, the headmaster, and the farmers refusing to reorganize labor relations to facilitate new techniques) have opted for familiar arrangements of structural properties rather than for new paradigms. By contrast, the next set of cases demonstrates that this is not always the case and that changes in the associations or paradigms that produce structural properties can and do occur.

Ceramic Production

Kono potters are always women. I was fortunate to have been able to work with two of the last remaining potters in Soa Chiefdom during my fieldwork in 1982–1984. The oldest, Yai, died in 1986. When I knew her, she was an elderly woman with knurled, arthritic hands and failing eyesight. She lived in a relatively large town several miles off the main road running from Koidu to the Guinea border. People say she was over ninety when she died. During one of my discussions with her she recounted her memories of "warrior times," beginning with stories of her warrior father's bravery. She remembered that one of her older sisters had been kidnapped during the wars and never seen again. As a child, Yai herself was also kidnapped, but her family found her some time after paramount chieftaincies were established in the area, presumably in the early 1900s. Yai married and had one child, but the child died. Her husband was also dead by the time I knew her and she was living with a sister, her granddaughter, and several great grandchildren. Yai learned pottery-making from her mother who had, in turn, learned from her own mother.

The second potter I interviewed, Finda, had been Yai's apprentice. Yai had also taught Finda's mother to work with clay, but when the mother died she began to work with Finda. Today, Finda is a younger, more agile woman in her late forties or early fifties. By 1984 her training had advanced to the point where she was capable of doing all the work herself, possibly with more facility than Yai. But it was still Yai who was recognized as the master potter and Finda who was considered the student. In fact, Finda did not work alone but only with Yai. When I returned to the area in 1988 after Yai's death, Finda was being recognized as a potter in her own right. She had not taken on an apprentice but hoped to in the future if she could find someone willing to do the work.

In other Mande areas, potters typically marry blacksmiths. The Bamana associate both pottery making and blacksmithing with people who control dangerous powers of transformation (McNaughton 1979, 1988). In interviews with Kono blacksmiths and potters, it was difficult to determine if marriages between the two had been a preferred marriage pattern in the recent or distant past. Kono do not talk of it being a norm, but it was apparent that it sometimes happens. Neither Yai or Finda were married to blacksmiths, but Yai's grandfather had been a smith.

Locally produced ceramic ware is rapidly disappearing in rural Kono areas. It is being replaced by more durable objects made of tin and other metals and, more recently, by plastics (all imported from Europe, China, or other African countries). Metalware began replacing ceramic ware between 1910 and 1925.[7] This occurred with the construction of a railway that eventually ran from Freetown to Bo, Kenema, and Pendembu, almost to the Guinea border. Like people in other areas, entrepreneurs in Kainkordu began transporting agricultural products to the railheads (a 30- or 40-mile walk). The earliest dates I have collected for this trek are 1918 to 1920, although it may have started a few years earlier. On their return trip to Kainkordu, the traders brought trade cloth, metalware, and other imported goods for sale in the rural areas. By the mid-1940s a growing system of roads replaced the necessity of trade by foot and contributed to the development of numerous market centers throughout the country. As imported goods became more available, locally produced wares became increasingly scarce, particularly in the market centers. Today, local ceramic production and pottery have almost totally disappeared in the more urban Kono areas. In the Koidu market between

1982 and 1984 the only ceramic vessels for sale were those brought from Guinea. In rural Kono it is still possible to find a few women who produce ceramic ware.

When Yai was a girl, ceramic pots were used in rituals and for cooking and water storage. Now, with the introduction of aluminum buckets and cast-iron cooking pots, ceramic pots (*boda*, literally, dirty mouth) are used only in certain ritual contexts. Medicines for a newborn are cooked and stored in a ceramic pot, bodies of the dead are washed with water from a ceramic pot, and other kinds of ritual or medicinal washings are done with a ceramic pot. There are also rituals specific to twins that use a particular pot known as *fen da,* or twin pot. In addition, ceramic vessels are also used in Poro initiation rituals. Substituting metalware in any of these ritual contexts invalidates the rituals or medicines.

In order to discuss the behavioral idioms apparent in pottery making and the ways in which they lead to the emergence of structural properties, it is necessary to describe the process of ceramic production, the associations behind aspects of production, the final pot form, and the use of pots.

Kono potters tend to be older women past childbearing age, partially because of the prohibition against sexual intercourse while working with clay. As in other Kono pursuits, if the laws (*sawa*) associated with particular activities are broken, the endeavors will fail. For this reason, potters are often widows (in the sense of women whose first husbands have died and whose second, or subsequent husbands, have no sexual interest in them). There is also a prohibition against menstruating women working with clay.

In contrast to most other production activities, pottery making is not a cooperative enterprise. Single individuals are quite capable of carrying out the entire process by themselves and, in fact, often do so. It is significant that potting, a task done alone, is allotted to elderly women, specifically women who are no longer able to participate in child bearing and agricultural production, the main cooperative enterprises of Kono life.

Ceramic production is a dry season activity and is similar to ceramic production in other areas of West Africa. Clay is dug from deposits and dried. Once dried, the potter spreads the clay on a board and pulverizes it with a short pestle. Stones are picked out of the mass, water is added, and the mass is beaten and mixed to ensure an even consistency. During this process the potter sits on a low bench in front of a wooden board that rests on the ground. The clay is placed on the board and the short pestle is held with both hands. The pestle leaves a circular impression in the clay.

While ceramic production is not a cooperative activity, some of the techniques used in it can also be found in other domains of production. Beating, for example, is a commonly used technique in husking rice, processing palm oil, and preparing food. Cassava leaf, okra, peppers, tomatoes, and other foodstuffs are all beaten into a pulp before being added to sauces that are served over rice. Beating also is associated with cleanliness and, as in many other places, cleanliness has moral overtones. As women return from initiation ceremonies in other towns, they often dance through town in order to beat the dust of the journey from their feet. Clothes are also beaten when they are laundered.

When the clay is ready to be worked, the potter rolls it into a ball and puts it in a shallow dish lined with leaves called *poponyamba* (*piper umbellatum*), which are commonly used to wrap kola, tobacco, and other things to keep them moist. The dish is one that has been discarded from kitchen use and varies in size, depending on the desired size of the final piece. Kono potters used a modified pinching technique.

To begin construction, the potter makes a hole in the top of the clay ball. The clay dug out is put on the top edge of the hole to make the form taller. As this is done repeatedly, the sides are pressed to make them thinner and to increase the diameter of the pot. I would expect that this choice of technology (as opposed to coil or slab techniques) to be significant, but I have no data as to the reason. Once the desired height has been reached, the potter smoothes the mouth of the pot with her fingers. This is the initial step in emphasizing the roundness of the mouth of a pot. At this point the potter sets the pot, still in its shallow pan, in direct sunlight to begin drying.

Before the pot reaches a leather-hard state, it is worked again to form the shoulder. The potter uses a scraper to trim the clay from the outside while holding the left hand inside the vessel. The scraper is used in one diagonal direction to form the shoulder and in the opposite diagonal direction to form the lower part of the pot. In addition to the scraping, the hand on the inside helps to shape the shoulder. There is an emphasis on keeping the mouth round here as well. At the end of this stage, the two women (Yai and her apprentice Finda) would ask each other whether or not the mouth was round (*A tindane a ne?*). This was the only discussion of the quality of the construction during the entire process. When the potters were asked if the mouth had to be round, I was told it would not be a *boda,* or pot, if it was not round. At this point the pot is put in the sun to dry again.

Next, the top portion of the pot is decorated by incising a series of parallel vertical or horizontal lines between the shoulder and lip or mouth with a short stick. The bottom is still hidden by the pan it was shaped in. Again the pot is put in the sun to dry. The quality or nature of the design is not something that potters comment on while working or that plays a part in decisions to buy particular pots.

The potter lifts the pot from the pan, turns it over, and scrapes the underside to remove excess clay and to smooth the bottom. Any irregularities in shape are adjusted by applying pressure from the inside. Once the shape is satisfactory, the inside is also smoothed. The potter adds decoration to the lower part of the pot by dipping a small piece of rope in water and rolling it over the clay, moving from the shoulder and progressing downwards, away from herself, making a series of ridges. Once again, the pot goes out in the sun to dry.

At the leather-hard stage, the potter uses a rag and burnishing stone to smooth the inside of the pot and the mouth. The rubbing removes surface irregularities and produces a natural sheen.

All of these steps are accomplished in a day. A potter works on several pieces at a time, using drying times to begin construction on new pieces. The pots are then left to dry for several days or weeks until enough pots are prepared to warrant a firing.

When the pots are dry enough to be fired, the potter collects brush and piles it in a low mound somewhere on the outskirts of town. Pots are carefully placed on top of the mound and more brush is packed around and on top of the pots. The firing that I witnessed included 10 pots, all about 6 inches high with diameters ranging from 6 to 10 inches.[8] The mound for the firing was about 5 feet in diameter and 3 feet high. The potter lights the mound with embers from a cooking fire in town, placing them in the brush and fanning them until they flame. The fire burns down to the point where the pots are sitting in coals and ash. The potter then lifts the pots out of the mound with a long stick and places them to one side where she splashes them with water in which the root of a particular tree has been soaking. This adds a slight sheen to the areas that the water touches and may help in making the pots more waterproof. Before firing, the pots are a light tan color, but once fired they become a dark chocolate brown. The entire firing process takes about two hours and the pots themselves are relatively low fired.

For Kono potters, a *boda* is good (*a nyi*) if it is a good container. As I have already discussed, associations with containment are common in the Kono world. A pot's ability to contain is related metaphorically to containment in the human body. I have already described the use of a pot to notify a woman of her son's death during initiation into Poro (Chapter 4). There are other associations as well. Pots are made from earth (*gbo*) and bodies are known to return to earth upon burial. There might also be a connection between physiological processes and decorative techniques. One individual told me, for example, that the rope decoration on the outside of the pot may be a reference to menstruation, although I was unable to confirm this with the potters themselves. Some methods of birth control utilize an analogy between the uterus and ceramic ware, suggesting that the womb's ability to contain is metaphorically linked to ceramic ware and its ability to contain. The mouth of a pot (*da*) also refers to the mouth of the body (*da*). Knowledge of what goes into a pot for medicinal purposes is often guarded, as is knowledge of what goes into the making of a person, as seen in the secret rituals of Sande and Poro, the ambiguous associations of individuals with their ancestors, and other ways in which identity is controlled and obscure. The mouth of the pot also refers to the door of a house (*da*), which separates public from private space and divides what is known from what remains ambiguous or obscure.

A successful pot is also one that does not crack or break in construction or firing, a pot that will eventually be able to contain. As has been noted previously, success in other domains also uses the metaphor of containment. A successful person is one who contains individual intention by balancing personal goals or aspirations with the expectations of others. A successful dance occasion is one in which individual intention remains physically contained by others. A successful woman is one who is able to conceive. On the other hand, an unsuccessful pot is one that breaks during construction or firing. Breakage during firing can be used as a sign that the potter has a witch, just as witches are suspected when a woman is unable to conceive (essentially when her uterus will not contain) or when an individual is unable to control emotions or intentions in acceptable ways. Managing the body and the emotions contained within it, then, is metaphorically similar to managing clay. This metaphorical relationship is further emphasized by the word *gbo*, which refers to both body and clay, as well as to skin, the element that physically contains the body when someone is behaving in a socially accepted way.

The list of these kinds of associations could continue and may be refined as more fieldwork is carried out. What they suggest, however, are patterns for action and patterns for conceptualizing objects and essences in the world. They refer to the relationships among people, objects, and technological processes, as well as to the integration of elements across domains and in the construction of structural properties.

If it is accepted that, as suggested in previous chapters, structural properties emerge only through the repetition of action in a variety of contexts, the question of what happens when a particular context of production disappears, or is radically altered, must be asked. Here I want to focus specifically on changes in action. Do changes in action, in this case a decline in the practice of ceramic production, weaken the underlying patterns or the montage of associations that give meaning, relevance, and a sense of appropriateness to action in other domains as well? Does such a weakening clear the way for the construction of other kinds of associations? Here I am speaking not only about the production of specific material objects but also the ramifications such substitutions (either in technique or conceptualization) have in other domains, such as agricultural production, economic practices, rules of descent, ideals of personhood, and other social patterns.

In a now classic article, Sharp (1952) analyzed the wide-ranging effects of replacing stone with steel axes among the Yir Yiront of Australia. For the Kono, the substitution of metal utensils for ceramic ware has not been as disruptive. Instead, the process of change resulting from the introduction of metalware among the Kono has been and continues to be a gradual one. If one uses the metaphor of culture as fabric, the Yir Yiront are a case in which the fabric was torn apart. The Kono are a case in which the threads in the fabric have been stretched and weakened to the breaking point but other threads have been substituted, resulting in a gradual but continuous reweaving of the fabric.

The contrast between the two cases stems, in part, from differences in access to substituted objects. In the Yir Yiront case, steel axes were distributed virtually on demand. In the Kono case, metalware was acquired only when cash was available and, thus, the change was more gradual. Differences also stem from differences in the position of stone axes and ceramic ware within the cultural framework. In the Yir Yiront case the centrality of stone axes has been documented by Sharp. The axes were owned by men and, thus, women who wanted to use them had to borrow them from their husbands or male relatives. This dependance was an important aspect of male-female relations. The axes were also important in linking the Yir Yiront to other groups because the stone for the axe heads was not available locally but had to be traded for, which tied the Yir Yiront to other groups in the region. In the Kono case, ceramic ware, while important, is considerably less central to Kono social organization. Anyone can buy or trade for a ceramic vessel; thus, there are no set patterns as to who owns and who borrows a vessel, and the consequences of introducing metalware have been very different from the introduction of steel axes in the Yir Yiront case.

Among the Kono, the references associated with the use of metalware are of a different order than those associated with ceramic ware. First, the newly introduced metalware was far more efficient for cooking than a relatively low-fired, and thus fragile, ceramic vessel. Second, metalware was purchased with cash, which indicated access to currency and, in turn, signalled interaction with a newly emerging cash economy and foreigners. Metalware, then, was both durable and prestigious, which served as a powerful reason for altering choices when selecting new cooking pots.

I would suggest that, as a result of substituting metalware for ceramic ware, certain habitual actions and underlying configurations of associations that connected pottery and their production to other spheres have been weakened or realigned. Chief among these would be the association between human bodies and pots. My evidence for this is that ceramic ware remains a necessary component of domains related to the body and health while they are absent from more mundane contexts such as household labor. When all containers were ceramic, each context in which they were used held within it potential references to containment and all that term implies. Today, although references to containment are made in those contexts where ceramics are not imperative (those not related to health and the body), these references have the potential to create new sets of principles and associations. In other words, the actions that might be interpreted as containment might also suggest other meanings. For example, when cooking today women will usually try to have the cooked rice fill the pot to the brim. A half-filled pot is somehow incomplete and not living up to its full potential. Similarly, only young children are able to return from the waterside with half-filled buckets of water without being teased or otherwise chided. These examples suggest that the relationship between fullness and containment, which is found in conceptualizing pregnancy and maturation, still exists to some degree in contexts where metalware has been adopted. I would suggest, however, that these associations have been somewhat supplanted by the association of metalware with trade and cash. Plenty and fullness, then, in the context of domestic use has also come to refer to the accumulation of wealth and resources in new ways.

On the other hand, the imperative to use ceramic ware in contexts related to health and social well-being now reflects a choice between ceramic ware and metalware. Today, medicines for newborns, certain funerary rituals, and rituals that celebrate the power of twins must be done with ceramic ware. This norm or rule has emerged only with the contrast between the meanings of ceramic and metal containers, and this contrast sets in motion new meanings for each form.

It can be argued, then, that a distinction has emerged between the idioms and sets of conceptual associations or kinds of knowledge that are embedded in certain ritual objects and activities and those idioms that are likely to emerge in the world of everyday life. Metalware, except for the tangential references discussed, is not imbued with the same sets of symbolic associations that ceramic ware has retained. Neither the purchasing of metalware nor the substance metal itself lend themselves to adoption in contexts where ceramics are important today. Under these circumstances the idioms associated with each type of material probably select for the emergence of different, even competing, structural properties. Table 7 presents an outline of the shifts in these associations.

What this chart suggests is that new criteria for judging actions are entering the pool of possibilities from which judgments about people are made. While there is not a distinct or total break between the associations of ceramic ware and metalware, there is a potential for new ways of evaluating action to emerge. One set of evaluations, those related to ritual domains, reproduces associations between containment and morality. The other set, related to food preparation and the household, focuses on durability and allows for the interpretation of objects as a sign of wealth and status. An argument can be made then that demonstrations of wealth, resources, and individuality are entering the evaluative picture in new ways. While access to resources has always been one criterion for judgment, now cash specifically and what one can purchase with it are being worked into judgments of people, as can be seen in the success of the trader whose resources allowed him to obtain a degree of

TABLE 7

Comparison of Associatons in Pre- and Post-Metalware Contexts

Pre-Metal Contexts	Ceramics
Contexts:	medicine/ritual/household
Associations/Idioms:	clay=body=skin
References:	(a) containment
	(b) morality
	(c) good health/good death
	(d) fullness as maturation and reproduction

Post-Metal Contexts

	Ceramics	Metal
Contexts:	medicine/ritual	household
Associations/Idioms:	clay=skin=body	durability
References:	(a) containment	(a) access to new resources
	(b) morality	(b) morality
	(c) good health/good death	(c) fullness as reference to resources
	(d) fullness as maturation and reproduction	
Structural Properties	(a) complementarity	(a) individuality and amassing of resources to acquire goods
	(b) emphasis on identity through social groups	(b) emphasis on identity through objects, individual achievement

political control that would not have been available to him based solely on his position within his patrilineage.[9]

It is also tempting to identify the changes noted here as a trend toward new distinctions between secular and ritual domains, which results directly from the introduction of a market economy and a newly emerging emphasis on capitalism and goods. I return to these issues at the end of this chapter.

Cloth Production

Significant changes in the use of cloth over the last fifty years also provide insights into shifts in the paradigmatic associations that produce structural properties. The complementary character of cloth production was described in Chapter 5. As with ceramics, trade items have been incorporated into preexisting categories of cloth use, and consequently local cloth production is declining. Currently, trade or imported cloth is used for everyday clothing, marriage negotiations, and post-burial funeral rituals. Country cloth is necessary only in the initiation of girls into Sande, the burial of chiefdom elders, and the demonstration of status (through dressings) by chiefdom elders. There are several reasons why the Kono currently use, and even prefer, trade cloth in most contexts. First, there is less time to spin cotton and weave. Women spend much of their free time in the evenings (when they used to spin) making foodstuffs to sell on the following day. Moreover, women also say that there is little point in spinning since men won't agree to weave for them anymore. Younger women also tend to be less interested in learning to spin today.

As a result of the shortage of local cotton thread, some men began weaving with imported thread, but the shortage of foreign currency in Sierra Leone in 1982 to 1984 raised the price of all imported goods, including thread, making it far too expensive for most weavers to buy. At the time of my fieldwork, there was also a shortage of imported cotton carders throughout Sierra Leone, again as a result of the lack of foreign exchange. Women whose carders had worn out were unable to spin without borrowing carders from other women. Most women were reluctant to return to the traditional technique for carding thread, which involves a bow-like tool (*pumpwine*) and is much more time consuming.

Another reason why women today prefer trade cloth to country cloth is that trade cloth is more colorful than the off-white, soft brown, or indigo of country cloth and has more variety in designs. Trade cloth is also more lightweight and cooler and most current dress styles require a lightweight fabric. (The women in Figures 8, 14, and 18 are wearing trade cloth, while the man in Figure 17 is wearing country cloth.) At the time of my fieldwork, the only people who wore country cloth consistently were chiefs and elders. Younger men could occasionally be seen in country cloth shirts and caps. Occasionally an older woman could be seen in a country cloth *lappa* or with a country cloth blanket thrown over her shoulders. I do not recall ever seeing a younger woman wearing country cloth (with the exception of girls preparing to join Sande). Country cloth blankets, however, are still being produced, and a variety of these were used for bedding in many houses.

Trade cloth has been incorporated into the exchange systems already described for marriage and burial (see Chapter 5). In most of these cases, money itself could be substituted for trade cloth. In the process of incorporating trade cloth or cash, however, the nature of the exchanges has shifted, as has the identity of those likely to be involved in the exchanges. By his ability to purchase trade cloth, a man lessens his dependence on relatives, primarily his wives, sisters, or mother, who previously produced cloth for him. If he has access to cash and thus to cloth outside a production network, the family's influence over the choices he makes is weakened. Alterations also occur in future expectations and in the way that rights and obligations between individuals are gauged. To understand how this happens, it is necessary to diverge briefly to consider the impact of contemporary access to cash.

Access to cash is markedly different for men and women. While women rarely have access to land for cash cropping, most male lineage elders have plantations of coffee or cocoa. Coffee entered the central Kono area as a cash crop in the late 1920s and cocoa was introduced shortly thereafter. Transportation also improved about that time, making it easier to sell surplus rice, palm oil, and cash crops in nonlocal markets.[10] These changes coincided roughly with the beginning of diamond mining in nearby areas, which further increased access to cash. I have very little data on how much money is made each year through cash cropping, but it varies with climatic and other conditions that affect the size of harvests and with transportation costs. All individuals involved with cash cropping in the Kainkordu area are also engaged in rice production. Some men also have access to cash through wage labor, either by migrating to the diamond fields or by working as agricultural laborers in the Kainkordu area. As mentioned earlier, men with little chance of inheriting property from their fathers are likely to migrate to the diamond areas. Men whose relative status is less certain (middle sons, for example) and who have not yet married are likely to remain in Kainkordu where they might become involved in wage labor and stay with the hope that eventually their lineage will agree to help them marry. Only one or two Kono men from Kainkordu are currently involved in trade (there are several other traders who are not Kono); these men are also involved in rice production and cash cropping, and the labor for these various enterprises is coordinated through family and lineage networks. Access to cash also comes through government posts. Teachers, chiefdom leaders, and the government dispenser all draw salaries from the national government. Some of these individuals, especially chiefdom leaders, are also involved in cash cropping, and all of these salaried individuals are likely to produce rice as a subsistence crop if they are married.

Women's access to cash is, for the most part, on a considerably smaller scale. Their access to land for cash cropping is, for all intents and purposes, nonexistent, although wives will usually be given a small percentage of profits from their husband's crops if they have helped in the production process. Small-scale marketing is the most common avenue to cash for women. There are two levels to this marketing. At one level, local women sell surplus produce from their own gardens to entrepreneurs (usually women) who will transport the produce to Koidu to sell. These entrepreneurs return with commodities, such as salt, bouillon cubes, tins of tomato paste, medicines, and kerosene, that they will sell in Kainkordu or at the weekly market in Manjama. Women use most of the money made from marketing to purchase clothing and other household necessities. With the high transportation costs and the relative lack of surplus produce, most women appear to earn enough cash to purchase excess goods for their families but not enough to allow them to accumulate the resources necessary to engage in large-scale marketing. Many women also are involved in preparing and selling cooked foods, such as beans, fried potatoes and sauce, and boiled cassava and corn. Here, too, profits are relatively small and are used primarily for clothing or household necessities.

Since the introduction of trade cloth, the social networks that facilitate marriage, burials, and other life-cycle events have begun to shift. In cases where an individual does not have ready cash for cloth, the alternative is to borrow from family members. This tends to follow the same lines previously used by men to obtain country cloth, with one important exception. Because women tend not to have access to cash to the same degree as men, the result is that women's influence on the actions of sons or male relatives is diminished, while that of male relatives, who have access to cash, may increase.

Trade cloth and its use, then, plays an active role in realigning basic social relationships. In specific cases people make choices based on the resources available to them. Over time these choices become patterned.

They hold the potential of shifting social relationships away from the reciprocal or complementary structure inherent in male/female relationships that is a necessary part of cloth production. Specifically, that realignment is associated with the changing values of certain kinds of resources. When country cloth was a preferred commodity, the production of that commodity included both men and women. With the introduction of trade cloth, access to cloth was more likely to be attained through male relatives. As this pattern is repeated, the complementarity between men and women is devalued, and a woman's influence on the actions of sons or other male relatives is replaced by the influence of those with access to valued resources. This is another case of changes in idioms or patterns of behavior affecting structural properties as the techniques and specifics of one form of production fall out of use. As that occurs, the efficacy of the elements of social organization upon which production was based are likely to become less operative in other domains as well. For example, in the case described by Rosen (1981, 1983), the women of Njaiama Nimi Koro contested the fact that they were not given access to farm lands; only then did it become possible for women to conceive of themselves in new ways. While they lost the actual court case, the seeds of dissension and redefinition had an effect on the subsequent actions of both women and men. These transformations and shifts are both manifested in and facilitated by aesthetic evaluation for it is in specific contexts of evaluation that arrangements of idioms are both perceived and judged. The consequences of such judgments allow for shifts in the structural properties that will guide future action.

When I first began working with my data on cloth, I was looking at cloth production and the division of labor inherent in it as a metaphor or representation of social order on a wider scale, a crystallization of ideas about the way things are or ought to be. This position followed from the work of many anthropologists and others who have dealt with nonwestern art as an element of culture that reflects cultural principles (see, for example, Gerbrands 1971 and Schneider 1971). I think it is apparent from the data I have presented here, however, that for the Kono decisions made in the production and use of cloth have aided in the transformation of people's thinking about cloth and about the social relationships that previously underlaid cloth production. The point to be made here is that objects that we might classify as art or craft do not necessarily reflect cultural principles but actually play a role in the construction of social and cultural forms. In cloth production, changes in the types of cloth available have altered the idioms inherent in production and use in such a way that shifts are occurring in the arrangement of structural properties. These shifts will potentially effect future action in numerous domains of life—from agricultural production and dance performance to household organization and economics. As similar alterations become apparent and, thus, efficacious in more and more contexts, the contingencies of action begin to form new patterns within, as well as across, contexts. As that occurs, new norms, new sets of knowledge, and new associations emerge. This process of association is especially important for the ways in which structural properties are constituted because, as Karp (1978a:2) and others note, "different aspects of given societies are changing at different rates." What this means is that the arrangement of the resources from which meanings and interpretations, and thus structural properties, are constructed are always shifting.

How such shifts or realignments occur can be illustrated through a discussion of the two contexts in which country cloth is still preferred over trade cloth. What becomes clear is that changing patterns of interaction suggest that certain categories of people are still constrained by notions of complementarity, while other categories seem to be released from such constraints. First, young girls are still required to have an all-white strip cloth *lappa,* or skirt, when they join Sande. This is in addition to other new clothing that may be purchased, depending on the wealth of the girl's family. Usually a girl's mother spins the thread for the *lappa* and arranges for the weaving to be done by the girl's father or uncle. If the mother cannot spin the thread, she asks one of her female relatives to do it.

It is significant that the emphasis on connections to others, which is required in the production of country cloth, is being maintained in a ritual context in which the primary participants (the female initiates and their mothers) have restricted access to cash and, thus, to trade cloth. This interdependence among relatives is reminiscent of that prior to the introduction of a cash economy. In contrast, in other kinds of situations, such as marriage or a couple's return to a sexual relationship after the birth of a child, new forms of relationships or dependencies are emerging. Specifically, in these arrangements men find themselves more dependent on those with cash, typically other men, while they find themselves less and less dependent on female relatives for the production of locally made cloth. As these shifts occur, women find themselves with less capital (symbolic or otherwise) and less able to make their demands heard.

Thus, women find themselves more dependent on their husbands, while their husbands find themselves less dependent on their wives or female relatives. Such changes have important consequences for the principles of complementarity that have been discussed throughout this book.

It is also significant that, to my knowledge, boys who are initiated into Poro are not required to have country cloth. They are given new clothes before initiation, but these are made of trade cloth. Thus, even though it is primarily mothers who arrange for both their son's and daughter's clothing for initiation, they make those arrangements in different ways. Young women and their mothers are required to reproduce complementarity in their actions, while young men are not. I would attribute this divergence, to some degree, to the changing nature of male-female roles and the changing access to power and authority. Young women are trained in Sande to take their places in society as wives and mothers. Part of that training includes how to behave towards others. In the pre-cash economy, the power and authority allotted to women of childbearing age came through the withdrawal of services to a husband's patriline. Withdrawal was an effective tool for voicing grievances in a subsistence economy based on a division of labor that required reciprocity and coordinated labor between husband and wife. At the same time, male power and authority came through the manipulation of resources in patron-client relationships. Neither male nor female roles have changed, but the resources used by men in patron-client relationships and the actual composition of patron-client relationships is changing. Where previously women, slaves, and rice or other subsistence needs were traded for support, today's patron-client relationships revolve around cash, favors, and the hope of obtaining positions in government or business. By requiring young women to have country cloth at initiation, then, women reproduce the sets of relationships based on reciprocity and complementarity appropriate to them, even though this mode of behavior is becoming increasingly ineffective as the Kono move further into a cash economy. While the objective definitions of women and their capacities have not changed, the power embedded in such definitions has been devalued as men's roles and capacities have changed. In essence, because the resources that women once traded for power are no longer as effective, women are becoming marginalized in some decision-making contexts.

There are, of course, alternatives to marginalization, but as the following case shows, the costs for such actions in moral terms can be extreme. During my initial fieldwork I met a woman of about thirty-five who belonged to a minor patrilineage in the area. At the time, she was not married but she had a child from a previous marriage. She had returned to her natal home after a divorce and, although she had a number of lovers, she seemed to have no intention of marrying again. She became a small-scale trader and, as she put it, without the responsibilities of a husband she had a degree of freedom of movement that most Kono women do not have. This allowed her to travel freely, buying produce in Kainkordu, selling it in Koidu, and returning with goods for sale. After several years she stopped trading and entered into an agreement with an unrelated landowning family to farm a section of their upland brush. She used money saved from trading to hire laborers to do the heavy brushing for her, but she also did much of the brushing herself, to the amusement of other townspeople. After she planted her rice crop, she asked her mother and other female relatives to help with the weeding, bird scaring, and other tasks, although she had to hire workers again to help with the harvest.

As a result of her switch of gender roles, she became the brunt of numerous jokes and her character was constantly being questioned. She was called *musu kai* (woman man), and people referred to her laughingly as the woman who wears pants. When I talked to her at the time, it was clear that she was uncertain if she would be able to survive the first year and she was not entirely certain she had made the right decisions. It was also clear that she was not sure if she would even get a rice crop, much less make any money from it that first year. What she hoped to do was to grow enough rice not only to feed herself and her child but also to have as a surplus to sell at a high price during the hungry season the following year. Then, she hoped to farm on the same land the following year (which meant that she had fewer costs for labor because the brushing would be minimal), grow a second rice crop, and again sell it for the highest price. In the third year she hoped to brush an even larger farm and increase her profits. At that point she wanted to use the profits from the rice to enter large-scale marketing. She was not sure exactly what commodities she would trade, but she was certain that the key to success was having enough money to buy in large quantities in rural areas and sell in Freetown.

When I returned to the area in 1988, the woman's plan had been successful. She had entered marketing, and her mother ran a small store while she travelled to buy and sell. Since I had known her in the early 1980s, she had also remarried. She was the fourth wife of a man who had "put kola" for her. As she explained it, both of them were busy "finding money." In the rainy season they farmed, but in the dry season they travelled to various dances in smaller towns to sell cloth, medicine, and other imported goods. When I spoke with her in 1988, it was clear that she was satisfied with her life at that point and felt that all the ridicule she had endured when she was farming alone had been worth it. Although she and her husband kept their money separately at that time, eventually she assumed that they would begin to pool their resources. It was clear that they loaned money back and forth when one of them needed to make a purchase. In fact, when I talked with her, she was travelling to meet her husband to loan him money to buy seed for their rice swamp, a sum of approximately $70 in 1988 U.S. dollars. When I asked her if she thought other women would begin to do as she had done because she had been so successful, she answered that she did not think so. Her life had been hard, both physically and emotionally, during the years she was making a farm by herself, and she knew of no other women willing to sully their reputation as she had.

In Njaiama Nimi Koro, the chiefdom headquarters of another Kono chiefdom, Rosen also reports that the costs for behaving in ways not categorized as female are sometimes extreme. According to Rosen (1981:159), women of childbearing age who are successful at marketing, for example, face accusations of "various moral offenses including child neglect, adultery, prostitution and drunkenness" similar to those "associated with accusations of witchcraft in traditional Kono society." Women in Njaiama Nimi Koro who attempted to shift to full-scale marketing risked being blamed for the misfortunes that might befall their households. Rosen (1981:161) writes that these "women, in the context of witch-finding rituals, were accused of abnormal role performances and demands were made upon them to renounce any involvement in cash cropping or marketing and return to the 'normal' role of wife and mother." The normal role in Njaiama Nimi Koro, as in Kainkordu, is one that emphasizes complementarity between men and women. While I did not see such direct accusations against Kono women in Kainkordu, the ridicule attached to the woman farmer described above is enough to stop most women from pursuing goals outside culturally objectified female roles. Even in this case, however, the woman returned to a relationship of complementarity once she had enough resources to demand a husband's cooperation and respect.

The second context in which country cloth is still important is that of leadership. The only men to consistently wear country cloth today are paramount chiefs and village or chiefdom elders. Even today, chief's cloth is of a different nature than other country cloth. Chief's cloth tends to have more colored thread and fewer white stripes than other cloths. The colored threads are made by dyeing with indigo (*kaa*), which gives two shades of blue, and by using a strain of cotton that produces thread with a soft brown color (*duu*). Because of the profusion of stripes in a chief's cloth, it takes considerably more time and requires more skill to dye and weave. Chief's robes are also made with more lengths of cloth than the shirts that ordinary men might wear. The large quantity of cloth and the use of many dyed threads allude to the power of the chief and his ability to capitalize on the labor of others. Many of the cloths a chief wears are gifts from individuals in neighboring towns or petitioners asking for favors.

Chiefs were also traditionally buried with country cloth. I was told stories about up to 200 cloths being given by a chief's supporters and clients for burial with him. Although I did not witness such a burial, I was told that this is still the custom today. Towns and villages under the control of the paramount chief supply the cloth for the burial. The number of cloths used in these demonstrations denotes the respect in which people held the chief. The burial cloth also serves as an indication of the position a chief will have among his ancestors. Things buried with the dead are thought to follow them to the next life, and cloth is one of the resources the chief will trade for patronage in his new setting. In short, lack of support in this life translates into a life of clientage rather than patronage in the next world.

In the case of cloth for chiefs and Sande initiation, then, it is possible to see shifts in the configurations of associations among actions from a range of contexts—the effect of action on structural properties as well as the effect of structural properties on action. Changes at the level of action—specifically, the increased use of commercial cloth and the decrease in county cloth production—have led to the production of new idioms and new configurations of structural properties. The result is a deemphasis of the complementary relationship between men and women in cloth production. By extension, this has led to a deemphasis on relations of complimentarity in contexts such as marriage arrangements and childbearing, in which country cloth was used in the past. In the case of chiefs, however, country cloth has been retained as a sign of control and support. Thus, chiefs, as well as women, have retained particular patterns of interaction or sets of idioms while other groups of individuals have replaced these patterns with new alternatives or sets of paradigmatic associations. Each of these categories of persons—chiefs, elders, women, and those without resources—find themselves dependent on others in ways that those with freer access to resources, usually men, are not.

Within the contexts of ceramic, metal, and cloth production, structural properties have been resorted in several ways. First, in terms of the introduction of metalware, it is possible that a new association of morality with trade goods is emerging. This new association involves an evaluation of what one has as well as how one acts. In terms of the context of cloth production, it is clear that changes in cloth production are tied to shifts in the nature of relations of complementarity. For women, relationships with husbands and family remain infused with complementarity. By contrast, for men, relationships of complementarity with women are diminishing in such a way that responsibilities towards wives are no longer as much a part of marital relations. Relationships of complementarity among male relatives (those with access to cash), however, are being reproduced, but in slightly new ways. Lastly, chiefs are still entwined in relations of complementarity with their subjects. Here, it is not just what the chief or elder has but also what others are willing to contribute to the creation of his status. These shifts suggest that what is considered capital or resources in patron-client relationships is expanding for men; for others (chiefs and elders), it is remaining static; and for women, it is becoming more and more limited.

The potential shifts in idioms and, thus, structural properties that can be teased out of the contested forms discussed earlier in this chapter shed light on the direction that these changes are likely to take in the future. In the thanksgiving dance, the potential changes include the possibility of evaluating dance on formal, rather than experiential, criteria with a more distinct separation between performer and audience, and more emphasis on the performer as individual. What this implies is a new set of criteria for evaluating performance or action in general. The new criteria emphasize elements other than the experiential, the building of consensus, and relations of complementarity. The nature of the contestations in the town meeting also suggest the potential shift in power relations in some contexts away from relations of consensuality and complementarity toward more rigid and hierarchical control of community members by a small elite made up of government employees, such as schoolteachers and court officials.

Exactly how particular domains will interpenetrate or serve as metaphors for others in the future is uncertain. What this analysis suggests, however, is a picture of Kono society as one in which the consequences of contemporary action are moving towards the formation of structural properties that allow for: (1) the accumulation of resources in new ways by particular individuals; (2) judgments of action and character based on evaluations of adherence to principles such as complementarity and containment as well as material possessions; and (3) a shift away from the circulation of possessions, resources, and capital to the accumulation of capital, at least for certain individuals. As a result, there is a subtle shift in the behavior of those without access to resources, most noticeably women, toward more dependence on those with resources, except in the case of chiefs and elders, who remain in relations of complementarity with their followers.

STRUCTURE AS CONDITION AND CONSEQUENCE

So far in this chapter I have explored variations in perception and interpretation, the ways in which variations in interpretation link aesthetics and power as certain interpretations of action and paradigmatic associations become accepted over others, and the ways in which such processes produce new or transformed sets of idioms and structural properties. Implicit is the idea that there are multiple and changing ways in which various domains interpenetrate; as those penetrations shift so, too, do the various structural properties that shape evaluation and future action. It is critical to point out that these penetrations or the perception of analogies or redundancies across domains is an ongoing and continually changing process that is activated and realized with each evaluative judgment. This brings us to Giddens' (1979) last component for a theory of action—an understanding of how structure acts as both a condition and a consequence of action—and a discussion of the dialectic between structure and action. To explore the dialectic, it will be useful to consider the relationships among structural properties, idioms that manifest structural properties, and action, which has remained rather implicit throughout this book. It is apparent that action, idioms (as the behavioral manifestations of organizing principles or structural properties), and structural properties are analytic concepts—useful tools of analysis but absent in reality. It should also be apparent that the boundaries between these three levels are blurred, both in analysis and in actuality. As a result, any distinctions that do exist are quantitative questions. The more particular actions or idioms are repeated or perceived, the closer they come to solidifying the principles they represent as structural properties and the more likely they are to be reproduced over time. Essentially, I would argue that it is through evaluative action and, more specifically, through the consequences of confrontations between habits of action and the conditions of action in specific contexts that structural properties emerge. This process is activated by the perceived associations between contexts or domains that recognize and give shape to idioms or habits of action and serve as the basis for evaluating action. In Giddens's (1979) terms, structure produces some of the conditions of action, which in turn interact with other conditions of action (including idiosyncratic aspects of personality or experience and the exigencies of situations) to produce action. One consequence of action is the perception of habits of action across contexts or over time and the construction of paradigmatic associations or idioms that manifest structural properties. With repetition these paradigmatic forms become the habits and traditions that structure future action; thus, they can be labelled structural properties. As actions change, then, so will structural properties and the use of structure in evaluation.

In this model, changes in structural properties can occur in at least two ways. The first springs from actual changes in action and the spaces that such changes open up as new patterns of action and interpretation are incorporated into already-known patterns of action. A second source of change stems from the possibility of new emphases in or sortings of paradigmatic associations and shifts in the importance or arrangement of idioms that make up paradigmatic associations.

In short, the resources that people use to evaluate and construct the world around them are constantly shifting. As they change, so will questions of value and morality. While such shifts are, to many, most obvious in objective forms, the same process informs shifts in social forms as well. The battleground between change and reproduction lies in the realm of human action, specifically aesthetic evaluation. In the impossible task of meshing or reconciling tradition, culturally objectified norms, and social expectations with personal goals, the contingencies of everyday situations, and the idiosyncracies of personality, individual actors make choices that often have unintended consequences for future action. Such choices are evaluated, both by the individual agent and others, and particular arrangements of paradigmatic forms are given primacy or import over others. While structural properties inform or shape these choices, they do not determine action or evaluation. Rather, the idioms that manifest structural properties are flexible, infinitely malleable frameworks that are in constant negotiation. It is this fact, coupled with the important role of aesthetic evaluation in mediating between structure and action, that lends dynamic tension to culture and social life.

9

THE AESTHETICS
OF ACTION

Defining an Anthropology
of Aesthetics

I began this book with two goals. The first was
to provide an ethnographic account of the Kono of eastern Sierra Leone.
The second was to locate the study of aesthetics more centrally within
social theory. While there has been an increasing interest in studies of
aesthetics in anthropology over the last few years, as evidenced by a new
body of writings on the topic (see, for example, Feld 1988; Forrest
1988), there has been little attempt to see how these various studies fit
together or whether or not they provide a coherent view of an anthropology of aesthetics.

Currently, there are two fundamentally different approaches to aesthetics. One emphasizes art as a universal category; the other focuses on
affect and implicitly looks at art as only one category of aesthetic phenomena. Both positions have been constituted through historical processes and have political consequences. The universalizing approach
places certain limits on studies of aesthetics. Practitioners of this approach consider it possible to find and analyze art in societies that do not
have an indigenous category of art. They do this by focusing on forms
that commonly fall within the boundaries of Euro-American categories
of art (e.g., dance, sculpture, painting, music, and sometimes weaving,
ceramics, body decoration, and architecture). While they may explicitly
state avoidance of these categories, in fact, much of their research

implicitly reproduces these categories (see, for example, Anderson 1990 and Hardin 1991). Studies of aesthetics from this perspective focus on how these sets of forms are produced or used, how they are evaluated, and how they intersect with religion, politics, and other sociocultural forms. By limiting the scope of research to specific forms, as this approach does, cross-cultural comparisons are relatively straightforward (see, for example, Anderson 1990; d'Azevedo 1973a; Vogel 1986).

Criticisms of this approach stem from the fact that one is hard-pressed to find categories of art in many parts of the world (both Western and non-Western) that mirror that of Euro-American elite culture. In effect, then, operating from predetermined categories reproduces Western notions of aesthetics, "high" art, and an evolutionary perspective that implicitly ranks aesthetic systems by their closeness to an ideal. In essence, this approach predetermines the focus of research by assuming that the Western category of art is "natural," and thus universal. The naturalness of the category is further reified by the limits it sets on research. Basically, this approach predetermines the location of divisions between affect (or potent, emotionally charged experience) and emotions related to art. As a result, several important questions are effectively ignored. These include where divisions between affect and aesthetic exist (if at all) in a specific setting, what relevance specific ways of dividing affect and aesthetic have for particular social and cultural forms, and what role affect, aesthetics, and value play in contexts that are defined as nonartistic. With only part of the picture visible, the idea that art (as construed in elite Euro-American contexts) is a universal is reinforced. Predetermining the boundary between affect and art also inhibits the analysis or critique of the Euro-American high art world and the history of its particular use of aesthetic sensibility, especially the ways in which aesthetic sensibility has been used as a tool of exclusion.

The second general approach to aesthetics focuses more on affect and implicitly looks at art as only one category of aesthetic phenomena. This group of work, however, can only be pieced together from a growing body of research that questions the reliance on Euro-American categories in studies of aesthetics and anthropology. See, for example, d'Azevedo (1958) on the importance of subjective experience in aesthetics; Feld (1988) on Kaluli aesthetic concepts; Forrest (1988) on aesthetic concepts of a tidewater community in North Carolina; Kaeppler (1978) on homologies and evaluation in Tongan music; and Riesman (1975) on his efforts to locate Fulani aesthetic criteria. These studies widen the focus of aesthetics by taking into account local categories of production and experience, sources of aesthetic evaluations, concepts of creativity, and the political consequences of aesthetic evaluations. In addition, they use field research to explore the boundaries, if indeed any exist, between affect and aesthetic. Focusing on indigenous frameworks opens the way for considering the particularities of how and under what circumstances people attach value to action, form, and experience. In this approach, aesthetics is linked more closely to systems of preference and value than to "art" per se, and art (in its Euro-American sense) becomes a subcategory of aesthetic experience, one that probably emerges under specific political and economic circumstances. The category of art, then, has relevance only in particular kinds of sociocultural formations. This may be a predominantly elite Euro-American setting, but certainly it does not rule out other particular historical or geographic settings where "art" is a category of experience or production distinct from other domains of life.

There are two main criticisms of this approach. The first is that such studies tend to be so context specific they make more general theory-building difficult. The second, and more vocal, criticism is that this approach allows anything to be perceived as art. Essentially, this criticism is a return to the position that aesthetics be limited to "studies of art," as art is defined in the Euro-American "high" art sense. Critics also suggest that once the categories of analysis are expanded in ways that include forms and activities not necessarily considered "art," cross-cultural comparisons become impossible. Implicit in this criticism is a denial that the link between aesthetics and art (again, as defined in the Euro-American "high" art sense) is culture specific and, thus, tenuous and related to specific cultural and historical circumstances. This criticism also assumes it is impossible to formulate cross-cultural comparisons using other than formal criteria.

In my view, what is needed to bridge the impasse between universalist and context-specific studies of aesthetics is an approach that will allow us to do two equally important things. The first is to discuss the social and cultural significance of value and criticism in contexts as seemingly disparate as, for example, "lowrider" culture in an Hispanic community in Texas and the latest exhibition of installation works at New York's Museum of Modern Art; or the emergence of a new dance form in the Kono area of Sierra Leone and the emergence of abstract expressionism in the United States; or the forms of dress and speech that British youth use to resist inclusion in upper class society and the objective and behavioral forms that a Kono youth manipulates to present himself as both a good and successful person. To do this, it is necessary to establish a body of theory and methods that will allow researchers to go beyond the particular and culturally constructed Western definitions of art and aesthetics and to consider what questions of value and choice can reveal about culture in general, no matter what kinds of forms or experiences they are directed towards.

The second is to discover a way of revealing, in indigenous terms, the culture specific forms and foci of aesthetic evaluation, or what Maquet (1986) termed the aesthetic locus. Those objects and forms chosen for aesthetic evaluation in a particular time and place are not always similar to those that might be chosen by Western art markets or critics. But how do we discover what those forms are; more importantly, how does the abandonment of Western categories allow us to begin to understand the role played by aesthetic experience in the very construction of culture.

Recent work in social theory suggests ways of moving beyond the universalist and context-specific approaches that have created the current deadlock in studies of the anthropology of aesthetics. The approach outlined in this volume borrows heavily from current questions about the relationship between structure and agency and recent research into issues of personhood and embodiment. One important outgrowth of bringing these literatures to bear on questions of aesthetics has also been a consideration of aesthetics and change.

SUMMARY OF THE ARGUMENT

I began this volume by suggesting that, because it is impossible to find distinctions between commonly accepted definitions of affect and aesthetic in some contexts, perhaps an anthropology of aesthetics should begin from another vantage point, one that is more likely to avoid the trap of allowing Western or elite definitions of art to intrude on research agendas. My starting point has been local categories of experience, production, and evaluation, with the hope that it may be possible, at some future time, to explore how these elements might be compared across societies in ways that say something meaningful about culture and human behavior. Specifically, I am interested in exploring how ideas about what constitutes appropriate form and action are produced and how they change over time.

Following Bateson (1972a) and others, I suggested that at least part of what goes into the construction of value has to do with redundancy, that recognizing something (a function of repetition) produces pleasure or acceptance in and of itself. It is important here to realize that aesthetics is not necessarily a question of pleasure but more a question of acceptance, in the way that certain West African masks are not necessarily pleasurable to look at (indeed, they can be quite frightening), nor are Picasso's *Guernica* or countless other masterpieces of Western art pleasant to look at. What I have suggested is that the sense of pleasure or acceptance stems from the repetition of forms in a range of domains.

As descriptions of the domestic and jural domains have shown, it is clear that Kono social life is patterned in certain ways. Furthermore, the patterns of action or idiomatic forms of, for example, the domestic domain can also be found in dance performance and agricultural production. As the analysis of the dance performance described in Chapter 5 indicated, when a particular set of idioms is successfully repeated in an event, that event and a particular set of idioms will be deemed appropriate or aesthetically pleasing.

While the perception of patterns across domains of experience provides the background against which actions are judged, there are several other levels to my analysis. The idioms in question are actually manifestations of arrangements of what Giddens (1979) calls structural properties, the properties that shape tradition, value, and objectively or culturally defined notions of personhood and appropriate behavior. Although not critical to my argument, it is helpful to think of structural properties as universal aspects of human society that are potentially present everywhere. The arrangement or weighting of structural properties in any particular place and time, however, is what distinguishes one lifeway from another. Karp and Maynard (1983:100) describe these structures as "universal proclivities of social practice" that "have no existence independent of the cultural idioms whose pattern of order they exhibit." I would add to this that they have no existence outside the points at which particular arrangements of idioms are contested and judged. For example, the structural properties that are foregrounded in Kono life include such general patterns as complementarity, containment, a contrasting of clarity and obscurity, and an emphasis on action. At the same time I have argued that in certain contexts structures that emphasize individuality are competing for primacy with ideas of complementarity. Even a cursory look at a series of ethnographies from around the world will show that these structures emerge in many places. What is culture specific is the particular arrangement of structural properties at any point in time. In other words, what is uniquely Kono has to do with when complementarity, as opposed to individual action or intention, is important and under what conditions various structural properties switch from foreground to background. The second thing that is culture-specific are the idioms that give shape to structural properties. These too, however, are the result of judgment and contestation. While complementarity is found in many agricultural communities, the exact shape it takes or the ways it links domains in the Kono area are relatively unique. Much of Kono complementarity, for example, is manifested in idioms of boundedness. When these idioms are successful at producing or maintaining complementarity, as they sometimes are in dance performances, then the performance itself is deemed appropriate or pleasing. What players are in relations of complementarity, under what circumstances complementarity or any other structural property is important, and at what times and for what ends is complementarity subverted then become questions about Kono culture specifically, but they also point the way for new ways of comparing aesthetic systems across cultures.

I would like, at this point, to review the Kono material more specifically. This volume began in Part I by focusing on what I consider to be only half of the problem, the ways that such structures as complementarity shape action. Complementarity is manifested in the conflicts between the obligations and sentiments engendered by rules of descent, on one hand, and the sentiments attached to matrifilial ties on the other. Just as much of Kono emotional life is caught up in meshing or coming to terms with this conflict, individuals are inextricably involved in finding ways of melding their own subjectively construed goals and aspirations with objectively derived ideas about what it means to be a moral and just person in Kono terms. Only by coming to terms with the complementarities of each pair of contrasts—descent and matrifiliation, obligation and sentiment, and personhood and individuality—is identity established. The rules and obligations of descent, the sentiments associated with matrifilial ties, and ideas of what constitutes a good and moral person, then, are all idioms that manifest complementarity. As the idioms themselves change, the emphasis on complementarity in Kono life will also shift. Other structures, such as the modulation of clarity with obscurity, allow for alternative ways of establishing identity, but in ways that still emphasize complementarity. Obscurity, for example, is manifested in parts of the descent system, such as the relationship between brothers, that individuals can manipulate to improve their social position. Clarity, on the other hand, is manifested in other parts of the descent system. People gain knowledge about others by knowing their genealogies or through participation in such public events as life-cycle rituals that constantly mark individuals' social position. Both of these aspects of the descent system temper individuals' claims to identity.

In subsequent chapters of Part I, I traced the ways in which structural properties shape action in other domains of Kono life. In agricultural production, complementarity is manifested in the division of labor, in men's access to land, and in the conceptual distinctions between forest space and farm space. In cloth production, it is also possible to see similar idioms manifesting complementarity. The division of labor makes both female and male participation important in cloth production. The fact that women control the finished cloth allows for the projection of complementarity back into the domestic domain in several ways. Before the introduction of trade cloth, young men who wanted to marry used locally produced cloth as part of their brideprice; it was also an important part of the post-burial ceremonies that ended relations between patrilineal and matrifilial relatives of the deceased. In both of these contexts, then, women played an important role in decision-making within the domestic domain.

In dance contexts, the structure of complementarity is equally important. Here, it is manifested in the ways in which the reputations of singers and dancers are established. It is also manifested in the spatial arrangements of the dance. To be contained is to be socially controlled, to be recognized, and to be achieving reputation in a morally acceptable way. To be uncontained is to delve into forces outside human control and to contest the importance of complementarity. Essentially, such actions are metaphorically associated with other uncontained spaces, specifically the unpredictability of forest areas and the possibilities for amoral and uncontrolled activities by individuals away from their natal home who are able to escape the constraints that obligations of descent relations imply.

It is more difficult to describe the ways in which tempering clarity with obscurity is manifested in agricultural and cloth production or dance performance. Essentially, however, obscurity provides gaps in the framework that allow some individuals a degree of manipulation and freedom from constraint. In most cases, however, the point at which clarity emerges, while probably open to negotiation and contestation, places limits on the activities of individuals. For example, it is relatively unclear who is dealing in witchcraft for their own advantage. However, when rumor reaches the point where it can no longer be ignored, individuals are identified, their activities become known, and their future actions will be suspect.

Finally, in the last chapter of Part I, I discussed the process by which actions are sorted or associated across domains in ways that reproduce particular arrangements of structural properties over time. I argued that the logic behind distinctions among categories of production and appreciation are idiomatic manifestations of various structural properties. Thus, distinctions between activities that fall under the categories of *nyane* (to make), *gbuo dia* (body or stomach sweetness), and *koo che* (speech thing) are made on the basis of how they manifest complementarity and other structural properties. In addition to referring to the production of physical things, those activities considered to be *nyane* suggest an emphasis on complementarity through the division of labor inherent in particular activities. In contrast, those activities that fall within *gbuo dia* or *koo che* rely on the coordination or the development of a consensus to produce complementarity. As is clear in Table 6, some of the distinctions among forms of criticism, such as *a nyi* (it is good), *a di* (it is sweet), and *a kosan fa* (he/she knows it) rely on the same contrasts between the production of physical and ephemeral forms and between complementarity and consensus. What is important here is that the very ways in which people conceive of production can be related to particular arrangements of structural properties. This suggests that, as people use a particular conceptual framework to think about an activity, they are, in fact, reproducing a particular arrangement of structural properties.

In closing Part I, I argued that when action reproduces the particular arrangements of idioms that correspond to the arrangement of structural properties guiding action at that point in time, it is deemed appropriate. This is, however, only the first half of the analysis of aesthetics. The second half focuses on the ways in which action affects structural properties. Without this focus, values and tastes would remain unchanged over time.

It is possible to see the dialectic between structure and action by considering the factors of variation, agency, and contestation. The dialectic is operationalized in evaluation—in the decisions individuals make as to which actions are correct and appropriate. My analysis, then, incorporates three elements: structural properties that tend to shape action over time; the idioms that manifest structural properties in particular contexts; and the actions of individuals or patterns of action that have the potential to construct new idioms and arrangements of structural properties (see Karp and Maynard 1983 for the original use of this triad). As patterns of action are increasingly practiced, they become more apparent and more idiomatic in that they become more easily perceived in a variety of situations. As such paradigmatic associations are established, they become increasingly important resources for structuring meanings and perceptions and for constituting particular arrangements of structural properties. In turn, structural properties guide (but do not determine) future action, but at the same time action has the potential to affect the emergence of future arrangements of structural properties.

The element that makes change possible, then, is agency and, specifically, actions associated with evaluation. While structural properties guide action, the potential for new arrangements of structural properties is embedded within action itself. In the analysis presented here, agency has two facets. The first is that the very perception of idioms or paradigmatic associations is an individualized act. It is guided by subjectively defined interests and goals, personal experience and the skills that an individual might have, other personal or idiosyncratic elements of the psyche, and the contingencies of particular situations. Surrounding these subjectively charged forces are, of course, objectively defined ideas of personhood, morality, and appropriate behavior. As individuals are pulled in what are often conflicting directions, the possibility emerges of perceiving redundancies and evaluating action in new ways. It is the very act of evaluation that actualizes or validates particular perceptions of idioms.

The second facet, which emerges from the first, is that the perceptions of some individuals, for a variety of reasons that change over time, are given more weight or are evaluated more positively than others. When this happens, new or alternative sets of idioms or paradigmatic associations are validated and put into play. Here, too, the result is a potential resorting of associations across domains and a reshaping of idioms. The result can be a reorganization of the very structural properties that shape action and culture.

My argument here is that aesthetic evaluation plays a central role in the very production of culture. Aesthetic preference is related to three things: redundancy and the habits of action that crosscut domains of life; agency and the individualized basis for recognizing habits of action, analogies, or paradigmatic associations across domains of experience;

and finally, power, in the form of judgments as to whose perception of paradigmatic associations is given more weight at any particular point in time. A primary focus of an anthropology of aesthetics, then, is exploring the conditions under which evaluation occurs and the consequences of that evaluation.

CAN AESTHETIC SYSTEMS BE COMPARED?

As noted earlier, a major question of the new context-based studies of aesthetics is how they can be compared to consider the role of aesthetic evaluation in culture in more general terms. The next question that must be considered is whether or not the model described in this volume has relevance for more than the Kono situation. I think it does, but the comparison moves far beyond questions of form and function to the larger issues of value, agency, and the power that expressive culture has in the process of constructing culture. Numerous studies in the social history of European and American aesthetic forms have begin to consider some of these larger issues. Baxandall (1972) has discussed how the skills of the marketplace intersect with Renaissance painting. In his view such skills as the ability to gauge the volume of a commodity and to calculate proportion were necessary for participation in the business world. Baxandall (1972:87) writes:

> ... to the commercial man almost anything was reducible to geometrical figures underlying any surface irregularities—the pile of grain reduced to a cone, the barrel to a cylinder or a compound of truncated cones ... the brick tower to a compound cubic body composed of a calculable number of smaller cubic bodies ...

Baxandall goes on to write that the entrepreneur's habit of analysis was very similar to the painter's analysis of appearances. "As a man gauged a bale, the painter surveyed a figure" (Baxandall 1972:88). This is not necessarily to imply that one skill causes the other, although the importance of the Quattrocento businessman as a patron of the arts might suggest a causal relationship. Rather, it is more useful for our purposes to explore what Karp and Maynard (1983:491) called the consistency of these relationships between domains and to suggest that both painting and the marketplace draw upon the principles of a particular kind of cognitive style that probably ordered numerous domains of fifteenth-century Italian life. The recognition of similarities across domains and the implicit focus on the ways in which such perceptions potentially shape culture is the same kind of perceptual and shaping process that I have traced in the Kono material. What becomes important for a cross-cultural approach to aesthetics is consideration of the ways in which particular skills interpenetrate in ways that have significant consequences for the shape of future action. This raises questions as to why particular skills and habits of action emerge as important at particular points in time and connects questions of aesthetics to questions of social formations, power, politics, and economics in new and useful ways.

Another example of the ways in which the model of investigation into aesthetics that I have employed with the Kono material can be used in another context can be seen in briefly looking at the rise of the New York School or abstract expressionist movement in the United States just after World War II. In general these art works formed part of the idioms that reinforced themes or structures of individuality, freedom, and class distinctions in ways that were historically important at mid-century and are still resonating in American culture today. I have chosen this movement to show that the approach I am taking to non-Western and non-elite art forms is equally valid and revealing when considering a Western art movement.[1]

Much of early twentieth-century American art traces its roots to European schools and forms, particularly the works of French artists. Debates about the nature of abstraction were an important part of the European art world prior to World War I. On one hand were those, like Mondrian, who searched for universal beauty in forms free of any suggestion of representation. In this kind of abstraction, it was important that the artist "frees himself from individual sentiments and from particular impressions which he receives from outside, and that he breaks loose from the domination of individual inclinations within him" (quoted in Osborne 1970:96). In this way the "great hidden laws of nature," or the "true content of reality" were revealed (quoted in Osborne 1970:98). On the other hand were those, such as Kandinsky, who wrote in 1912 that there is an "innate affinity between pictorial elements and emotional states" (quoted in Osborne 1970:269). Art, in this view, is about the direct perception of emotional states, rather than an escape from individual to universal sentiments. In defending his brand of abstraction in later years, Kandinsky wrote in 1938 that "[t]his art creates alongside the real world a new world which has nothing to do with *external* reality. It is subordinate *internally* to cosmic laws" (quoted in Osborne 1970:95) and is directly related to emotion. The debate between Mondrian's emphasis on objective laws or universals and Kandinsky's emphasis on metaphysical and individual realities was only one of many that guided the shape of abstract art in Europe and, by extension, in America. Many of these debates ended with World War I as artists, in reaction to the massive destruction of the war, began to search for a new relevance for their work and in doing so returned to more realistic styles. The trend toward realism carried over to America as well. Rose (1967:113) writes that "[d]uring the disillusioning post war period, many [American] artists felt that their only choices were to give up abstraction, give up art, give up society, or give up life."

In the movement toward realism, American artists began searching for a style that might be called uniquely American. The work of Grant Wood, Thomas Hart Benton, and others, which focused on somewhat romanticized images of American life, demonstrates this search (Rose 1967:115). This search was also somewhat political, as seen in Benton's emphasis on the democratization of art. He wrote (cited in Rose 1967:121) that "only by our own participation in the reality of American life ... could we come to forms in which Americans would find an opportunity for genuine spectator participation."

Another example of the newly emerging American style is the work of Stuart Davis. Although he rejected the pastoral scenes of Woods and Benton, Davis's focus became the restless and ever-changing qualities of urban life. While he considered himself a realist, he relied on abstraction as a vehicle to portray the city (Rose 1967:118). Edward Hopper's works also exemplified American realism, but his work focused on the loneliness and pathos of daily life in the city (Rose 1967:124).

Realism carried with it the potential of communicating political messages in ways that abstraction could not. This tendency was further emphasized with the onset of the Great Depression, when many American artists began to participate in the Works Project Administration (WPA) projects around the country. The links between politics and art were further solidified in 1936 when about 350 artists formed the Artist's Congress, which was dedicated primarily to anti-fascist activities (Rose 1967:128).

With the beginning of World War II, a new series of concerns emerged. People were forced to come to terms with new definitions of humanity, morality, and human capacity after the brutalities of the holocaust and the horrifying images of what atomic weaponry could do. The search for new definitions of humanity were sought in Jung's work on archetypes and the collective unconscious (Rose 1967:164). At the same time, the Cold War was beginning and the threat of communism, real or imagined, loomed large. In 1948 George C. Marshall proposed a recovery program designed to stabilize European nations by rebuilding a safe business environment. Americans feared that without such a program more of Europe would fall into communist hands (Czechoslovakia had recently moved into the communist bloc, and the American government was worried about possible communist victories in upcoming elections in France and Italy) (Guilbaut 1983:167). Closer to home, Henry Wallace decided to run for the presidency as a progressive candidate against Harry Truman. Adding to the rhetoric that helped establish the cold war, President Truman announced universal military training, further suggesting that a war against communism was a real possibility. Then, in 1950, the Korean War broke out and the House Committee on Un-American Activities began its work.

Events in the art world shifted along with concerns in the wider society. With the threat of communism and the growing anti-communist sentiment in the United States, artists turned away from political commentary. By the late 1940s, art was viewed as an aesthetic creation, separate from political or commercial considerations. This was emphasized in 1943 with the founding of the Federation of Modern Painters and Sculptors, a group that saw itself in opposition to the political goals of the Artists Congress (Cockcroft 1974:40).[2] One critic wrote "a work of art, being a phenomenon of vision, is primarily within itself evident and complete" (from *Tiger's Eye,* quoted in Guilbaut 1983:166). The parallel with Kandinsky's earlier emphasis on internal emotional states is evident here. In this atmosphere, the work of certain artists moved to the forefront. Chief among these were artists who had moved away from realism and had merged abstraction with some of the techniques and symbols of the surrealists. One technique, automatism, was particularly suited to the new emphasis on internal states. Early exemplars of this new emphasis included Arshile Gorky and Willem de Kooning who were both concerned with the release of energy and emotional expression. Another was Jackson Pollock, whose concern with ordering raw feeling translated into large canvases covered with randomly dribbled paint (Rose 1967:173).[3] Pollock's work was described as showing a new kind of sincerity, and it became a symbol of the regeneration of American art that artists had been looking for since the move away from European models in the 1920s. In an early commentary Clement Greenburg predicted that the new avant-garde would be a very personal art that focuses on the externalization of interior states (cited in Guilbaut 1983:170). Pollock himself described his painting in the following way: "When I am painting I have no knowledge of what I am doing. Only after a moment of 'returning consciousness' do I become aware of what I have been doing" (quoted in Pellegrini 1969:119). An article in *Life* described Pollock's work in the following way:

> Sometimes he dribbles the paint on with a brush. Sometimes he scrawls it on with a stick, scoops it with a trowel or even pours it on straight out of the can. In with it all he mixes sand, broken glass, nails, screws or other foreign matter lying around. Cigaret ashes and an occasional dead bee sometimes get in the picture inadvertently (quoted in Guilbaut 1983:186).

The picture of Pollock painting is one of frantic activity, of emotion externalized, ordered, and made public. Judgments of this new painting style were based, among other things, on the quality of finish. While French paintings of the day were seen as infinitely finished, abstract expressionist work was evaluated on its unfinished quality. At a symposium in 1950, American artist Robert Motherwell compared French and American styles by saying "[t]hey (the French) have a real 'finish' in that the picture is a real object, a beautifully made object. We are involved in 'process' and what is a 'finished' object is not so certain" (quoted in Guilbaut 1983:177). In discussions and debates over issues such as this, American abstract art was transformed into the representative style of "Western culture" and "French taste and finish gave way to American force and violence as universal cultural values" (Guilbaut 1983:177).

Another component in the success of abstract expressionism was the way that political and cultural institutions used the work as a demonstration of the values of freedom and capitalism, as opposed to communism, fascism, and other forms of totalitarianism. It is no secret that the Central Intelligence Agency and the Museum of Modern Art (which was then funded primarily by Rockefeller and Whitney money) collaborated to organize numerous major exhibitions for European audiences after World War II (Cockcroft 1974). In a book on the history of the Museum of Modern Art, Russell Lynes writes that these exhibitions were used "as a way of letting it be known especially in Europe that America was not the cultural backwater that the Russians, during that tense period called the 'Cold War', were trying to demonstrate that it was" (quoted in Cockcroft 1974).

In this atmosphere, American painters who were still following European models or working in American realism fell out of fashion. Such previously well-known artists as Romare Bearden and Stuart Davis were redefined as secondary talents and were lost in the reshuffle. Presumably their works dropped markedly in value as well. A new definition of the avant-garde, prefigured by Clement Greenberg's earlier comments, moved to the foreground. "The intrasubjective artist invents from personal experience, creates from an internal world rather than an external one. He makes no attempt to chronicle the American scene, exploit momentary political struggles, or stimulate nostalgia through familiar objects. He deals, instead, with inward emotions and experiences" (Samuel Kootz, quoted in Guilbaut 1983:178).[4]

These dramatic shifts in the American art world did not occur without debate and contestation. Some critics called abstract expressionism irresponsible, incoherent, and simplistic. It did not appeal to large segments of the rapidly growing ranks of the post-World War II middle class. More importantly, it found its most enthusiastic supporters among members of the middle and upper classes who had achieved their positions before the war. In essence, then, abstract expressionism also served as a vehicle for clarifying class distinctions. Liking abstract expressionism and all it stood for became a marker of distinction, as did disliking it or claiming not to understand it. By identifying with abstract expressionism, America's liberal bourgeoisie rejected political art and pre-war images of America in favor of a new image (Guilbaut 1983). In an atmosphere of convergent interests, this new image fostered an emerging international art style, as well as America's newly emerging international economic and political presence. Such connections were made not only in the name of modernity, taste, and class but also because of America's leading role in the Cold War. In this way abstract expressionism linked values that were part of the dominant ideology with the avant-garde and the ideology of the Cold War. In the tensions between an encroaching middle class and a dominant elite, artists had to be anti-political, especially anti-communist, to succeed as well as to save high culture from both the threats of communism and the rising tide of the new middle class (Guilbaut 1983).

Although abstract expressionism was overtly apolitical, it in fact served as a powerful political instrument. Abstract expressionism, because of its apolitical character and emphasis on individual emotions and views, became a powerful vehicle for post-World War II liberals in fighting what were perceived as the most serious threats of the day—fascism and communism. Because each "ism" was seen to threaten a way of life based on an ideology of freedom, the interior and individualized view of abstract expressionism provided a potent symbol for celebrating the freedom of the individual.

But what does this have to do with aesthetics? The rise of abstract expressionism is a good illustration of the phenomenon that what people praise is integrally tied to their own interpretation or perception of the cultural forms that emerge around them at any point in time. This perception comes both from the structures that guide action and from an individual's interests and goals in particular situations. The rise of the New York School reinforced the structures of individuality and freedom at a time when ideas of human nature were being revised in American society. The idioms that helped in this process included the texts and paintings that focused on the externalization of internal emotions. Along the way, the interests of artists in identifying an American style and the interests of patrons in distinguishing themselves from the rapidly growing post-World War II middle class were served. Also served were the interests of artists, most of whom found that it was difficult to exhibit and sell work that was overtly political during this era.

While interpreted as a new vision or new way of making art, in fact the abstract expressionists demonstrate continuities with or transformations of European abstraction, surrealism, as well as American cultural forms. The parallels with Kandinsky's discussions of abstraction have already been discussed. There are also continuities in terms of the emphasis on an ideology of independence and individual freedom. In addition, it is important to point out that many of the abstract expressionists studied with the American realists. Jackson Pollock, for example, was a student of Thomas Hart Benton. Many of the abstract expressionists also show the marks of having worked with the WPA during the depression era. The large-sized canvases that Pollock and others painted were first used in the 1930s by the muralists commissioned to produce large format works for public buildings.

All of these influences merged to produce a rearrangement of structural properties that emphasized idiomatic ways of including, excluding, and otherwise emphasizing distinctions between individuals, the importance of interior vision and emotion, an ideology of individualism and freedom, and the maintenance of a particular political and economic status quo. What I want to suggest in comparing the Kono and American cases is that the process of producing aesthetic effect is similar, if not identical, in each. People respond to forms based on what they "know" from experiences that occur or have occurred in other domains of their lives. Even when the forms themselves masquerade as avant-garde, they are intimately connected to experiences in other domains of life. The abstract expressionist artists of mid-twentieth century America, though perceived as individualists and avant-garde, were in fact closely tied to elite values and the status quo. Appreciation of their efforts and financial support of their work was directly connected to their abilities to carry out this task. The difference between the contexts and forms of appreciation found in these two cases is not the way appreciation is structured but the content of the idioms and the structural properties they give rise to. It is not the forms alone that are applauded as much as their accuracy in presenting or restructuring sets of broader structures or principles that, in turn, guide future action. The nature of the principles, the forms to which they are applied, and the meanings attached to particular forms may vary between cultures, but I would suggest it is this very adherence to and re-presentation of principles from the culture at large that elicits positive aesthetic response.

There are three factors that are important in this kind of analysis: (1) identifying the idiomatic forms or habits of action that crosscut domains of experience, (2) describing the forms of debate and contestation that surround judgments as to whose paradigmatic arrangements of habits of action are given more weight in the production of structural properties, and (3) some consideration of the consequences of particular arrangements of structural properties for future action. When examined in this way, it is clear that aesthetic judgments are more about a process than about particular forms or content and that this process is present in contexts that are defined as "art" or "artistic," as well as in a range of other contexts. To explore this process thoroughly, it is as important to see it working in contexts unrelated specifically to Western categories of art as it is to study it in art contexts.

From this perspective it becomes possible to explore a set of questions that have yet to be fully considered. These center around defining the parameters of particular aesthetic systems and considering what kinds of distinctions can be drawn among them. Several questions come immediately to mind, for example: Under what conditions do categories of "art" emerge? And under what conditions are aesthetic judgments likely to support or counter the status quo? Other research questions will emerge as more comparisons become apparent.

IMPLICATIONS FOR AN ANTHROPOLOGY OF AESTHETICS

The model of analysis presented here suggests ways in which an anthropology of aesthetics might escape the Western categories inherent in most of the fields that traditionally study art and aesthetics. Doing so takes questions of aesthetics into a range of issues that have tended not to be associated with studies of art and aesthetics. From the perspective presented here, art, aesthetic evaluation, and expressive culture (meaning those areas of culture that are evaluated) can no longer be seen as a reflection or mirror of cultural processes. Rather, expressive culture must be taken as a fundamental part of the very construction of social and cultural forms. Focusing on the constructive aspects of expressive forms leads, by necessity, to a consideration of agency and the relationship between structure and action. One of my conclusions has been that aesthetic evaluation is one of the mediating forces in the interplay between structure and action. In other words, as agents evaluate they are forced to reconcile ideas of appropriate behavior with interests, abilities, and the contingencies of particular situations. Embedded within this process is the potential for new ideas about what constitutes moral or appropriate behavior and new arrangements of structural properties.

Positing connections between morality and aesthetics raises important questions about the manipulation of aesthetic evaluations for political or economic ends and the role of aesthetic evaluations in constructing and maintaining social distinctions. Another aspect of aesthetic evaluation, then, is power—the power of critics and the impact their judgments have on the construction of new or alternate arrangements of structural properties and, thus, social and cultural forms in general.

The perspective or analytical framework described in this book can be applied to changes in any Western art form and to the analysis of behavior in settings outside the Euro-American elite art world. Such a wide range of applications, however, depends on beginning from local categories of experience. This is a perspective that can be applied to those contexts that have explicit definitions of art or aesthetics as well as to contexts that do not have such definitions. It is in the latter contexts, however, that researchers must be willing to focus on forms that may not be part of their taken-for-granted ideas of what art or aesthetic evaluation is all about. Only by beginning with local categories is it possible to discuss the molded ceramic figurine found on the mantelpiece of a lower middle-class American home in the same breath as a Kono dance form, compliance with the obligations inherent in the Kono descent system, or the sculptures of a contemporary American artist such as Nancy Graves. These forms live in different worlds, but all are the focus of aesthetic evaluation and all work to construct the specific social and cultural frameworks within which they are found. All four forms speak of agency and structure, power and identity, but in very different ways. The perspective described in this volume shifts an anthropology of aesthetics towards an analysis of the ways in which forms as seemingly different as these operate in the construction of social and cultural forms and away from a comparison of the forms themselves. It is this potential focus that distinguishes an anthropology of aesthetics from the treatment of aesthetics in other fields.

APPENDIX A

1982 Upland Rice Yields

Household	Bushels Planted	Laborers	Yield (Bushels)	People Eating	Bushels Needed*	Plus/ Minus**
1	3	4	16.5	5	15	+ 1.5
2	2.5	4	14	5	15	− 1
3	3	2	18	12	36	−18
4	2	3	11	5	15	+ 4
5	3	3	16	4	12	+ 4
6	4	5	24	16	48	−24
7	2	3	5.5	4	12	− 6.5
8	2.5	4	7	6	18	−11
9	3	6	21	12	36	−15
10	2	7	18	14	42	−24
11	1.5	3	9	4	12	− 3
12	4	7	27	9	27	—
13	3.5	11	23	15	45	−22
14	2	4	18.5	6	18	+0.5
15	4.5	12	32	17	51	−19
16	2	3	17	8	24	− 7
17	3	8	22	11	33	−11
18	3.5	9	21	9	27	− 6
19	4.5	10	20	18	54	−34
20	1.5	3	4.5	4	12	− 7.5
21	3	4	10.5	5	15	− 4.5
22	3	6	9	8	24	−15
23	3.5	5	10	7	21	−11
24	3	4	10.5	5	15	− 4.5
25	3	5	11	6	18	− 7
26	5	4	17	7	27	−10
27	1.5	2	9	2	6	+ 3
28	3.5	4	13	4	12	+ 1
29	4	3	19	5	15	+ 4
30	3	3	13	4	12	+ 1
31	3.5	3	20	16	48	−28
32	3	3	9	4	12	− 3

*calculated at 3 bushels per person per year
**bushels over (+) or under (−) household's estimated needs.

APPENDIX B

1983 Upland Rice Yields

Household	Bushels Planted	Laborers	Yield (Bushels)	People Eating	Bushels Needed*	Plus/ Minus**
1	2.5	3	19	6	18	+ 1
2	2	2	21	3	9	+12
3	3.5	5	34	7	21	+13
4	2.5	2	31	4	12	+19
5	1.5	1	20	2	6	+14
6	4	5	38	8	24	+14
7	6	4	52	5	15	+37
8	8	9	74	12	36	+38
9	6.5	5	74	9	27	+47
10	3	3	32	8	24	+ 8
11	2	2	31	3	9	+22
12	8.5	6	82	12	36	+46
13	2	2	32	4	12	+20
14	5	4	62	7	21	+41
15	4.5	5	72	9	27	+45
16	1.5	2	31	3	27	+ 4
17	3	3	55	4	12	+43
18	3.5	5	50	7	21	+29
19	4	3	58	4	12	+46
20	3	2	60	4	12	+48
21	4	2	72	4	12	+60
22	3	2	49	5	15	+34
23	1.5	3	30	4	12	+18
24	3.5	3	63	5	15	+48
25	1.5	3	40	4	12	+28
26	3	3	57	5	15	+42
27	3	3	54	6	18	+36
28	4	4	72	7	21	+51
29	5	6	62	9	27	+35
30	3.5	3	52	5	15	+37
31	4.5	3	81	6	18	+63
32	4	3	75	7	21	+54
33	3	2	58	3	9	+49

*calculated at 3 bushels per person per year
**bushels over (+) or under (−) household's estimated needs.

GLOSSARY

bain den moe: Literally "mother's brother's child person," refers to the mother's brother and his descendants.

baama: Outside or public space.

baffa: Farm structure where women cook the main meal of the day, where rice is stored, and where people come to rest during the work day.

beeboe: Literally "to give." This is the second part of post-burial ceremonies. During this part of the ritual the *fa den moe* and *bain den moe* of the deceased exchange goods to formally close the relationship that was established between them by the marriage of the parents of the deceased.

bemba: Grandparents or ancestors.

bien gai: Term for one's spouse's father and elder brothers. Contrast with *bien musu* and *nimoti.*

bien musu: Term used to refer to a spouse's mother and elder sisters (contrast with *nimoti* and *bien gai*).

boda: A ceramic vessel. Literally "earth" (*bo* or *gbo*) and "mouth" (*da*).

bwi or *bui:* Translates as medicine, which has two dimensions. The first refers to things that cure illnesses, and the second includes those things, such as charms or masked figures, that can empower individuals or groups.

chekugba: Warrior.

chima: Cold, malaria.

da: Mouth.

da si: Advice.

de: Mother, always used with a pronoun such as *n de* (my mother).

di: Sweetness.

diiboe: Literally "to pull the cry." This is the first part of Kono post-burial ceremonies, often called the "forty days," and includes formalized wailing that helps to open the way for the deceased to join the ancestors. The plural is *diiboenu.*

dunuya: This world.

fa: Father.

faa yonda: Literally "spoiled" (*yone*) "heart" (*faa*). Refers to sadness or disappointment.

faa chima: Literally "cool" (*chima*) "heart" (*faa*). Refers to the absence of malice.

fa den moe: Literally "father's child person," refers to a child's father and his relatives (the patrilineage of the child).

fande: Cotton.

fiao: Forest.

filiation: Relationships created by the fact of being recognized as the legitimate child of one's parents (see Fortes 1969:253). Matrifiliation refers to relationships with mother's relatives, patrifiliation refers to relationships with father's relatives.

fondon: Quarters or neighborhoods of a Kono town.

fufu: Fence.

gbako: Big man.

gbaseia: One of the Kono words for power, it refers to an individual's ability to control resources.

gbo or *bo:* Body, skin, and earth.

gbuo dia: Literally "stomach sweetness," refers to a sense of satisfaction.

harmattan: Late dry season winds that are said to sweep into West Africa from the Sahara. Probably an Arabic word.

idiom: Habits of action that manifest cultural principles or structural properties.

kai or *gai:* Man.

koa don: To warp a loom.

koa sa: To weave.

koo che: Literally "speech thing," refers to spoken activities.

kosan fa: To understand or to know how to do something.

kwee: Rice.

lappa: Rectangular piece of cloth that women tie around their waists and wear as a long skirt (this term is used in much of West Africa).

matrifilial: Refers to relationships created through being the child of one's mother. For the Kono the most important relationship established through matrifiliation is with the mother's brother and his descendants.

mbain: Term of address for one's mother's brother.

musu: Woman.

nyane: To make.

nimoti: Term used for one's spouse's younger brothers and sisters.

nyi: Goodness.

patrilineage: Subset of a clan in which all claim membership by virtue of direct descent (through the male line) from a known ancestor.

plasas: Krio word for the sauce that is served over rice.

Poro: Male initiation society found throughout the Central West Atlantic region of West Africa.

saama: Rainy season (March to September).

Sande: Female initiation society found throughout the Central West Atlantic region of West Africa.

sara: Sacrifice (probably from Arabic).

seneo: Farm (*sene*) place (*o*).

si sa: Singing.

sinyuenu: Kono domestic unit.

songo songwe: Noise, refers to the confusion of shouting matches or other verbal disagreements.

structural properties: The resources and rules used in the construction of action (from Giddens 1979). Also referred to as "principles" throughout this volume.

swin chea: Useless activity.

structural properties: Ever-changing set of rules and resources that people use to construct and evaluate action.

tamba tina: Literally "spear" (*tamba*) "place" (*tina*). This is the ritual center of a rural Kono town. Members of a town are linked to their patrilineal ancestors through rituals done at this spot.

tana: Food prohibition shared by all members of the same clan.

tehma: Dry season (October to February).

tendu: Individual responsible for remembering amounts of bridewealth paid during marriage negotiations.

tindane: Round.

togbai: Term of address for men who have joined Poro at the same time.

tombo baama: Literally dance public, refers to the central area of a dance procession.

tombwe: Dance.

tombweo: Dance (*tombwe*) place (*o*).

tombwe don: To enter the dance.

wai chea: Productive activity.

yisi: Thread.

NOTES

I AESTHETICS AND CHANGE

1. The difficulty in defining art even within American society is demonstrated by recent debates over the role and financing of the National Endowment of the Arts in the United States.

2. Forrest (1988, forthcoming) makes a similar argument about the problems of relying on Western genres or categories in research on aesthetics.

3. Merriam's components were drawn from Western philosophical and art historical writings and thus reflect the interests of what can be called elite concerns about aesthetics. They included psychical distance, manipulation of form for its own sake, attribution of beauty to the art product or process, purposeful intent to create something aesthetic, and presence of a philosophy of an aesthetic (Merriam 1964:259-67).

4. In my usage, the production of objects is integrally related to the production of social forms, and the phrase "production processes" relates both to the production of material and to behavioral forms.

5. Throughout this volume I am using the word "domain" to mean a particular sphere or context of activity.

6. This triad is adopted from Karp and Maynard's reconsideration of Evans-Pritchard's *The Nuer* (Karp and Maynard 1983).

7. I have consciously chosen to focus on these perceptions of likeness as analogy rather than homology because the word homology implies likeness because of common origin. While this may be the case for some of the analogies discussed, as when elements of social organization and dance performance can be assumed to stem from some features of agricultural production, such historical connections can not be assumed in all cases. Additionally, focusing on homology implies the primacy of particular domains, something that I hope to avoid in this analysis. Rather, my interest is in the process of perceiving similitude, an act that not only may reflect structures or principles over time but that also may contain within it the possibility of new perceptual schema and serendipitous possibilities.

8. In an analysis that is in some ways very similar to the one presented here, Beidelman (1986) uses "moral imagination" to discuss the process by which Kaguru cosmology is shaped, used, and conceptualized. In Beidelman's terms, imagination alludes to the means by which people "measure, assess, and reflect upon the reality of their experiences" and "offers the possibility of questioning some aspects of the version of the system in which imagination itself is rooted" (Beidelman 1986:4,5). He goes on to write that it is through social interaction that appropriate or moral ways of behaving are conceptualized or imagined. An important part of Beidelman's analysis is also the role of metaphor and analogy and the ways that patterned action construct possibilities and cosmology. My work differs from this approach in two ways. First, I am interested in the specific ways that evaluations of action affect structure. In this way I consider aesthetic evaluation to be one aspect of imagination. Second, to do this I have relied on Giddens's model of structuration as a way of grounding my analysis.

2 THE REGIONAL SETTING

1. Government airplane service was stopped sometime between 1984 and 1988 as spare parts for planes became increasingly scarce and fuel prices increased.

2. The journey between Koidu and Freetown is increasingly difficult to negotiate as the highway, built by a German aid project in the mid-seventies, has fallen into disrepair.

3. The Sierra Leone Government hopes to switch to kimberlite mining, a technique that requires tunneling and the search for diamonds below the ground, sometime in the future. This process will require fewer workers, can continue year round, and will undoubtedly have a major effect on labor migration in the area.

4. Syrian traders, immigrants from the Ottoman Empire, began immigrating to Sierra Leone in the 1890s. Gradually they were given priority over Creole traders in the Sierra Leone protectorate (Fyfe 1962:159). Today, the Lebanese traders continue this tradition, controlling much of the business and foreign exchange throughout the country.

5. In fact, I saw what was probably the last Datsun sedan to make the journey to Kainkordu early in my fieldwork in 1982. The extent of rising transportation costs in rural Sierra Leone can be demonstrated in my own rising costs. In 1982 transportation between Koidu and Kainkordu was 4 to 6 leones (about $.36 to $.54 in 1982 U.S. dollars). By the time I left in 1984 the cost for the same trip was 16 to 20 leones (about $.40 to $.50 in 1984 U.S. dollars). In comparison, most secondary school teachers were earning about 25 leones a month between 1982 and 1984, and salaries did not go up in response to inflation. When I returned in 1988, costs for the trip between Koidu and Kainkordu had risen to between 30 and 40 leones, while teachers's salaries had only risen slightly above 1984 levels.

6. A maternity clinic was opened in 1987 in Manjama, three miles from Kainkordu. It currently provides prenatal and postnatal care, treatment for minor medical emergencies, venereal diseases, and childhood illnesses.

7. Sande and Poro are the two main initiation societies in the area. Young women and men are initiated into Sande and Poro respectively in adolescence. Membership remains an important source of identity and allegiance throughout an individual's lifetime.

3 IDENTITY IN TIME

1. This emphasis on the two dimensions of personhood mirrors the work of Fortes (1973) and Mauss (1939). The importance of these two dimensions for theories of agency was recently discussed in Jackson and Karp (1990).

2. Parsons (1964:xii) identifies the mountain as Kono-su, which he says is located about fifty miles northeast of the Kono area.

3. Given Mende proximity to the Kono and the fact that each group was responding to similar threats, it is not surprising that Mende accounts of warfare are similar to those related by elderly Kono individuals.

4. It is possible that this political change reinforced patrilineality in ways that made patrilineal affiliations stronger and more important, particularly in ruling families, than they had been in the pre-Colonial period.

5. Rosen suggests that the Kono make a distinction between clans as large agnatic units, which share the same *tana*, and more local territorial clan units, known as *dambi*. He (Rosen 1973:32) writes that historically *tana* were not exogamous but *dambi* were and that, while those sharing the same *tana* might make war on each other, groups sharing the same *dambi* would be less likely to do so. The Kono descent system is very similar to that which Jackson (1974, 1977) describes for the Kuranko. One major exception is Kuranko clan hierarchies. Kuranko clans are identified as ruler and commoner clans, traditionally Muslim clans, and clans that are occupation-specific. Such distinctions do not exist for the Kono. While the Kono do recognize certain clans as original landholders and founders of villages or chiefdoms, which implies preference in terms of land tenure today, these hierarchies tend to be chiefdom-specific in ways that Kuranko clan hierarchies are not. In addition, there are no specifically Muslim clans among the Kono, although all clans may have members who have converted to Islam. Most importantly, in terms of the Mande literature, the Kono do not have hereditary occupational specialists such as the weavers, leatherworkers, blacksmiths and others known as *nyamakala* among other Mande groups (see McNaughton 1988).

6. Given the current tendency for young men to migrate for wage labor, there is not a noticeable shortage of agricultural land in Soa Chiefdom. There is, however, intense competition for land that is close to towns and villages. Disputes between lineages over the control of specific tracts of land are frequent. There is also a tendency to decrease fallowing periods between crops in areas closest to towns. While most farmers admit that land should lie fallow ten to fifteen years, the average in the Kono area is from three to seven years. This change may be attributed to a shortage of land near living spaces as well as to a tendency to avoid the intense labor required to clear land that has remained fallow for ten or more years.

7. While I was told this was a yearly event, in fact it is not held every year. I witnessed it in 1982, but it was not held in 1983. In addition, there were few people present in 1982 who had seen the event before.

8. Fortes (1970) distinguishes between the external domain of political-jural relations and the more internal or domestic domain that is characterized by ties of sentiment and affect. Here, I am referring to the external domain.

9. Citing the Sierra Leone National Archives, Rosen (1973:57) reports that Gbenda was the only Kono paramount chief to meet with the governor of Sierra Leone at the time he was installing the paramount chiefs of Kono.

10. Fortes (1969:253) describes filiation as "the relationship created by the fact of being the legitimate child of one's parents."

11. I do not have actual figures on the divorce rate. Those presented here are estimates.

12. These terms may be similar to *fakor* (near the father) and *ndikor* (near the mother) used by Rosen (1973:40) to refer to patrilineage and mother's agnates, respectively.

13. Children may also adopt the *tana* of a legal father should a man other than their biological father tie kola for their mother in the future.

14. The closeness of the terms *fa den moe* and *bain den moe* to the Bamana distinction between *fa den ya* and *ba den ya* cannot be ignored, especially given the fact that *ba* is mother in Bambara but it appears in *bain den moe* (the Kono word for mother is *de*). The Kono terms may, indeed, be remnants of this distinction, but caution should be used in applying the Bamana material as a whole. Bird and Kendall (1980) write that children compete with their patrilineal ancestors (*fa den ya*) to establish their own individuality in the form of personal renown. On the other hand, it is the recognition by one's mother and her relatives (*ba den ya*) which pulls the individual back under the control of the social group. According to Bird and Kendall (1980:15), "since ideally one cannot refuse the request of one's *ba den,* an individual's wishes must be subordinated to the interests of other members of his group." The goal is to impress one's *ba den,* which means the adventuring individual must first have adventures and then return to tell about them and be recognized by the *ba den* to achieve status. Recognition often is contingent upon the dispersal of resources gained outside. Thus the system remains somewhat in equilibrium by sending individuals out to achieve but bringing them back to invest in their home communities. Without returning, the movement out becomes meaningless, their deeds go unrecognized, and the individual is forgotten (Bird and Kendall 1980:2).

For the Kono, the concepts of *fa den moe* and *bain den moe* do not contrast individualism and efforts to surpass the deeds of patrilineal ancestors with group centeredness and triumphal returns to the group for recognition. In some ways the Kono situation is the reverse of that of the Bamana. While for the Bamana it is patrilineal associations that push toward individuality and achievement, for the Kono it is matrifilial ties that allow some individuals an escape from the identities and control of the patrilineage. On the other hand, patrilineages are only too happy to recognize and reward achievement with social status and resources if it is felt this individual will be advantageous to the lineage. This is clearly demonstrated in the land dispute involving the foreign-trained individual cited earlier in this chapter. Before this similarity in terminology can be explored further, however, more comparative research must be done.

15. Wives are usually inherited by a brother of the deceased.

16. This year-and-a-half period coincides roughly with the postpartum ta-boo on sexual relations between husband and wife after the birth of a child.

17. It is interesting to note here that the tensions between those who have attended school and those who have not have been evident from the first in-troduction of primary schools (the first government-run schools were intro-duced in the Protectorate between 1910 and 1920). When paramount chiefs were first invited to send their sons away to government schools, it was com-mon for them to send the son of a slave instead. As a result, certain low status individuals were actually far better educated than the sons of chiefs and were in the pool of individuals first chosen for employment with the British.

18. In 1988, it was clear that the economic situation in the country as a whole, especially for government employees such as teachers, was such that many individuals were returning to farming at least part-time to make ends meet. In some ways this is fostering a renaissance of interest in farming. Teachers in secondary schools, especially those that have a curriculum similar to an American technical school, develop small farms near their school posts, sometimes even on school lands, and use these as demonstration plots to grow rice and test new agricultural techniques. It is currently uncertain how these efforts will change attitudes towards agriculture.

19. A presentation of red kola by itself, without white, is a sign of ill will or of bad news.

4 MANAGING SUBJECTIVITY

1. Fortes's (1973) ideas are similar to those of Mauss (1939) who distin-guished between *moi*, as awareness of self, and *la personne morale*, the rules, roles and representations that are part of ideology. For a discussion of these two approaches to personhood and their application to contemporary theories of agency see Jackson and Karp (1990).

2. Parsons (1964) translates Bii or Bili as "to circumcise."

3. Bush refers to the place, usually a short distance from town, where the initiates are secluded from family and friends for the initiation. The period of seclusion was once several months long but today instruction may only last a few weeks.

4. Kono medicine (*bwi* or *bui*) has two aspects. It can cure and it can also empower. For example, medicines of empowerment are used to enhance status, to protect oneself from the challenges of others, and to turn someone into an adult.

5. There are also other small but apparently growing exceptions to universal initiation into Poro or Sande. The most prominent are fundamentalist religious groups, such as "God Is Our Light," who refuse to initiate their children because they feel the initiation societies undermine Christianity.

5 THE AESTHETICS OF PRODUCTION

1. I do not have statistics on the size or acreage of farms, other than in terms of the bushels of seed rice used.

2. See Ben-Amos (1976) for an early discussion of the contrasts between civilization or town space and the uncivilized nature of forest space in African symbol systems.

3. I often heard women threatening to withdraw from the labor pool when talking among themselves. I knew of three cases of actual withdrawal during my two years in the area. One case involved Fiya and Tamba, who were described in Chapter 3. Two cases lasted for most of the growing season, and the other was resolved relatively quickly.

4. These groups may be remnants of the communal work groups found in other Mande areas, although there is very little local evidence to suggest this.

5. Kaeppler (personal communication 1986) has suggested dance movement itself may demonstrate contained versus uncontained elements, or that laterality signifies a lack of social control, while verticality and the crowd pressure that produces it may represent social control over the individual. In considering this, it became apparent that the participants outside the performance area use what could be described as contained movement—arms at sides, legs relatively straight with small swaying movements from side to side, and very little up and down movement. The impression I had was of a series of columns swaying in unison. In contrast, the dancers entering the performance arena exhibited much more freedom of movement, with more expansive gestures in both the vertical and horizontal planes.

6. Even in contemporary politics a paramount chief is relatively ineffective without the support of his constituents, even though he legally maintains his office for life.

7. Understanding the link between exchange and knowledge in this area is critically important for Peace Corps volunteers and other development workers and agencies.

8. The limits of redundancy as a positive force have to do with the boredom that overly repetitive stimuli can induce (see, for example, Berlyne 1971

and Winner 1982). Awareness of this fact is important, but exactly where the divisions between lack of comprehension, recognition and excitement, and boredom are located is a question better left to cognitive psychologists.

9. The process I am describing here is also similar to that which Beidelman (1986:2) attributes to imagination when he writes that " . . . imaginative exercise constitutes means for criticism, for distortion, even subversion, of the social order. It offers the possibility of questioning some aspects of the version of the system in which imagination itself is rooted."

7 POWER, AUTHORITY, AND ACTION

1. Power here, and throughout this chapter, refers more to the constructive and transformative possibilities of human action than to the controlling or determining aspects of action. Karp (1986), for example, writes that "[a] different view of power is exhibited in African societies than in Western social science. The stress in Africa is not on the element of control but on the more dynamic aspect of energy and the capacity to use it." Power, here, then is treated as a "social resource" (Arens and Karp 1989) that enables some individuals to have more impact than others on the construction of social and cultural systems. See also Foucault (1980) on the construction of right and Parkin's (1982) discussion of "semantic creativity."

2. Karp (1978a:2–3), for example, writes that "different aspects of given societies are changing at different rates" and that explanations of change must include an analysis of the relationship between various cultural domains or subsystems.

3. For the most part, anthropologists have used linguistic models to deal with action, implying that specific movements or action sets can be examined as units of specific meaning (Birdwhistle 1970; Ekman 1972; and others). This approach has been criticized by a number of scholars (Crick 1976; Jackson 1983; Williams 1982:173). In one critique, Williams (1982:173) has suggested using linguistic analogy as a means of examining action. One thread in this approach builds on Saussure's recognition of the importance of contrast in language processes, the implication being that actions in themselves are not meaningful, but, instead, it is the distinctions that action sets up that provide actual meaning. Thus, action has meaning because it refers to other action sets—past, present, and potential. Meaning, then, is associational and it varies with situations.

One approach to this perspective has been the notation of movement systems. The notations are then analyzed to develop grammars of movement and the contextual or relational associations surrounding specific movements. Implied in these studies is the notion that an adequate understanding of the semantic uses of the body have eluded researchers because movement is nonverbal expression. The remedy for this problem has been to present movement systems in notated form. Thus, "the same status is accorded to transcriptions of bodily acts as to vocal acts" (Williams 1982:162). Notation has been relatively successful when it is applied to highly structured, formally learned performance movement systems (see, for example, Farnell 1986; Puri 1981; and Williams 1982). It is less successful when applied to streams of everyday behavior where the distinctions between units of movement or between movement and action are less clearcut. While Saussure's (1960) interest in meaning, as it relates to distinctions or contrasts, obviously still applies, eliciting and notating the constituent features of specific units of movement is problematic. Even if such notation was possible, the resulting analysis would provide little indication of the richness of the meanings engendered through everyday movement.The emphasis on notation, however, gives priority to structure over action. Implicit in this weighting is a distinction between synchrony and diachrony—that systems or structures are static and thus capturable at specific moments in time (Giddens 1979). Emphasizing structure masks questions about the relationship between structure and action, about how transformations or changes in social and cultural formations take place over time (Karp 1986), and about how varying interpretations of action are reconciled. An overemphasis on structure also gives primacy to the observer's knowledge at the expense of the participant's knowledge.

4. Tricula is an imported defoliant that was used in swamp rice development programs but has been outlawed.

5. Clothes are laundered in streams by wetting them, working in soap, beating them against a rock in the stream, rinsing, and drying. In Krio, the term for beating clothes against a rock is "to knock."

6. As young girls spend less and less time in the Sande bush, it may be that the emphasis on experiential learning diminishes because of the lack of time. While older Kono women talk about being in the Sande bush during initiation for six months to a year, it is not uncommon today for girls to remain under the control of Sande elders for less than a month.

7. A further example of experiential learning comes from Holsoe's (1980:101) report that initiation into Sande in the Vai area includes actual demonstrations of intercourse with a wooden penis. Whether or not this occurs in the Kono area is uncertain.

8. Undoubtedly, if the younger and obviously stronger girl had been the one to make the initial curse, the reaction of the adults would have been

different. In cases where a stronger child tries to take advantage of someone weaker, older women will step in to stop the abuse.

9. To my knowledge, there is no Kono word for this behavior. The expression *N da o gba*, "my mouth is dry," meaning the person is so upset they have nothing to say about the matter, also implies a kind of withdrawal. When a wife withdraws from a husband's farm labor force (as described in Chapter 3), it is done in a similar way, with the wife moving around town in a slight daze, not really explaining why she did not go to the farm that day.

10. Country cloth refers to fabric that is made from handspun cotton thread that has been woven by hand. Warrior shirts are worn very infrequently. During the two years of my initial field work, I remember seeing them on only two or three occasions.

11. McNaughton (1979) describes similar challenges of the leaders of the Komo society among the Bambara.

8 AESTHETICS AND CONTESTATION

1. Karp and Maynard (1983) have discussed the importance of cultural idioms in their analysis of the Nuer. Their view of cultural idioms is that these are properties of culture that are named and tend to be constant over time. While this is often the case, I would suggest that idioms, while they may be named, may also be more fleeting and less enduring; in addition, they are as likely to exist in the way people move through or conceive of the world as they are to exist as named or linguistically marked entities.

2. This critique is similar to Karp's (1986) comments that Bourdieu fails to take account of the agent's knowledge of situations. My comments on Bourdieu are based on his earlier writings, especially *Outline of a Theory of Practice* (1977). His later writings suggest a view of habitus that is less rigidly structured, but even in these writings it is unclear how habitus is shared and, more specifically, who shares in habitus (see, for example, Bourdieu 1990:12–17).

3. Mimesis has been primarily studied as it occurs in infants and as it relates to facial expression. It is the process by which children learn about their own musculature, particularly facial, and begin reproducing the actions of others. There is the implication, however, that there is much more to it than this. Sarles (1975:26) has described the production of symptoms in an observer-interactor's body in an "essentially uncontrollable way." His examples include changes in body rhythms and pulse rates related to shared movement. Other research has demonstrated the modification in and mimicking of hormonal

levels among individuals sharing close psychological or environmental spaces. Clearly, the means by which bodies interact outside the awareness of mental processes is still a relatively uncharted area of psychobiology. The important point here is that this is not necessarily (and, in fact, is probably rarely) a conscious imitation or copying. Such interactions, however, are capable of triggering affect, and this quite likely plays a role in the interpretation of action.

4. In addition to highlighting appropriate modes of behavior, this elderly woman had her own interests in praising me over another foreigner.

5. Some 17,000 Sierra Leoneans enlisted in the Sierra Leone Regiment during World War II. Most served in combat or service positions in East Asia or Burma (Fyfe 1962:170).

6. See Siegmann and Perani (1976) for a description of an agricultural fair in the Mende area of Sierra Leone.

7. While there is evidence of a tradition of locally smelted ore for the production of metal objects in the area around Kainkordu, very little is known about this today. When I use the term metalware here, I am referring to imported goods.

8. Large water jars (2 or more feet in height) are no longer made. The largest pot I saw being made was approximately 8 inches in height.

9. The fact that he lost his position once his resources were gone and he was reduced to poverty does not necessarily suggest that claims to power and control through lineal affiliations may be slightly more enduring. As discussed in Chapter 3, old age is also likely to strip power from those whose claims to resources are based on lineal affiliations.

10. Oil palms have not been grown as cash crops on plantations in this area, except for a single government pilot project that failed. Instead, the surplus from household production may be sold for cash in the markets of Koidu. This oil comes from uncultivated oil palms that grow throughout the forest.

9 DEFINING AN ANTHROPOLOGY OF AESTHETICS

1. For the purposes of this comparison, I am using secondary sources since I have not done original research on the New York School.

2. Cockcroft (1974) develops an argument that ties abstract expressionist artists and the content of their work directly to government attempts to export ideas of individual freedom to the rest of the world during the Cold War. Artists who were suspected of harboring communist leanings or who had been

associated with radical political groups during the 1930s found it difficult to have their works included in art exhibitions sent to Europe through American government agencies. Cockcroft suggests that the personal content of the abstract expressionists work made their canvases perfect vehicles for the themes of individual freedom and capitalism that the government was interested in exporting.

3. Michael Leja (1987) discusses the process by which the various styles of this group of relatively diverse artists came to be recognized as a school, as well as the process by which the artists themselves came to stress their commonalities.

4. The ebbs and flows of the American art world and aesthetic judgments within it can be illustrated by the fact that the Museum of Modern Art has recently held a retrospective of Stuart Davis's work that restored him to the ranks of major twentieth-century American artists—a fitting end to the Cold War period.

REFERENCES CITED

Abraham, Arthur
    1973   Mende Influence on Kono. *Africana Research Bulletin*
           3(2):44–46.

Adams, Marie Jeanne
    1973   Structural Aspects of a Village Art. *American Anthropologist*
           75:265–79.
    1977   Style in Southeast Asian Materials Processing: Some Implica-
           tions for Ritual and Art. In *Material Culture: Styles, Organiza-
           tion, and Dynamics of Technology,* Heather Lechtman and
           Robert S. Merrill, eds. pp. 21–52. New York: West Publish-
           ing Co.

Anderson, Richard L.
    1990   *Calliope's Sisters: A Comparative Study of Philosophies of Art.*
           Englewood Cliffs, New Jersey: Prentice Hall.

Arens, W., and Ivan Karp
    1989   Introduction. In *Creativity of Power: Cosmology and Action in
           African Societies.* W. Arens and Ivan Karp, eds. pp. xi–xxix.
           Washington: Smithsonian Institution Press.

Arnoldi, Mary Jo
    1986   Puppet Theatre: Form and Ideology in Bamana Performance.
           Empirical Studies of the Arts 42(2):131–50.

Atherton, John H.
    1979   Early Economies of Sierra Leone and Liberia: Archaeological
            and Historical Reflections. In *Essays on the Economic Anthro-
            pology of Liberia and Sierra Leone*. Vernon R. Dorjahn and
            Barry L. Isaacs, eds. pp. 27–43. Philadelphia: Institute for
            Liberian Studies.

Bateson, Gregory
    1972a   Style, Grace, and Information in Primitive Art. In *Steps to an
            Ecology of Mind*, pp. 128–58. New York: Ballantine Books.
    1972b   Social Planning and the Concept of Deutero-Learning. In *Steps
            to an Ecology of Mind*, pp. 159–76. New York: Ballantine
            Books.

Bateson, Gregory, and Margaret Mead
    1942   *Balinese Character: A Photographic Analysis*. New York: New
            York Academy of Sciences, Vol. II.

Baxandall, Michael
    1972   *Painting and Experience in Fifteenth-Century Italy*. London:
            Oxford University Press.

Beidelman, T. O.
    1963   Kaguru Time Reckoning: An Aspect of the Cosmology of an
            East African People. *Southwestern Journal of Anthropology*
            19(9):9–20.
    1966   Swazi Royal Ritual. *Africa* 36:373–405.
    1986   *Moral Imagination in Kaguru Modes of Thought*. Blooming-
            ton: Indiana University Press.

Ben-Amos, Paula
    1976   Men and Animals in African Art. *Man* 11:242–52.

Berlyne, D. E.
    1971   *Aesthetics and Psychobiology*. New York: Appleton Century
            Crofts.

Bird, Charles S., and Martha B. Kendall
    1980   The Mande Hero. In *Explorations in African Systems of
            Thought*. Ivan Karp and Charles S. Bird, eds. pp. 13–26.
            Bloomington: Indiana University Press.

Birdwhistel, R.
    1970   *Kinesics and Context. Essays on Body Motion and Communi-
            cation*. Philadelphia: University of Pennsylvania Press.

Bledsoe, Caroline
  1980   *Women and Marriage in Kpelle Society.* Stanford: Stanford
          University Press.

Bourdieu, Pierre
  1977   *Outline of a Theory of Practice.* London: Cambridge University Press.
  1990   *In Other Words: Essays Towards a Reflexive Sociology.* Stanford: Stanford University Press.

Cockcroft, Eva
  1974   Abstract Expressionism, Weapon of the Cold War. *Artforum.*
          June 1974:39–41.

Conteh, Sorie
  1976   *Diamond Mining and Kono Religious Institutions: A Study in
          Social Change.* Ph.D. dissertation, Department of Anthropology, Indiana University.

Crick, Malcolm
  1976   *Towards a Semantic Anthropology: Explorations in Language
          and Meaning.* London: Malaby.

d'Azevedo, Warren
  1958   A Structural Approach to Esthetics: Toward a Definition of
          Art in Anthropology. *American Anthropologist* 60:702–14.
  1962   Some Historical Problems in the Delineation of a Central West
          Atlantic Region. *Annals of the New York Academy of Sciences*
          96(2):512–38.
  1973a   Introduction. In *The Traditional Artist in African Societies.*
          Warren d'Azevedo, ed. Bloomington: Indiana University Press.
  1973b   Sources of Gola Artistry. In *The Traditional Artist in African
          Societies.* Warren d'Azevedo, ed. pp. 282-340. Bloomington:
          Indiana University Press.

Durkheim, Emile
  1915   *The Elementary Forms of the Religious Life.* New York: The
          Free Press.

Ekman, P.
  1972   *Emotion in the Human Face.* New York: Pergamon Press.

Evans-Pritchard, Edward
  1940   *The Nuer.* New York: Oxford University Press.
  1956   *Nuer Religion.* Oxford: Clarendon Press.

1960   Introduction. In *Death and the Right Hand. Essays by Robert Hertz*. pp. 9-24. Glencoe: The Free Press.

Fagg, William
1973   In Search of Meaning in African Art. In *Primitive Art and Society*. Anthony Forge, ed. pp. 151–68. London: Oxford University Press.

Farnell, Brenda
1986   Problems with Spoken Language Models in the Analysis of Sign Languages. Paper presented at the American Anthropological Association annual meeting, Philadelphia.

Feld, Steven
1988   Aesthetics as Iconicity of Style, or 'Lift-Up-Over Sounding': Getting into the Kaluli Groove. *Yearbook for Traditional Music* 20:74–113.

Fernandez, James
1971   Principles of Opposition and Vitality in Fang Aesthetics. In *Art and Aesthetics in Primitive Societies*. Carol Jopling, ed. pp. 356–73. New York: E. P. Dutton and Co.
1973   The Exposition and Imposition of Order: Artistic Expression in Fang Culture. In *The Traditional Artist in African Societies*. Warren d'Azevedo, ed. pp. 194–220. Bloomington: Indiana University Press.
1976   *Fang Architectonics*. Philadelphia: Institute for the Study of Human Issues.

Forge, Anthony
1970   Learning to See in New Guinea. In *Socialization: The Approach from Social Anthropology*. Philip Mayer, ed. pp. 269-91. London: Tavistock.

Forrest, John
1988   *Lord I'm Coming Home: Everyday Aesthetics in Tidewater North Carolina*. Ithaca: Cornell University Press.
forthcoming Analyzing Forms through Appropriate Contexts: A West African Example. In *Studies in Third World Societies*.

Fortes, Meyer
1958   Introduction. In *The Developmental Cycle in Domestic Groups*. Jack Goody, ed. pp. 1–14. Cambridge: Cambridge University Press.

1969   *Kinship and the Social Order: The Legacy of Lewis Henry Morgan*. Chicago: Aldine Publishing Company.

1970   Descent, Filiation and Affinity. In *Time and Social Structure and Other Essays*. London School of Economics Monographs on Social Anthropology No. 40. pp. 96–121. New York: Humanities Press Inc.

1973   On the Concept of the Person among the Tallensi. In *La Notion de Personne en Afrique Noire*. Germaine Dieterlen, ed. pp. 283–319. Paris: Editions de Centre National de la Recherche Scientifique.

Foucault, Michel

1977   *Discipline and Punish*. New York: Pantheon.

1980   Truth and Power. In *Power/Knowledge*. Selected Interviews and Other Writings, 1972–1977. Colin Gordon, ed. pp. 109–33. New York: Pantheon Books.

Fyfe, Christopher

1962   *A Short History of Sierra Leone*. London: Longman.

Geertz, Clifford

1976   Art as a Cultural System. *Modern Language Notes* 91:1474–99.

Gerbrands, Adrian

1971   Art as an Element of Culture in Africa. In *Anthropology and Art: Readings in Cross-Cultural Aesthetics*. Charlotte M. Otten, ed. pp. 366–82. Garden City, New York: The Natural History Press. First published 1957.

Giddens, Anthony

1976   *New Rules of the Sociological Method: A Positive Critique of Interpretive Sociologies*. New York: Basic Books.

1979   *Central Problems in Social Theory: Action, Structure and Contradiction in Social Analysis*. Berkeley: University of California Press.

Guilbaut, Serge

1983   *How New York Stole the Idea of Modern Art: Abstract Expressionism, Freedom, and the Cold War*. Chicago: University of Chicago Press.

Hardin, Kris L.

1991   Review of Calliope's Sisters: A Comparative Study of Philosophies of Art. *Journal of Anthropological Research* 47(1):116–20.

n.d.   The Wives of Sande: Deep Politics in a West African Masquer-
            ade. To appear in *The Image of Women in Religious Art.*
            Tanya Luhrman, ed.

Hardin, Kris L., Mary Jo Arnoldi, and Christrand Geary
n.d.   Efficacy and Objects. In *How To Do Things with Objects:
            Contemporary Issues in African Material Culture Studies.*
            Mary Jo Arnoldi, Christrand Geary, and Kris L. Hardin, eds.

Hebdige, Dick
1979   *Subculture: The Meaning of Style.* London: Methuen.

Hertz, Robert
1960   *Death and the Right Hand.* Glencoe: The Free Press.

Hill, Matthew
1971   Towards a Cultural Sequence for Southern Sierra Leone. *Afri-
            cana Research Bulletin* 1(ii):3–12.

Hobsbawm, Eric, and Terence Ranger
1983   *The Invention of Tradition.* Cambridge: Cambridge Univer-
            sity Press.

Holsoe, S. E.
1980   Notes on the Vai Sande Society in Liberia. *Ethnologische
            Zeitschrift, Zurich* 1:97–109.

Jackson, Michael
1974   The Structure and Significance of Kuranko Clanship. *Africa*
            44(4):397–415.
1977   *The Kuranko: Dimensions of Social Reality in a West African
            Society.* London: C. Hurst and Co.
1983   Knowledge of the Body. *Man* 18:327–45.
1990   The Man Who Could Turn into an Elephant: Shape-shifting
            among the Kuranko of Sierra Leone. In *Personhood and
            Agency: The Experience of Self and Other in African Cultures.*
            Michael Jackson and Ivan Karp, eds. pp. 59–78. Washington:
            Smithsonian Institution Press.

Jackson, Michael, and Ivan Karp
1990   Introduction. In *Personhood and Agency: The Experience of
            Self and Other in African Cultures.* Michael Jackson and Ivan
            Karp, eds. Washington D.C.: Smithsonian Institution Press.

Jones, Adam
1981   Who Were the Vai? *Journal of African History* 22:159–78.

Kaeppler, Adrienne
    1978   Melody, Drone, and Decoration: Underlying Structures and Surface Manifestations in Tongan Art and Society. In *Art in Society: Studies in Styles, Culture and Aesthetics*. Michael Greenhalgh and Vincent Megaw, eds. pp. 261–74. London: Ducksworth.
    1986   Aesthetics: Evaluative Ways of Thinking. Una's Lectures in the Humanities. Unpublished lecture series.

Karp, Ivan
    1978a   *Fields of Change among the Iteso of Kenya*. London: Routledge and Kegan Paul.
    1978b   New Guinea Models in the African Savannah. *Africa* 48(1):1–17.
    1980   Beer Drinking and Social Experience in an African Society: An Essay in Formal Sociology. In *Explorations in African Systems of Thought*. Ivan Karp and Charles Bird, eds. pp. 83–119. Bloomington: Indiana University Press.
    1986   Agency and Social Theory: A Review of Anthony Giddens. *American Ethnologist* 5(13):131–38.

Karp, Ivan, and Kent Maynard
    1983   Reading *The Nuer. Current Anthropology* 24(4):481–503.

Kratz, Corinne
    n.d.   "We've Always Done it Like This . . . Except for a Few Details": "Tradition" and "Innovation" in Okiek Ceremonies. Forthcoming in *Comparative Studies in Society and History.*

Leach, Edmund
    1954   Aesthetics. In *The Institutions of Primitive Society*. E. E. Evans-Pritchard, ed. pp. 25-38. Oxford: Blackwell.

Lechtman, Heather
    1977   Style in Technology—Some Early Thoughts. In *Material Culture: Styles, Organization, and Dynamics of Technology*. Heather Lechtman and Robert S. Merrill, eds. pp. 3–20. New York: West Publishing Co.

Leja, Michael
    1987   The Formation of an Avant-Garde in New York. In *Abstract Expressionism: The Critical Developments*. Michael Auping, ed. pp. 13–33. New York: Harry N. Abrams.

Lienhardt, Godfrey
    1961   *Divinity and Experience: The Religion of the Dinka.* Oxford:
            Clarendon Press.

Little, Kenneth L.
    1948   Social Change and Social Class in the Sierra Leone Protector-
            ate. *American Journal of Sociology* 54(1):10–21.

Maquet, Jacques
    1986   *The Aesthetic Experience: An Anthropologist Looks at the Vi-
            sual Arts.* New Haven: Yale University Press.

Mason, Peter
    1990   *Deconstructing America: Representations of the Other.* New
            York: Routledge.

Matturi, Aiah M.
    1973   Appendix A. In *Diamonds, Diggers and Chiefs: The Politics of
            Fragmentation in a West African Society.* David M. Rosen. Ann
            Arbor: University Microfilms.

Mauss, Marcel
    1939   Une Categorie de l'Esprit Humaine: La Notion de la Personne,
            Celle de Moi. *Journal of the Royal Anthropological Institute*
            68:263–82.
    1966   *The Gift.* London: Routledge and Kegan Paul. (First published
            in 1954)
    1979   Body Techniques. In *Sociology and Psychology: Essays.*
            pp. 95–123. London: Routledge and Kegan Paul. (First pub-
            lished in 1950)

McNaughton, Patrick
    1979   *Secret Sculptures of Komo: Art and Power in Bamana (Bam-
            bara) Initiation Associations.* Philadelphia: Institute for the
            Study of Human Issues.
    1988   *The Mande Blacksmiths: Knowledge, Power and Art in West
            Africa.* Bloomington: Indiana University Press.

Merriam, Alan P.
    1964   *The Anthropology of Music.* Chicago: Northwestern University
            Press.

Moore, Sally Falk
    1978   *Law as Process.* London: Routledge and Kegan Paul.

Mudimbe, V. Y.
    1986   African Art As a Question Mark. *African Studies Review*
            29(1):3–4.

Munn, Nancy
    1973   *Walbiri Iconography: Graphic Representation and Cultural
            Symbolism in a Central Australian Society.* Ithaca: Cornell Uni-
            versity Press.

Needham, Rodney
    1963   Introduction. In *Primitive Classification*. Emile Durkheim
            and Marcel Mauss. pp. vii–xlvii. Chicago: University of
            Chicago Press.
    1983   *Against the Tranquility of Axioms.* Berkeley: University of Cali-
            fornia Press.

Osborne, Harold
    1970   *Aesthetics and Art Theory: An Historical Introduction.* New
            York: E. P. Dutton
    1972   Introduction. In *Aesthetics*. Harold Osborne, ed. pp. 1–24.
            London: Oxford University Press.

Parkin, David
    1982   *Semantic Anthropology.* New York: Academic Press.

Parsons, Robert T.
    1964   *Religion in an African Society: A Study of the Religion of the
            Kono People of Sierra Leone in its Social Environment with
            Special Reference to the Function of Religion in that Society.*
            Leiden: E. J. Brill.

Pellegrini, Aldo
    1969   *New Tendencies in Art.* New York: Crown Publishers.

Puri, R.
    1981   Polysemy and Homonomy, and the Mudra "Shikara": Multiple
            Meaning and the Use of Gesture. *Journal for the Anthropologi-
            cal Study of Human Movement* 1(4):269–87.

Riesman, Paul
    1975   The Art of Life in a West African Community: Formality and
            Spontaneity in Fulani Interpersonal Relationships. *Journal of
            African Studies* 2(1):39–63.

Richards, Paul
    1985   *Indigenous Agricultural Revolution: Ecology and Food Produc-
            tion in West Africa.* Boulder, Co.: Westview Press.

312   References

Rose, Barbara
    1967   *American Art Since 1900: A Critical History.* New York: Frederick A. Praeger.

Rosen, David Michael
    1973   *Diamonds, Diggers and Chiefs: The Politics of Fragmentation in a West African Society.* Ann Arbor: University Microfilms.
    1981   Dangerous Women: Ideology, Ritual and Knowledge among the Kono of Sierra Leone. *Dialectical Anthropology* 6:151–63.
    1983   The Peasant Context of Feminist Revolt in West Africa. *Anthropological Quarterly* 56(1)35–43.

Rubin, Arnold
    1975   Accumulation: Power and Display in African Sculpture. *Artforum* 13(9):35–47.

Sahlins, Marshall
    1981   *Historical Metaphors and Mythical Realities: Structure in the Early History of the Sandwich Islands Kingdom.* Ann Arbor: University of Michigan Press.

Said, Edward
    1979   *Orientalism.* New York: Vintage Books.

Sarles, Harvey B.
    1975   A Human Ethiological Approach to Communication: Ideas in Transit Around the Cartesian Impasse. In *Organization of Behavior in Face to Face Interaction.* Adam Kendon, Richard M. Harris and Mary Ritchie Key, eds. The Hague: Mouton.

Saussure, Ferdinand de
    1960   *Course in General Linguistics.* London: Peter Owen.

Schneider, Harold
    1971   The Interpretation of Pakot Visual Art. In *Art and Aesthetics in Primitive Societies.* Carol F. Jopling, ed. pp. 55–63. New York: E. P. Dutton.

Sharp, Lauriston
    1952   Steel Axes for Stone-Age Australians. *Human Organization* 11(2):17–22.

Sieber, Roy
1985   Stunning, But is it Art? Talk presented at Midwest Art History Association meetings, March 1985, Bloomington, Indiana.

Siegmann, William, and Judith Perani
1976   Men's Masquerades of Sierra Leone and Liberia. *African Arts* 9(3):42–47, 92.

Simmel, Georg
1968   On the Third Dimension in Art. In *Georg Simmel: The Conflict in Modern Culture and Other Essays*. Peter Etzkorn, ed. pp. 86–90. New York: Teachers College Press.

Thomas, Armand C.
1983   *The Population of Sierra Leone: An Analysis of Population Census Data*. Freetown: Demographic Research and Training Unit, Fourah Bay College.

Thompson, Robert Faris
1973   Yoruba Artistic Criticism. In *The Traditional Artist in African Society*. Warren d'Azevedo, ed. pp. 19–61. Bloomington: Indiana University Press.

van der Laan, H. L.
1965   *The Sierra Leone Diamonds: An Economic Study Covering the Years 1952–1961*. Oxford: Oxford University Press.

Vogel, Susan
1986   *African Aesthetics: The Carlo Monzino Collection*. New York: Center for African Art.

Willans, R. H. K.
1909   The Konnoh People. *Journal of the Africa Society* 8:130–44, 288–95.

Williams, Drid
1982   Semasiology: A Semantic Anthropologist's View of Human Movements and Actions. In *Semantic Anthropology*. David Parkin, ed. pp. 161–82. London: Academic Press.

Williams, Raymond
1981   *Towards a Sociology of Culture*. New York: Schocken Books.

Willis, Paul
    1977   *Learning to Labour: How Working Class Kids Get Working Class Jobs.* New York: Columbia University Press.

Winner, Ellen
    1982   *Invented Worlds: The Psychology of the Arts.* Cambridge: Harvard University Press.

Wylie, Kenneth C.
    1969   Innovation and Change in Mende Chieftancy 1880–1896. *Journal of African History* 10(2):295–308.